Black Plays: Two

The Dragon Can't Dance by Earl Lovelace, **A Ro**
Blood, Sweat and Fears by Maria Oshodi and Jo

The Dragon Can't Dance is an adaptation of a novel by Earl Lovelace, first published to critical acclaim in 1979. The play has not yet received its stage première in the UK.

A Rock in Water was first staged by the Royal Court Young People's Theatre in 1989. It tells the story of Claudia Jones, the American Black rights campaigner who was deported from the United States in 1955 for un-American activities and settled in London where she became the proprietor of the West Indian Gazette and a moving force behind the Notting Hill Carnival. 'Winsome Pinnock is on a new wave of Black British writing that is answering back to Mustapha Matura and Michael Abbensetts. Ideas of homeland and justice are now entangled in a complicated skein of women's stories across three or four generations.'
Michael Coveney, *Financial Times*

Blood, Sweat and Fears, focusing on the problems of 10 per cent of Britain's Black population suffering from sickle cell anaemia is 'an absorbing play about the pain and courage of a young man reluctantly coming to terms with a still relatively ignored illness. Although this is the central theme the problems of youth are also tackled with wit and warmth.' *City Limits*. It was first staged in a touring production in 1988.

Job Rocking, first staged at the Riverside Studios, London in 1987, is the first play by Rastafarian poet Benjamin Zephaniah. It is set in and around a new-style 'Job Club' designed, in true late 80's fashion, to sell the idea of work to the unemployed as a substitute for the real thing. Zephaniah's 'portraits of out-of-work youngsters (and one deeply depressed older man), constructed through lively verbal arias and ensemble passages, are packed with insights and observations . . . an exhilarating piece of theatre . . .' Malcolm Hay, *Time Out*

YVONNE BREWSTER has worked extensively in theatre, film, television and radio both as an actress and director. In 1965 she began her career as a director by co-founding The Barn, Jamaica's first professional theatre, with Trevor Rhone. The Barn is dedicated to staging new plays from the Caribbean and Africa and celebrated its 21st anniversary in 1986. For the past fifteen years, Yvonne Brewster has lived in England working primarily as a director. Recent productions include: C.L.R. James's *The Black Jacobins* for Talawa Theatre Company, Dennis Scott's *Echo in the Bone* and *School's Out* by Trevor Rhone. In 1986, she became Associate Director at the Half Moon Theatre, London, where her first production was *Flash Trash* by Barbara Gloudon. Yvonne is at present Artistic Director of Talawa Theatre Company for whom she recently directed *The Importance of Being Earnest* by Oscar Wilde with an all black cast.

Methuen Theatrefiles and **New Theatrescripts** series offers frontline intelligence of the most original and exciting work from the fringe.

Black Plays: Two

The Dragon Can't Dance
Earl Lovelace

A Rock in Water
Winsome Pinnock

Blood Sweat and Fears
Maria Oshodi

Job Rocking
Benjamin Zephaniah

Edited by Yvonne Brewster

Methuen Drama

A Methuen New Theatrescript

This collection first published in Great Britain as a paperback original in 1989 by Methuen Drama, Michelin House, 81 Fulham Road, London SW3 6RB and distributed in the United States of America by HEB Inc, 70 Court Street, Portsmouth, New Hampshire 03801.

British Library Cataloguing in Publication Data

Black plays II.
  1. Drama in English. Black writers, 1945–
  Anthologies
  I. Brewster, Yvonne
  822'.914'080896

ISBN 0-413-61470-0

Printed in Great Britain by
Richard Clay Ltd, Bungay, Suffolk

Contents

Introduction

Although the first Black play to be published in England, Kobina Sekye's **The Blinkards**, appeared in 1907, it was the 1970's before anything approaching a major body of such work began appearing in print. Of course there were people writing in the intervening years and some work was indeed published: Errol John, **Moon on a Rainbow Shawl** (Faber, 1958), Derek Walcott, **Ti Jean and his Brothers** (Farrar Stauss and Giroux, 1958), Barry Record, **Skyvers** (Penguin, 1964). It is true to say, however, that the great bulk of this work remained unpublished.

In the 1970's plays which were, along with those mentioned above, to have an enormous influence on contemporary Black British playwrights, received welcome but belated publication: C.L.R James', **The Black Jacobins** adapted from his novel of the same name in 1935 and performed in London with Paul Robeson as Toussaint L'Ouverture in that year, was published in 1976 and Roger Mais', **George William Gordon** about the nineteenth-century Black Jamaican revolutionary was seen in print 30 years after it had been successfully produced.

Also in the 70's some Black playwrights began to see their work published relatively quickly. Two important examples are: Wole Soyinka, **Shuttle in the Crypt** (Methuen, 1972), **Collected Plays Volumes One and Two** (Oxford University Press, 1973). **Damwood on Leaves** (Methuen, 1973), **Death and the King's Horseman** (Methuen, 1975) and Derek Walcott who has had all his work published by both American and English firms.

James, Mais, John, Record, Soyinka and Walcott all had one thing in common: the British Colonial experience. They were all educated in the English system: European and English History, Literature and Geography took precedence. In all cases the struggle for the liberation of the natural voice was intense; in the rhythms of Walcott, the humour and satire of Soyinka, the vision of Mais and the politics of James. These voices overcame in spite of or maybe because they were written in perfect but conditioned English. The exception was John. His play **Moon** uses the dialect of his native Trinidad, and when it won the coveted *Observer Playwrights' Prize* in 1956, it struck a blow for the dignity and beauty of West Indian dialects, and continues to do so.

It is also true to say that these playwrights concerned themselves with African or West Indian themes: none were writing about English concerns. Michael Abbensetts with his first play **Sweet Talk** (Methuen, 1973) did. The frustrations of a talented black 'migrant' from the West Indies, condemned to live in a cold water, paraffin-heated Britain exploded onto the theatrical scene, and later on television. Mustapha Matura's emphasis shifted regularly, and still does, between the West Indies and England. His **As Time Goes By** (Calder & Boyars, 1972) and **Nice** should be compulsory reading for the social anthropologists trying to make sense of the Black British psyche! Alfred Fagon's **11 Josephine House** (1971) attacked with bravado the sham of respectability which blind adherence to the demands of a religious household placed on the newly immigrant.

Jamal Ali broke away from the idea of the well-made play and produced one of the first 'street-cred' dramas **Black Feet in the Snow** (1972) which pulsated to the fear, dread and threat of the London Street post-Notting Hill riots. The Black British voice was beginning to emerge.

INTRODUCTION

The SS Windrush which brought the first really sizeable contingent of West Indian Black people to take up residence in England in the 1950's has now produced her children and grandchildren. It is they who are now writing in every area of theatre. They are taking up the challenge of being seen as 'rather uncivilized', of the belittling of the Black oral tradition, the taunts of not belonging etc. and are examining these manifestations and producing work which breaks with tradition and is often surprising. In this work there is a strong pulse which continues to search for the cultural roots of this community of writers, which challenges and presupposes nothing.

It is this challenge and variety which this volume attempts to celebrate in some way, setting the three plays by Black British writers against a background of possibly the best recent development of the traditional West Indian yard play **The Dragon Can't Dance** by the distinguished Trinidadian man of letters Professor Earl Lovelace. **Dragon** has been adapted for the stage from the author's well known novel of the same name. His plays have a surreal and experimental quality about them and are never to be taken at face value. **Jestina's Calypso** offers immense acting challenges as it examines the concept of ugliness, while **The New Hardware Store** is allegorical and political in its use of the Carnival figure of Robber and the almost mythological Che to discuss materialism. In **The Dragon Can't Dance** Lovelace uses the power and persuasion of the Carnival as the driving force of the play, omnipresent like some gift from a demanding God. The lives of the characters unfold in all their universality both petty and grand. The play is universally apt too with its hero fighting the sponsorship mania which is overtaking the creativity of this most West Indian of art forms, Carnival. Another Lovelace novel, **The Wine of Astonishment** has been adapted for the stage and recently received an acclaimed production in Trinidad.

Another play in this volume **A Rock in Water** by Winsome Pinnock also explores the power of the Carnival, but from a completely different vantage point. This play was commissioned by the Royal Court Young People's Theatre, to examine the life and work of Claudia Jones. Playwright and company worked on the project for a year and the resulting play has a simple majesty which eschews tricks and speaks straight to the heart. The story of this indomitable woman whose early life steeled her into something akin to a one-woman army springs to life. After spells in prison for un-American activities in the MacCarthy era she ends up in Britain as colonial flotsam, but succeeds in energising the first black British newspaper, and in her spare time, being the spirit behind the first London Street Carnival now the largest in Europe. The writing is economical, and there is a good feel of period in the dialogue and in the situations. The humanity and frailties of the characters make this play special. Winsome in her short career of writing plays has an impressive body of varied work. Her play **A Hero's Welcome** draws on the traditional West Indian yard play format and is stylistically interesting. In Errol John's **Moon on a Rainbow Shawl**, the prototype of such plays, the communal yet separate existences within the yard react to the outside influences, both American and English, which pull the people down and away. It is interesting to see a young British playwright of West Indian parentage examining a similar scenario 30 years or so later. Her **Picture Palace** takes a very detailed look at the fantasies to which some women are prone, and reveals a lot about female interaction.

Sickle cell anaemia is a blood disorder which mainly affects Black people. Too little is known about Sickle Cell although there is much more research being conducted at the present time than in the preceding decades. In Maria Oshodi's **Blood, Sweat and Fears** the subject is unquestionably Sickle Cell. The outstanding success of this play is in its approach, which is one hundred per cent theatrical. If you are educated, inspired to do something to help, or simply entertained, all to the good – but the play refuses to be simplistic or to patronise with well-meaning pity. Its wit, humour and lack of overkill strike a telling blow at much larger prejudices. In this zany, fast-moving play the punch and accuracy of the dialogue is particularly commendable, and the situations keep the action on the boil, focusing on the central theme throughout.

I first saw Benjamin Zephaniah perform his work in a pub in Brixton. His skill was as impressive as the 'dub poetry' he delivered – reciting was not the word! Now, very few years later, he has been a candidate for a visiting fellowship at Trinity College, Cambridge! This whirlwind of energy recently had his first radio play **Hurricane Dub** produced by the BBC and has performed at the Queen Elizabeth Hall with Union Dance Company, while attending closely to the many socially significant projects which he undertakes. Much of Benjamin's personal directness is present in **Job Rocking**. Although it is an issue-based play he has not structured it predictably , leaving the issues to float atop the sea of rhythm. A Job Club is formed to persuade its out-of-work members to come to grips with the unemployment realities of the 1980's. It uses the jargon of modern computerized soft sell, injecting it with deliberate hard-nosed job facts and is written in a serious street beat. This is compulsive reading.

The Black voice in theatre is certainly stronger now, becoming more difficult to ignore and as the Black British playwrights continue to explore their unique sounds and rhythms it will soon be impossible to ignore this voice of Britain.

Yvonne Brewster
June, 1989

The Dragon Can't Dance

EARL LOVELACE was born in Toco, Trinidad in 1935 and spent his childhood in Tobago and Port of Spain. He first worked with the Trinidad Publishing Company and later joined the Civil Service, serving first in the Forestry Department and then in the Department of Agriculture. His first novel, **While Gods are Falling**, won him the BP Independence Literary Award. It was followed by **The Schoolmaster**, a novel which drew on his experiences of rural Trinidad. These novels of the 60's were followed by **The Dragon Can't Dance** and **The Wine of Astonishment** which, West African magazine argued, 'put him on the front rank of Caribbean writers'. These were followed by a collection of plays, **Jestina's Calypso** (1984). His latest work, **A Brief Conversion and Other Stories** groups together twelve of the author's best short stories. Earl Lovelace lives in Trinidad where he works in the Folk Theatre and teaches creative writing at the University of the West Indies.

Author's Preface

The present playscript of the **The Dragon Can't Dance** has emerged out of the novel, from which it was adapted, through staged readings held in Trinidad in 1979, in New York's Black Theatre Alliance in 1980, in Barbados at The Caribbean Festival of Arts in 1981, in workshop at the Eugene O'Neil Theatre Centre, Connecticut in 1984, and, finally, the play which ran in Port of Spain during Carnival 1986. The present script owes many debts: to Errol Jones, the distinguished Carribean actor, who insisted that the novel be adapted into a play; to Earl Warner, the director both of the dramaturgy at The Eugene O'Neil Theatre Centre and of the play in Port of Spain; to Andre Tanker for his music and his assistance with lyrics; to the dramaturgs at the Eugene O'Neil Centre, and to the many actors who at various stages managed to bring to another life the granduer of these ordinary people who inhabit the world of the play.

Earl Lovelace

Characters

Aldrick *the Dragon*

Sylvia *a young girl of 17*

Fisheye *a bad John*

Pariag *an East Indian*

Dolly *Pariag's wife*

Basil *Boy*

Mr Guy *Rent Collector*

Philo *Calypsonian*

Cleothilda *Mulatto woman*

Olive *a woman in the yard – Sylvia's mother*

Reds *a steel bandsman*

Yvonne *a narrator, Fisheye's Woman*

Proprietor/Magistrate

Proprietor's Wife

Pa *Pariag's father*

Synco
Crowley } *Rebels at the Corner*
Smalls

Setting

Calvary Hill, a depressed section of Port of Spain. The set should suggest the hill with shacks stacked like medieval shields, with the precipitous and winding road leading up to the hill and the yard in which **Sylvia**, **Cleothilda**, **Miss Olive**, **Guy** and others live. Upstairs in separate apartments are **Cleothilda** and **Guy**. There is a verandah. Downstairs are **Cleothilda**'s parlour, **Olive**'s rooms and in a separate addition **Pariag**'s rooms. **Aldrick** has a shack somewhere in the yard.

Prologue

A few days before Carnival.

Aldrick is in his little shack working on his partly finished dragon mask. Around him are tools and materials related to his task, paint, tin, scales of metal which he will sew onto the cloth of the dragon costume mask.

He works with ceremonial solemnity as he sews scales onto the body of the dragon, each scale significant, some part of the story.

Lights go up on Alice Street, Calvary Hill, East Port of Spain. In the background its shacks are stacked like medieval shields. The road leading up the hill. The yard in the foreground.

Sylvia, the teenage beauty, goes down the hill past the steel band **Fellars** at the corner. They love her: each one of them wishes to have her jumping up with him in the band for Carnival. She dodges through them teasingly, playfully.

Fellar Sylvia, I hope this year you playing in the band.

Sylvia dodges away from **Fellars**, smiling, teasing.

Sylvia I ain't even have a costume yet.

Cleothilda, the mulatto woman, Queen of the Band, is coming up the hill, serious faced. She has a basket in one hand and a bit of material for her costume in another. She walks disdainfully almost past the **Fellars**. They watch her silently as she and **Sylvia** cross paths.

Sylvia Morning, Miss Cleothilda.

Cleothilda Morning.

Cleothilda continues uphill.

Fellars had been leaning on street corner in different poses of rebellion. After **Cleothilda** goes past them, they assemble themselves, and, harmonising with a mouth band, they troop up the hill.

Enter **Taffy**, the shouters' leader, followed by his flock. They are singing a hymn. **Taffy** speaking the words and the followers taking them up and singing.

Taffy (singing) I heard the voice of Jesus say
Come unto me and rest
Lay down my weary one lay down
thy head upon my breast.

Philo (to rapso beat, the mouth band of the **Fellars** as backup) This is the hill tall above the city, where Taffy a man who say he is Christ put himself up on a cross one burning midday and say to his followers.

Taffy Crucify me. Let me die for my people. Stone me with stones as you stone Jesus. I will love you still.

Philo And when they start to stone him in truth he get vex and start to cuss.

Taffy Get me down, get me down. Let every sinner man bear his own blasted burden. Who is I to die for people who ain't have sense enough to know that they can't pelt a man with big stones when so much little pebbles on the ground.

The **Fellars** provide rhythm. Drum background.

Cleothilda (on her verandah with accompanying rhythm from **Fellars**) This is the hill, Calvary Hill, where the sun set on starvation and rise on pot-holed roads, thrones for stray dogs that you could play banjo on their rib bones, holding garbage piled high like a cathedral spire, sparkling with flies buzzing like torpedoes; and if you want to pass from your yard to the road, you have to be a high jumper to jump over the gutter full up with dirty water, and hold your nose. Is noise whole day. Laughter is not laughter; it is a groan coming from the bosom of those houses. No, not houses, shacks that leap out of the red dirt and stone. Come out again. Thin like smoke, fragile like kite paper; balancing on their rickety pillars as broomsticks on the edge of a juggler's nose.

Chorus – all as one, singing.

Voice One With Carnival coming, radios go on full blast, trembling these shacks.

Voice Two Booming out calypsoes, that announce the new rhythms for people to walk in.

Voice Three Rhythms that climb over the red dirt and stone,

Voice Four Break-away rhythms that laugh through the groans of these sights, these smells,

Voice Five That swim through the bones of these enduring people and they shout,

All Life! Life! Hurray!

Voice They drink a rum and say, fuck it!

Voice They walk with a tall, hot beauty between the garbage and dog shit.

All Dance, there is dancing in the calypso. Dance!

Voice The words mourn the death of a neighbour,

All dance!

Voice They tell the troubles of a brother,

All dance!

Voice Dance to the hurt!

All Dance!

Voice You ketching hell and the government don't care,

All dance!

Voice Your woman take your money and run away with another man,

All dance! Dance! Dance! Dance! Dancing wards off evil. Dancing is the chant that cuts off the power from the devil. Dance! Dance! Dance!

Voice (*singing*)
Wake up the people

All Carnival!

Shake up the people

All Carnival

Dance up the people

All Carnival

Lick down the devil

All Carnival

Dance the calypso

All Carnival

Prance the calypso

All Carnival

Shake out the devil

All Carnival

Beat back the evil

All Carnival

All Dance, dance, dance, dance
No time for grieving

All Dance

No time for screaming

All Dance

You woman gone away

All Dance

You ketching hell I say

All Dance
Dance, Dance, Dance

They dance.

All exit.

Act One

Cleothilda *comes out on her verandah with material for her costume.* **Olive** *goes to standpipe to wash clothes. She looks up at* **Cleothilda** *as she makes her way to the tub.*

Cleothilda (*singing with a section of the chorus*)
Carnival coming, everybody nice
The land is amazing, it is paradise
Everybody jumping, woman and man
And hear what they saying, all ah we is one

Voice All ah we is one in the island

Chorus All ah we is one

Voice All ah we is one in the island

Chorus Underneath the sun.
All ah we is one hear what we say
Drink drink and be merry, this is carnival day.

The **Chorus** *contrasts with* **Cleothilda's** *song almost despite itself, until they both blend into one tune.*

Cleothilda (*exultantly*) Carnival! Bacchanal! All ah we is one. (*Singing alone now*) All ah we is one in the island, all ah we is one. (*Calling.*) Miss Olive (**Olive** *looks up slowly, sullenly.*) Sylvia! Sylvia! (*Now entering yard.*) You see colours! (*Indicating the material of her costume.*) You see colours! And when I put on my plume and I fix up my cape . . .

Sylvia What masquerade you playing, Miss Cleothilda?

Cleothilda You don't have to ask that. Queen. I don't play nothing else. Queen of the band . . . And when I put on my plumes and I fix up my cape, and the music blast and I move my waist! Nobody to touch me, nobody to touch me.

Yvonne *enters from across the fence, goes to the standpipe.* **Olive** *makes room for her.*

Philo (*who has entered the yard flirtatious, goes towards* **Cleothilda's** *steps. To* **Cleothilda**) You don't want me to help you with your cape? I could do it right now. (*Making as if to mount the steps.*)

Cleothilda Miss Olive, like the Carnival season getting to Philo brain . . . (*To* **Philo**.) No darling. Don't come up these steps today. When Carnival come I coming down to meet you. Carnival coming; it ain't reach yet.

Yvonne *and* **Olive** *exchange glances.*

Philo Miss Cleothilda, why you punishing me so?

Cleothilda (*coyly*) Punishing you? I punishing you? Miss Olive, you hearing my troubles this morning?

Olive (*surprised at* **Cleothilda's** *performance of friendliness, exchanges glances with* **Yvonne**) Troubles?

Philo (*with self mockery, singing*)
I coulda choose Irene
I coulda choose Lillian
I coulda pick Doreen
But I choose the queen of the band.
Love is so wicked
Love is so hard
The lady that I love
Ready to throw me outa she yard.
Irene have a summons bed
Lilly have a radio
Doreen will keep him well fed
So you see he coulda do without Cleo
(How he stupid so)
But love is so wicked
Love is so hard
Is Cleo that he love
And she ready to kick him outa she yard.

All laugh.

Philo *exits in direction of* **Aldrick's** *shack.*

Cleothilda *exits into her house.*

Cleothilda (*to* **Olive**) Like Philo really going for the calypso crown this year.

Olive (*turning to* **Yvonne**) I wonder if Miss Cleothilda crazy?

Yvonne You don't see that this rush of friendliness is the first instalment on her masquerade for Carnival day.

Olive I getting too tired to fix a smile on my face that I don't feel, and pretend that she and me is friend when she come out on her verandah and shake her waist.

Yvonne So, Olive, you don't have eyes in your head to see that is because the woman skin lighter than yours and mine she feel she better than people on this Hill. All the friendly friendly thing she give off for Carnival is just a smoke screen to hide the wretch she really is. And Philo such a jackass at his age, up in the woman tail and she don't want him, you know.

Olive I know she don't want him. That woman like a sickness hook inside him.

Yvonne But, Olive, what it is that have you bowing to her so? What preventing you from putting she in her place? Or maybe you really think she is some kinda queen and ain't have the responsibility to live and be a human being? I tell you, you don't have to credit from her. The Chinese man at the corner will let you open an account with him.

Yvonne *exits.*

Olive (*leaving*) Yes, yes. I ain't taking no more foolishness from that woman. (*She turns to* **Sylvia** *who is still in the yard.*) And you? You going to stay there whole day looking up in the woman house? You ain't have nothing inside your own house to do?

Sylvia I was just looking at the costume.

Olive Costume, costume. That is all I hearing from you. Mr Guy coming for his rent this evening. I ain't even have it to pay. I don't know what I going to tell him, and you studying costume . . .

Sylvia Don't worry yourself with the rent, Ma. Mr Guy will wait.

Olive (*soft, scared*) Mr Guy . . . how you know he will wait?

Sylvia He does always wait.

Olive (*would like to comfort* **Sylvia** *and be herself comforted*) Watch yourself, you hear, watch yourself. (*Pauses, indicating* **Cleothilda**.) Of late I see you getting well taken up with her, like she is your friend . . . you see me how I live. Things hard, but I trying. Try. I don't know how you will make it though. Lord, it will be a miracle.

Sylvia *nods. They exit,* **Olive** *first,* **Sylvia** *following.*

Philo *emerging from* **Aldrick**'s *shack, sings. Chorus singing,* **Philo** *leading.*

Philo (*singing*)
Sylvia ain't have no man
She want a costume to play in the band (*Repeat.*)
The young fellars who begging she to play
Ain't have no money, ain't working nowhere

All (*Chorus*)
And Mr Guy, the landlord, watching and waiting
Sans humanite.

Aldrick
Sylvia's a woman now
Her breasts rising like two islands (Repeat.)
Her body is fire, her movement is sweet
See she toting water up and down the street

All
And Mr Guy like a spider watching
and waiting
Sans humanité.

Yvonne Monday is Carnival
The whole hill is fever, is bacchanal
(Repeat.)
Cleo playing friendly, Aldrick working
hard
Excitement rising inside the yard.

All
And Mr Guy and the young boys
watching and waiting for Sylvia to play
on Carnival day
Sans humanité

Chorus (*Singing*)
Sylvia ain't have no man
She want a costume to play in the
band
The young fellars who begging she to
play
Ain't have no money, ain't working
nowhere
And Mr Guy, the landlord, watching
and waiting

All Sans humanité

Sylvia *returns to yard, goes to standpipe
with a bucket. Enter Mr Guy, the rent
collector, coming down the steps of his
house. He moves towards* **Sylvia**, *and
stands with a calm sense of menace.*

Mr Guy Sylvia, I hope your mother
have the rent today.

Sylvia I don't know if she have it, you
know, Mr Guy.

Mr Guy Well, tell her I coming for it.
She have till this evening.

Sylvia *nods. He turns to go but now his
effort at casualness fades.*

Mr Guy Sylvia, you not playing in the
band?

Sylvia *adjusts the elastic at the waist of her
panties and turns off the tap.*

Mr Guy What costume you want?
(*With undisguised promise.*) What
costume you want?

Sylvia (*in confusion*) I . . . I don't even
know.

Mr Guy Well, just find out what
costume and just tell me, tonight.
Come upstairs tonight and I will, I will
give it to you.

Sylvia You making joke, Mr Guy?

Mr Guy I . . . I ain't joking. You want
to play a princess? A lady-in-waiting?
Anything. (*She steals a glance from him
up to his house. He looks at her body.*)
Tonight. (*Whispering, for* **Miss
Cleothilda** *has appeared on her verandah.
To* **Cleothilda**.) Eh! Miss Cleothilda,
what have you looking so nice this
morning?

Cleothilda Me? I have to try, Mr Guy.
I have to try. I ain't a young girl again.
Eh, Sylvia?

Sylvia (*with aggravating
innocence*) What you say, Miss
Cleothilda?

Cleothilda Nothing, girl. Just this old
man teasing me. (**Sylvia** *makes to leave,
but* **Cleothilda** *wants* **Miss Olive** *to
witness the scene of* **Sylvia** *and* **Guy**.)
Sylvia, wait! I think I have an old
costume here from last year that could
fit you . . . if your mother would let
you take it. (*Calling.*) Miss Olive! Miss
Olive! (**Olive** *enters.*) You mind if I
give Sylvia a costume?

Olive (*taking in the scene as* **Guy**
exits) Sylvia, you want the costume?

Sylvia Costume? Which costume? I
ain't see no costume.

Cleothilda Oh-oh. Why you don't
come upstairs and try it on.

Olive *exits.*

Sylvia (*with casualness*) Later.

Cleothilda (*with mischief*) I know you don't care for costume from me. A girl like you could get anything you want.

Sylvia *looks at* **Cleothilda**, *her youth like a shield about her. Also a vulnerability that makes her invincible.*

Night

The steel band humming over the hill. **Sylvia**, *like a dancer, barefooted and with nothing on under her dress. She moves stealthily, her eyes searching the yard to see who is about at that hour. Light move to* **Aldrick** *at the window of his little shack. He sees* **Sylvia** *and freezes.*

Aldrick (*to himself*) So your turn come. I wonder which of the young fellars is the lucky one.

Sylvia *pauses, clears her own throat lightly. An answering cough comes from* **Mr Guy**. *Lights pick up* **Mr Guy**. **Aldrick** *takes a cigarette from behind his ear, hesitates then lights it boldly.* **Sylvia** *turns to the sound and light, sees* **Aldrick**. *Grasping the hem of her dress around her knees, she approaches him boldly.*

Aldrick So?

Sylvia (*combative, hands on hips, head thrown back*) . . . So?

Aldrick So Guy is your man? (*Silence.*) I don't mind, you know. Do what you want, I don't care. I ain't going to say nothing.

Sylvia What you could say?

Aldrick I could say: a nice girl like you?

Sylvia A nice girl like me?

Aldrick Yes, a nice girl like you. You could get married.

Sylvia (*still aggressive*) You will married me?

Aldrick Me? Married? I can't afford woman. You don't see how I living? No chair, a little bed in a little room. A woman want things. I ain't have nothing here except my dragon costume to put on for carnival.

Sylvia (*softening*) But you always have woman coming here to you.

Aldrick Yes, but you never see any of them stay more than a night. I can't afford it. I . . . I ain't have nowhere to put them.

Sylvia You can't get a bigger place and buy some chairs? Even in there, you and somebody could live, if you love her.

Aldrick She will have to eat. I ain't working nowhere. (*Silence.*)

Sylvia You ever was in love, Aldrick?

Aldrick (*thoughtful pause*) No . . . Love is on the screen.

Sylvia Me neither. I like to see love pictures though . . . you feel those people real on the screen? Or is something they make up? I find it does look so real.

Aldrick You like Guy?

Sylvia He buying a costume for me. (*Long pause.* **Aldrick** *and* **Sylvia** *thoughtful.*) It ain't no big expensive costume either. Is just that I have to be there in the band when Carnival come. I have to play . . . you finish your dragon costume yet?

Aldrick Nearly.

Sylvia You lucky. You always have your costume. You don't get tired playing the same mas every year?

Aldrick Every year I make a new costume. The costume this year ain't the same one I had last year. When I finish I always throw them away.

Sylvia I know; but still, in a way is the

same costume, the same dragon. I wonder if I could do that.

Aldrick Do what?

Sylvia Play the same masquerade every year. I mean, every year you there with the same tin, the same scales, the same thread.

Aldrick Yes. Every year I do it again. Every threat I sew, every scale I put on the body of the dragon is a thought, a name, a chant that celebrate how I get here and how I survive on this Hill. Every year I trace my life again.

Sylvia (*marvelling*) I thought it was easy.

Aldrick (*proudly*) Look! (*Holding up a scale.*) This scale here is for my grandfather working that mountain and stone land.

Sylvia (*impressed*) I wish I coulda play a mas so.

Aldrick What costume you want?

She hesitates.

Aldrick Eh, what costume you want?

Sylvia It ain't no big expensive costume. You will laugh when I tell you. (*Bashfully*) A . . . a slave girl. You see, it ain't no big expensive costume . . . you feel I should play a princess or a slave girl?

Aldrick You is a princess already. Play a slave girl.

Pause.

Sylvia I could ask you a question. Don't get vex, you know.

Aldrick What could get me vex?

Sylvia How . . .? How you make out? I mean, how you manage not working nowhere and you always have woman coming to your place?

Aldrick I don't know.

Sylvia Well . . . you not so bad looking.

Aldrick You not so bad looking yourself.

Sylvia You feel . . . you really feel I is a princess in truth?

Aldrick You is a *princess*.

Mr Guy *coughs. Pause. Lights go on in* **Miss Olive**'s *house.*

Sylvia (*alarmed*) Oh God! My mother turn on the light. (*She moves very close to* **Aldrick** *as if wanting him to shield her.*) I better go (*Turns to go.*)

Aldrick Okay . . . Okay (*Turning away, not wanting to see where she is going.*)

Blackout.

Day

Lights up on **Aldrick**'s *shack. Boy hurrying down hill.*

Aldrick *working solemnly on dragon costume. The boy* **Basil**, *like an acolyte attending him, handing him material for his work with ceremonial solemnity as if* **Aldrick** *is the priest.*

Song from the yard – 'Dance Dragon':

Dance dragon, play mas
Dance dragon, but do not dance too fast
Dance dragon, play mas
This dance could be your last
The dragon ain't have no woman
The dragon ain't have no friend
The dragon is breathing fire
The dragon in the dragon's den.

Song fades away.

Aldrick (*to* **Boy**) Every day as soon as school over you reach here. You don't go home to eat?

Boy I like to come here.

Aldrick *searches for piece of material. The* **Boy**, *with great eagerness, finds it and gives it to* **Aldrick**.

Aldrick You learning fast . . . How you find we going?

Boy (*looking at costume . . . after pause*) Like magic.

Aldrick (*approving*) You will make a champion dragon.

Boy *hands* **Aldrick** *a scale*.

Aldrick Hold it careful. This is for my mother, rocking the last baby to sleep and waiting for my father, Sam. Sam Prospect, the Miracle man. (*Pause.*) Boy, the miracle of our surviving, the miracle of my mother bringing up five children and waiting . . . for that busy man. (*Pause.*) What was their gift to their children? Yes, this sense of miracle and man-ness, this standing up still on your own two feet to be somebody in a world where people is people only because of their property.

Pause.

Boy How you learn the dragon? Who teach you?

Aldrick My uncle Freddie. Cooler than water and smoother; never in a hurry, saying 'Take it easy! Take it easy!'

Reverently, the **Boy** *hands him another scale.*

Aldrick This is for you. Magic.

Mr Guy *locks his door and goes out. Sees* **Sylvia**.

Enter **Sylvia** *in shoes too big. Lips reddened. Long, ancient, almost bridal dress. Walking awkwardly. She stands before* **Aldrick**.

Sylvia I come.

Aldrick I see.

Sylvia I was passing and I see you.

Aldrick (*indicating the cluttered room*) You see what I mean. I ain't have no space even to invite you in. (*Indicating the dragon.*) You like how it coming? (*To* **Boy**.) Scissors. (**Boy** *hands him scissors; he makes a cut.*)

Sylvia (*waiting for his question*) You know I ain't get my costume yet. (*Happy to be able to say it.*)

Aldrick No? You mean you didn't . . . Guy didn't (*To* **Boy**.) Look. (*Taking money from his pocket and giving to the* **Boy**.) Go by Miss Cleothilda parlour and bring a pack of cigarette. Buy something for yourself too. (**Boy** *exits*.)

Sylvia (*triumphantly*) I ain't get my costume yet.

Aldrick (*to himself. First with relief as if now seeing her for first time; he holds back from commitment*) You is a princess, girl.

Sylvia (*eagerly*) I is what?

Aldrick You don't need those clothes and that lipstick. You is a princess just as you is every day. But I can't tell you that. That wouldn't be a compliment, it would be a proposal. I is a dragon.

Sylvia And that is why you didn't watch to see where I was going when I leave you last night? Why you didn't watch?

Aldrick (*pleading*) I is a hustler. I ain't working nowhere. The only responsibility I could bear now is to this dragon. This is my whole life here. (*Indicating the dragon.*)

Silence. **Sylvia** *waiting.*

Sylvia You know why I didn't get my costume. I didn't go for it.

She is vexed to tears; disappointed; she stomps off.

Aldrick Sylvia, listen. Sylvia. (*He*

*doesn't know what to say. She stops
expectant.*) Is only when this dragon
breathe fire that this city know that it
have people living here. (*She begins to
move again.*) If . . . if it wasn't for this
dragon, this island wouldn't even know
we is people here on top this hill . . .
Sylvia. Wait! Listen! (*She stops again.*)

*Enter **Philo** calling.*

Philo Aldrick! Aldrick!

Aldrick (*with relief*) Hail! Philo!

*Enter **Philo**. He is immediately attracted to
the overdressed **Sylvia**.*

Philo (*half joking*) Hail! Who is that so
dress up? That is you? No, that is not
you.

*He turns her round to inspect her. As she is
turned and facing him, she slaps his face
and marches off.*

Philo What wrong with her?

Aldrick You asking me?

Philo What wrong with her? (*Holding
his face where she had slapped him.*)

Philo How your dragon coming?

Aldrick (*sits to resume work on his
costume. He gets up*) Ah, to hell with the
dragon.

Mr Guy *goes up the steps.*

Philo It's Sylvia, not so? Why you
don't buy the costume for her?

Aldrick Is not even just the matter of
the costume, man. Is her eyes: the way
she look at me.

Philo Then buy her the costume. Buy
her the costume, then you could look
in her eyes, too. If I had money, I
would lend you, just for it to happen.

Aldrick T'ain't the costume alone.
She's a woman with all those woman
things in her; those woman
wantings . . . I mean, she not asking

for anything, but if you's her man, the
world is what you will want to give
her. And I . . . look at my life.

Philo So you serious then? I
thought . . . I thought she was just an
adventure, a little side thing. Guy. I
thought Guy was the serious one.

Aldrick Guy? What Guy could make
of that woman?

Philo What Guy . . .? Guy could
afford her, man!

Aldrick Afford her costume.

Philo Hi! You not serious about that
girl? Eh?

Aldrick Nah. I can't get serious about
no woman. She just have me thinking,
that's all. You know what I mean,
man?

Pause.

Philo You know, I used to say to
myself, Aldrick, you living the life. If it
have one man in the world living the
life is you: no wife, no child, no boss,
no job. You could get up any hour of
the day you want to, cuss who you
want. Anywhere you go people like
you. You's a favourite in the world.
Anybody will give you a dollar, just so.
And for Carnival you's the best dragon
in the whole fucking world.

Aldrick And now this girl, this girl . . .

Philo (*growing alarmed*) Have your
head on. I thought was just the
costume you wanted to give her. *You*
can't think 'bout no woman. You is the
dragon, the rebellion. Though
(*Softening.*) to tell the truth, that girl,
that Sylvia, more than any of the
hundred of females ripening on this
hill, is the most dangerous, because
she brings the most breathlessness.
You know, she have in her something,
a difference that does make me
wonder what miracle bring her here.

Like when I see a single pretty flower blooming on a dunghill or when I hear a piano or a violin coming out of a rubbish bin. I understand . . . she have in her a thing, a speed, a beauty, and at the same time something that could break and that could break you. She could make you throw over your whole life.

Aldrick She just have me thinking, that's all.

Philo (*leaving*) Have your head on.

Philo *exits, looks up the steps to* **Cleothilda**'s *verandah. She is watering flowers. He waves. She waves, keeping him at a distance.* **Miss Olive** *has been picking up clothes from the clothes line. Now she encounters* **Philo**.

Olive These steps high, high, you know.

Philo *says nothing to her. He passes her, then he speaks.*

Philo I will go right up those steps one day.

Exit **Philo**. *The* **Boy** *has returned.*

Aldrick (*turning back to his costume, sits, gets up, bursting out*) Wait! But what the hell I here worrying myself about? I ain't responsible for her. All I do is just see this girl going one night to meet a man, that's all. I don't even know what under her dress. Hi! (*Surprised at himself.*) Aldrick, you growing old, boy, you getting soft . . . and you (*To the* **Boy**.) it nearly dark, you ain't going home?

Boy I leaving home.

Aldrick Don't make that kinda joke with me. Not today. You leaving home? What you leaving home for? What *you* leaving home for?

Boy (*tearfully*) He beat me again. Every time he get drunk, he beat me. He beat everybody in the house.

Aldrick Who? Who is that beating you and everybody? Your father?

Boy He ain't my father. He living with my mother. Fisheye!

Aldrick (*with surprise*) Fisheye is your step-father?

Boy You know him?

Aldrick Well, maybe you do something wrong. Maybe you don't learn your lessons or something. I used to get licks for that too, and I never leave home.

Boy You don't know him when he get drunk. My big brother, Leroy, he beat Leroy so bad he break Leroy hand, and when they was carrying Leroy to hospital, he tell my mother to tell the doctor that Leroy fall down from a tree, else he going to break her hand too.

Aldrick He really don't make fun. But, I . . . I not going to encourage you to run away. Where you will go? You have anybody nearby where you could stay? 'Cause I . . . you can't stay here, you know. (*The* **Boy** *begins crying.*) You see how small this place is. Is not that I don't want you here, man; but, look at the size of this place. (*Pause.*) Look, this ain't my business. You understand? (*With softness and aggravation.*) This is family business. (*They fall silent.* **Aldrick**, *waiting for the* **Boy** *to leave.*) Okay, wipe your face and go, I can't do nothing. This is family business.

The **Boy** *leaves, backing out, dragging his feet, eyes filled with tears. He doesn't exit but remains behind the door out of* **Aldrick**'s *sight.*

Aldrick (*to himself*) Fisheye is a hell of a man. (*He walks to the door, sees the* **Boy** *standing there.*) Okay, okay (*With soft roughness.*) come, let's go. . . . I don't know where this softness coming from. I must be getting old in truth. Come!

Boy (*incredulous*) *You* going by Fisheye?

Aldrick Come. (*suddenly realizing*) (*Pause.*) Wait! What's your name?

Boy Basil.

Aldrick Come.

They exit.

Chorus *chant*
Mastifay mastifay
Meet me down by the quasay
Cutouter, cutouter,
Meet me down by Green Corner

Fisheye's *song.*
Enter **Fisheye**, *energetic, flag of his steelband in hand, singing. Also* **Reds** *and* **Yvonne**.

Fisheye
Yes, I Belasco from Moruga
I ain't 'fraid no man or he brother
I bad like a dragon
Strong like a lion,
A true true Bad John

Chorus
Mastifay mastifay
Meet me down by the quasay
Cutouter, cutouter,
Meet me down by Green Corner

Reds
That's the man they call Fisheye,
I telling you Managuy
He don't Managuy
With his cutlass in his waist
He setting the pace
He go show you how blood does taste.

Chorus
Mastifay mastifay
Meet me down by the quasay
Cutouter, cutouter,
Meet me down by Green Corner

Yvonne (*narrates*) He did never like the name Fisheye. In Moruga they would never think to give him such a name. He already had a name they knew, a name started long before he

was born, in his grandfather, Otway John, continued in his father, Samuel, a baptist preacher, who, when he raised his voice to preach, was heard in every corner of Moruga, and in his brothers, Clarence and Isadore and Dudley and Findlay and Silbert and Carlton, tall, strong men who could handle their fists, and who was good each one with a stick.

Chorus So that in Moruga they were a fearsome band and for all their bulging eyes, no one would have dared call them any name more derogatory than John.

Reds But when he came to Port of Spain, we didn't ask him his name: we gave him one.

Fisheye 'My name is Belasco, Belasco John!'

Yvonne But they refused to hear him: so he fought them over it.

Fisheye I was working on Marine Square as a truck loader for Laidlow Brothers, and working real hard too. I used to look across at the other fellars to see how they working, eyeing their muscles, comparing theirs to mine, measuring the amount of sweat they sweated and feeling kinda like I was tall and wide and big; and it didn't use to worry me that they were getting a bigger pay.

Enter **Reds**.

Reds (*admiringly*) Boy, you's a real devil for work, Jeez-us!

Pause.

Fisheye Is like all you leaving all the work for me?

Reds Well, we see like you feel you could kill work, so we say, okay, go ahead to see if work really going dead.

Fisheye Reds, you shouldn't a tell me nothing. What I go do with myself? I in this room alone, nobody to talk to; at night I can't sleep, just tossing. I feel like I useless. I feel like if I here and real life, somewhere far away. I feel that to make sure that I is myself I have to get up and go and burst a man head.

Reds Is the devil. The same thing uses to happen to me. You have to get a girl or some kinda thing to get you so tired that you can't think. You have to find something to do with yourself else the devil going to stay in your head. Why you don't play some football?

Fisheye It will go away, man, and anyway football ain't my game.

Yvonne (*narrates*) One day eating a bread and shark in a Port of Spain parlour, Fisheye suddenly decides not to pay for it.

Lights up on a little parlour. **Proprietor** *and* **Wife***: Proprietor, old, partly paralysed. Parlour will become court and the* **Proprietor** *the magistrate.*

Fisheye I ain't paying!

Proprietor You ain't what? You not what? You crazy or something?

The **Proprietor** *moves forward threateningly.*

Wife No Donald, don't put yourself in trouble for a bread and shark. Go on Sonny, take it and go. You don't know the devil everywhere? Leave him, he will get what he looking for.

Spectator A knife! A knife! Is a knife in his pocket!

Wife Go on, Sonny don't look for trouble. You done eat the bread and shark already. Go on. Don't make the police come and arrest you.

Yvonne (*narrates*) He stand up there very silly, not knowing how to pay the money and not knowing how to leave

and go. He tried to smile to make the old woman feel more comfortable. And while he there standing, with this silly smile on his face, trying to take his hands out of pockets to show that he was unarmed, he see this policeman in front of him, see the baton coming at his head and he saw one policeman fall and he heard the police whistle blasting and he had this baton in his hand and before he could decide what to do with it, he saw a whole crowd of grey-shirted policemen coming towards him – a whole army of them, like in 'Guns Across the River', and he was standing there with this baton in his hand swinging, and he tasted blood in his mouth and then he was floating down very slow, like he had all the time in the world to fall, and it would be the last thing he would do, forever and forever.

Fisheye *has mimed this action.*

Magistrate Six months hard labour. Jail is the only thing to straighten out you young hooligans.

Fisheye *shrugs.*

Fisheye Jail? All jail do is teach me time. My life ain't change, I feel myself wasting, marking time. My own strength stifling me. Is then Reds encourage me to come and join the Calvary Hill steel band. I was never no real musician. The only instrument I could play was the three note boom and I could beat iron.

Yvonne Those were the days when every street corner was a war zone and to be safe if you come from Belmont, you don't let night catch you in St James; if your home is Gonzales Place you didn't go up Laventille; and if you live in Morvant you pass San Juan straight.

MUSIC . . . MASTIFAY, MASTIFAY . . . Dance.

Yvonne That was the time I meet him.

Fisheye Those were glorious days. I had my girl, Yvonne, living with me; we had some real good times, real good times. Reds had his girl and Terry his and sometimes we all sit down over a bottle, just talking and playing all fours for water, losers drink or just off by myself, me and Yvonne, on the beach under a coconut tree like tourist, my foot in the water and the waves washing them sometimes, and Yvonne talking about things; the world. And I was lucky in gambling! One month I give her four hundred dollars to go and shop, and she went and buy all kinda nice things, things for the house and a shaving set for me and a bottle of aftershave cologne that I didn't want to use because man not suppose to smell so. That was my season.

Yvonne (*embracing him*) People love you, Belasco. You mean with all the love people show you and the power you have, is only fight you want to fight. You don't know is my cousin all you cut up in your fight with Desperadoes. Fifteen stitches the boy get. Suppose all you did kill him, Belasco?

Fisheye Is war, Yvonne, it coulda be me get cut.

Yvonne Why you have to fight one another?

Fisheye I don't understand that. I ain't have no grudge against Desperadoes. Is years we fighting one another, like brothers, like a tribe that split up to keep the warriors. Who we will fight then? Is war, Yvonne.

Yvonne You mean you will go on fighting one another? Why you don't join up? And make one army?

Fisheye And fight who?

Yvonne Fight the people who keeping down black people. Fight the government.

Fisheye Fight the government? All I want is to live, to be somebody for people to recognize, so when they see me they say, 'That is Fisheye' and give me my space and when they see you, they say, 'That is Fisheye woman!' and they know to leave my friends alone else I turn beat. I didn't think 'bout government and black people and all them kinda thing . . . Wait! . . . You know you talking sense . . . you talking sense . . . I could be a General in that army.

He crosses to **Reds** *at the corner.*

Fisheye Reds, we have to sign peace with the bands. We is all one army: Desperadoes, Invaders, Tokyo, Casablanca, Rising Sun; all o' we is one. We is the same people catching hell.

Reds Make peace and do what?

Fisheye Fight, fight the people that keeping us down. Take over the government.

Reds Take over the government? Ha! Ha! You will be the Premier? Fisheye, you crazy. You ain't hear what you saying . . . peace with bands and that ain't all, take over the government. The honourable Fisheye! . . . (*Mimicking.*) Premier I want a job for my brother . . . Premier, help me get a house for my sister.

Fisheye (*disappointed, sternly*) You know, you surprise me.

Exit **Reds**.

Yvonne What they tell you?

Fisheye Those fellars not serious. They just want to be bad johns that's all.

Yvonne Leave the band Belasco, leave it.

Fisheye Leave and go where? Leave and do what? Steel band is my life. (*Chuckling.*) Then, just like that the bands sign peace. Steelband yards become concert halls, warriors come to be critics of music. Even the white fellows open their own steelband. Now all ah we is one.

Yvonne And you vex?

Reds *enters.*

Fisheye (*heatedly*) Run them outa town, Reds. Let them feel the heat. Bust their head. Run them.

Reds Run who?

Fisheye Them white boys.

Reds Why? You don't see they helping to make steel band respectable, us, we, respectable.

Fisheye (*incredulous*) You mean *you* want *them* to accept you? You is a king, Reds.

Reds Fisheye, you like too much fight.

Fisheye (*disappointed*) Yes, Reds, I like too much fight.

Reds *exits and then* **Fisheye. Fisheye** *goes to the street corner. He stands one foot drawn up resting against the wall.* **Pariag** *enters with a basket of channa and peanuts which is what he sells.*

Fisheye Hey, Indian! You living up here?

Pariag Yes, is up here I living.

Fisheye Where?

Pariag Alice Street.

Fisheye You look like a okay fella. Gimme a shilling.

Pariag *gives it gladly.*

The police siren sounds. **Policeman** *enters.*

Policeman Move on! Move on! No loitering at this corner. This is the last

warning. Next time, straight inside the van.

Fisheye *moves sullenly.*

Yvonne If you don't do something with life, Belasco, life going to do something with you. If you intend to spend all your days as a bad john, I could get a decent man.

Fisheye *slaps her. He picks her up off the floor where his blow had sprawled her. He tries to comfort her and explain, but there is no yielding in her. She knees him in his crotch. He grimaces.*

Yvonne I going to have to leave you, Belasco. I can't go on so.

Fisheye And just so Yvonne go and sudden so everything turn sour.

Reds *enters.*

Reds Fisheye, the fellars in the committee want to talk to you.

Fisheye (*sullenly*) Me? What they want to talk to me for, two weeks before Carnival?

Reds It have people out there who want to help us.

Fisheye *is silent.*

Reds Companies want to sponsor us. New pans, new jerseys, jobs for us to play music in fêtes. All we have to do is put their name on the banner when we go on the road for Carnival. Desperadoes getting sponsored.

Fisheye You all not thinking about getting sponsors in this band?

Reds Fish, times change, man. We not bad johns again.

Fisheye What we is now, Reds? What we is now?

Reds The fellars serious. They want to suspend you if you can't behave.

Fisheye Suspend me? You want to

suspend me from Calvary Hill Steel band so your sponsors could come in and put their name on the flag? Reds . . . Reds, you know how I get to be in this band. Is you invite me. I had nothing, no life, no place, and I come up this hill and join the band. Out of old oil drums and rubbish bins and steel and old iron we make something to sing, to sound, to ring for everybody living here on top this hill. And I wave the flag for Calvary Hill Band. Through all the wars we had with Invaders and Tokyo and Desperadoes and Rising Sun, I wave this flag. I stand up, Reds, against the baddest men in this land, Mastifay, Barone, Zigilee, everyone of them had to respect me, and we walk fucking tall in this land. And little boys, little fellars, the people. If we didn't have nothing in Calvary Hill, we had this band. And now you telling me you want to put another name on this flag. For some fresh paint and free jerseys, you want me to agree to sell out Calvary Hill people band.

Reds (*angrily*) We ain't selling out nothing, man. All the other bands doing it.

Fisheye (*sternly*) This is Calvary Hill, man!

Reds The fellars serious. I tell them I will talk to you.

Fisheye (*with calm that moves to explosive vexation*) Reds, all of us is man, but, I telling you, all you going to have kill me to put a new name on this flag. I will mash up . . . I will mash up . . . I will mash up every pan. Tell them I waiting here. They know where I stand.

Reds *exits.*

Fisheye *doesn't move. Enter* **Aldrick** *and* **Boy.**

Aldrick Aye, Fisheye, what

happening? What the hell you doing there alone on the culvert, man? I just bring home your little son. I hear you does beat him for nothing.

Fisheye So what?

Aldrick So . . . so I come to warn you. If you beat him again I going straight to the gym and lift some weights and learn some jujitsu and come back for you.

Fisheye I ain't making joke tonight.

Aldrick If you think is joke I making, touch him.

Fisheye I ain't making joke tonight. That's what's wrong with this hill, we have too much people making joke. What it is you come to tell me?

Aldrick (*tone changing*) What I come to tell you?

Fisheye You, go inside. You coming home after dark and telling people how I beating you. Go inside. Later I will deal with you.

Aldrick (*serious now*) What I come to tell you? Nothing. I just bring your boy home; he was helping me with my dragon costume.

Fisheye You hear what happening?

Aldrick I ain't hear nothing.

Fisheye You ain't hear they putting me out the band?

Aldrick You? . . . Out the band?

Fisheye Their sponsors. They want musicians. They don't want men again.

Aldrick Well . . .

Fisheye Well, tell them for me, they better look out. they know me. I could be dead any time. Tell them . . .

Aldrick Tell them? Tell them? You know me, man. I ain't no messenger.

Fisheye I ain't know who one damn

soul is on this hill. I thought we had men, but now I don't know who nobody is.

Aldrick I still have to talk to you about the boy.

Fisheye You better don't talk that talk tonight.

Aldrick When I lift the weights I will talk.

Fisheye Lift plenty!

Fisheye *exits.*

Aldrick *walking home.*

Aldrick (*uneasily*) I had no right to get involved in the first place. Maybe I getting soft in truth . . . Sylvia . . . she ain't get she costume yet . . . you's a dragon, man, a dragon can't think 'bout these things.

Lights up on **Pariag** *rising out of the shadows.*

Pariag Hey, Aldrick!

Aldrick Okay.

Pariag You taking a stroll?

Aldrick Yes. How it going with you?

Pariag I just coolin' out . . . you want a cigarette? I have a whole pack.

Aldrick Thank you, I'll take one.

He takes the cigarette.

Pariag How your dragon costume coming?

Aldrick Okay, it coming okay . . . it kinda quiet tonight, eh?

Aldrick I sit down here listening to the steel band.

Aldrick Yes, with Carnival coming they practice till late . . . well, I going in . . .

Pariag All right. You could take a few cigarettes if you want, you know. I

have a whole pack.

Aldrick (*walking on*) Is okay.

Pariag (*to arrest him*) I name Pariag; I living right there. I does see you all the time but we never talk.

Aldrick No, we never talk.

Pariag I is a A-One card player. All Fours is my game.

Aldrick A-One?

Pariag I from New Lands, and it ain't have a better All Fours player there than me and Seenath. You does play All Fours?

Aldrick A little . . . well . . . I . . . going in now.

Pariag I see you playing a game on Sunday morning by the shoemaker.

Aldrick Those fellars could play you know.

Pariag If I had a partner all you could give me a invite. I would play.

Aldrick But everybody have their partner, and I don't know anybody . . . so . . .

Pariag I hope you ain't feel funny, I talk so much.

Aldrick (*as he walks away*) I find it strange that after living in the yard for two years, he choose tonight to talk to me. Wait! I never talk to him in two years either.

Pariag (*entering home*) Two years and I is still a stranger on this hill. And the main reason I come here to live is to join up with people, to be part of something bigger.

Flashback. **Pariag***'s father* (**Pa**) *enters.*

Pariag I leaving this village.

Pa This young generation! This young generation! Your uncle wouldn't like this, you know. He wouldn't like it at all. And your mother? You want to kill she? You want to send your mother to her grave? (*Changes to a more appeasing tone.*) They say you want to married. Okay. Okay. I know a man in Tabaquite with a daughter just to age.

Pariag All you making arrangements for me to married? I ain't ready to married yet. And besides, I want to choose the girl for myself. I is the one going to have to live with her.

Pa For yourself? For yourself? You think you getting married for yourself? You hear how you talking already and you ain't even leave this house yet.

Pariag But I never even see the girl, Pa.

Pa You will see her.

Indian ceremony – prelude to the wedding.

Dolly *enters. Sits. They go to see the girl.*

Pariag (*tough voice*) What you name?

Dolly (*trembling*) Dolly.

Pariag I is Boya. You ever . . . You ever go to Port of Spain?

Dolly No.

Pariag You going to have to live in Port of Spain.

Present time, **Pariag** *in house talking to* **Dolly**.

Okay, in the Savannah and on the street, people only see me with a basket of channa and peanuts, so my name is Channa Boy, okay. But, in the yard, here on Alice Street, they see me come into the yard and go out. They see my wife at the pipe, they see her hanging clothes on the line. They have to know I is somebody, a person. They never invite me to the All Fours game. They never say, 'Channa Boy' . . . okay, I know I ain't know nothing

about Carnival, but All Fours. All Fours . . .

Dolly You don't see, Boya, that you is Indian and they is Creole.

Pariag No, Dolly, no. It ain't that. They don't know me. They don't know the kinda man I really is. They not seeing me.

Dolly You have your uncle in New Lands. He will give you a work tomorrow morning. Why we don't go there?

Pariag I trying for myself. Let we try for weself. (*Optimistically.*) We will make it here. Look at Christmas. Ain't the lady upstairs send a piece of cake for you wrap up in nice, fancy paper? They know we here.

Dolly And what happen on Christmas Day? (*Silence.*) We was so glad for the appreciation that I make roti for them to eat when they come.

Pariag And I went and buy a bottle of rum . . .

Dolly Two bottle.

Pariag Two bottle. Yes. And I buy ice and put it in a bowl and while I was rinsing the five glasses, you was spreading out the new tablecloth that we never use . . .

Dolly 'Cause we never had visitors . . .

Pariag (*Christmas music up in background. Voices singing, 'Drink a rum and a puncha crema'*) And all the time hearing the music, hearing the merriment, and waiting. They didn't have no first class instrument. Was a toy flute and a mouth organ and somebody had a guitar and somebody had a shac shac and the rest was bottle and spoon. But it was nice.

Music in background.

Dolly And I plait my hair and press your shirt, and we wait.

Pariag They go upstairs by Miss Cleothilda, and they go by Guy and they come downstairs and I hear them by Aldrick and . . .

Dolly And we here alone, the two of us.

Pariag And they go by Miss Olive with her little preparation and her seven children and we hear the singing and the Merry Christmas and the glasses clinking and we wait 'cause we was sure they was leaving us for last because we new.

Dolly We wait.

Pariag We wait, with the ice melting in the bowl, and the curried mango getting cold and we hear the music fade away, fade away, fade away.

Silence.

Dolly They didn't come.

Pariag Is my fault. I shoulda invite them in. This is my place. I should go to the door and call them and say, 'Neighbour, come in. Come in and take a drink with me for Christmas. I is a Indian from New Lands and I ain't have no prejudice. We is all people. Come in.' How they will know I make preparations for them if I didn't tell them? How they coulda know that if they did come in here they wouldn't embarrass me because I didn't have a drink to offer them? They don't know me. They don't know the kinda man I really is. They not seeing me. (*Pause, with a sense of illumination.*) Maybe, if I had a car.

Dolly A car, Boya? Where we will park it?

Pariag A bicycle. A green bike with a carrier. We could use it to sell channa and peanuts and barra and double. And put a sign on it. And a bell, a big bell to ring. We will use the money that we have save up to buy it, eh?

(*Excitedly.*) Eh?

Dolly *nods, bowing her head many times.*

Pariag They must see me now. I bet they invite me to all the All Fours game.

With a daredevil's exuberance **Pariag** *rides his bicycle. One person darts out of his path. One person sees* **Pariag**.

Person Hey, look at that crazy Indian!

Others take up the chant.

Chorus (*chanting*)
Something new happening in town
The Crazy Indian coming down.
(*Repeat.*)

Cleothilda *makes the announcement to the yard.* **Olive** *appears.* **Cleothilda** *repeats.* **Olive** *repeats to* **Mr Guy**. *The yard picks it up.* **Pariag** *comes up the hill with his new bike walking.* **Fisheye** *is at the corner.*

Fisheye (*matchstick at the corner of his mouth, menacing look*) Channa Boy! . . . Come!

Pariag (*to himself, angered, seeking to establish a balance between proper respect and his own dignity*) Come? Come? He don't know is a big man he talking to. Come?

Fisheye How you passing me straight so today, man?

Pariag I . . . I didn't see you . . . I . . . I really didn't see you . . .

Fisheye You mean . . . you mean I so black you can't even see me in the day? . . . That will cost you two shillings, my friend.

Pariag (*hesitating, making of his hesitation a gesture of defiance, feeling in his pocket, trying to identify coins by touch*) I don't know if I have two . . . things hard these days . . . I have forty-two cents . . .

Holds coins for a long moment while
Fisheye's *hand remains extended. Smiles.*
Drops coins into **Fisheye**'s *palm.*

Fisheye (*pocketing the money*) You have a new bike!

Pariag I have to try.

Fisheye Just now you is a big shot, eh? Just now you going to start bouncing down people with your new bike, eh?

Pariag (*the beautiful exuberance flown from him, tries to force a swagger into his gait as he pushes bike into yard*) I wouldn't bounce you down, Fisheye. (*To himself.*) Straight to his face, I call him, Fisheye . . . straight to his face, for the first time . . . Fisheye! Fisheye! Fisheye! Let him try to stop me when I going down a hill, I wouldn't bounce him down at all!

He parks the bike carefully. Exits.

The yard. **Cleothilda** *on her verandah.*
Miss Olive *in the yard washing.*

Cleothilda (*singing in a thin, mournful voice*)
Rock of AA-ages
Cleft for me-e-ee . . .
Let me hide myself in thee . . .

Aldrick *enters and crosses, going to pipe to bathe.*

Olive Aldrick!

Cleothilda (*with an air of bereavement*) Olive! You see what happening?

Olive (*equally wounded*) Miss Cleothilda, I don't know . . . I don't know.

Cleothilda That is why I never trust them, they too sly and secretive. You could never know what going on with them. Turn, just turn your head, and they knife you in the back.

Olive But how? How we coulda ever

think to expect that from him?

Cleothilda Twenty years I live here, and if was one thing you could depend on was the equalness of everybody . . . Eh, Olive? Eh?

Olive Maybe somebody had a pot or two or a dress or two more than you; but everybody was one.

Cleothilda Not that we didn't have ambition, but nobody here look at things as if things is everything. If you had more money, you buy more food, and if is a holiday, you buy drinks for your friends, and everybody sit down and drink it out, and if tomorrow you ain't have none, you know everybody done had a good time, and all of we was . . .

Olive (*holding up a finger*) One! If a man had money he didn't go and buy things to show off. You, Miss Cleothilda, you buy nice curtains and you have radio and furnitures, but I don't call that showing off . . . you always had them. It ain't something that you buy, just to show off.

Cleothilda Who? Who in this yard like to show off?

Olive We come and meet you with what you have . . . I don't call that showing off.

Cleothilda Not a soul in this yard like to show off. You feel Aldrick can't buy a bicycle if he want to? You feel you, Miss Olive, if you really want a bike . . . really want one . . .

Olive What I going' do with bike, Miss Cleothilda?

Cleothilda No . . . I mean, you a little on the big side, is true, but if you really want to buy a bike, you can't save and save and buy one, you can't scrape and pinch and sell your soul to get one to show off with like the Indian boy do? . . . But, bike have it people . . . bike is not for you.

Olive I see the little Indian fellar with his basket o' channa. I say 'Good morning', I say 'Good evening', I say 'Howde do'. He so quiet and he little wife too. Who coulda imagine he was dangerous so?

Cleothilda Next thing he will want is to open a parlour.

Olive No! . . . No!

Cleothilda No? . . . If in . . . how much? If in two years he could buy a bike, why he can't open a parlour? I don't see how we could have him living in this yard . . .

Aldrick *completing bathing, crosses back to his room.*

Eh, Aldrick? Eh? . . . You not saying nutten at all.

Olive Aldrick, you not saying nothing?

Cleothilda Only in this yard, on this hill, this thing could happen.

Mr Guy *rushes down steps and crosses to Aldrick's room.*

Mr Guy Prospect! The Indian buy a bike!

Aldrick He buy a bike?

Mr Guy Brand new Humber . . . how you like that?

Aldrick How you want me to like it?

Guy How I expect you to like it? . . . No. You tell me how you expect me to expect you to like it. You tell me! Just now he will be buying a car, and after that a shop . . . just now he will own this whole street. You tell me how you like that.

Aldrick How you like my dragon?

Mr Guy Very nice . . . very nice. Sit down there and ask me how I like your dragon . . . your dragon is very nice, Mr Prospect . . . very nice. You don't care if he take over the whole hill, the whole town, as long as you play your masquerade, eh? You don't care.

Aldrick Listen! . . . Listen! . . . Listen!

Mr Guy Anyhow, you's your own man . . . you do what you want. I ain't come here to tell you what you must do. The rent! . . . the house rent, that's what I come for. Let the Indian take over Alice Street . . . you have the rent? The owner in my backside all the time, you know, people think I own these buildings. They feel I own them . . . the owner in my arse every day for his money.

Aldrick What about the rent?

Mr Guy What about the rent? Today is the tenth . . . that's what about the rent. The month end ten days ago. That's what about the rent.

Aldrick You have to give me a chance this month, Mr Guy . . . Carnival . . . I have to make my costume. You know how much this dragon costing me?

Mr Guy Your dragon! You want me to go and tell the owner about your dragon?

Aldrick You will have to give me a chance this month.

Mr Guy Chance? What chance you want me to give you again? The owner tell me, 'No more chance!' The owner say to give you all, all of you, notice to leave if you don't pay. Give you a chance? The Indian living here two years, you think he every one month ask for a chance? Eh?

Aldrick Listen! Listen! . . . I ain't have no rent today . . . okay? I don't have it . . . is nine years I living here, I can't owe you some rent?

Mr Guy How much rent you want to owe? Eh? Is ten months, man. Is ten months you ain't pay no rent, or you forget? What you want me to tell the owner?

Aldrick Okay, ten months . . . okay. I going somewhere? Eh? Everyday you get up an' look out, you see me here, not so? You think I going away to America or somewhere tomorrow morning? Eh? Well, what the hell you rushing me so for, this big Carnival week? When I get the money I will pay . . . well, what the hell going on in this place? What it is? I must be getting soft or something. I must be getting old. First they come fucking up my brain about the Indian; now this man come telling me about rent. Listen, man I is still Aldrick. I is still the dragon. I could turn beast in a minute.

Mr Guy That is what I say . . . the Indian must take over this place. You have your masquerade to play, so you can't think 'about nutten else. How you like that? How you like that?

Mr Guy *exits.*

Aldrick How I like that? Shoulda cuff-in his mouth from the start.

Philo *enters hastily, excitedly.*

Philo Aldrick! . . . Aldrick!

Aldrick Don't tell me you come to tell me that the Indian buy a bike too. Don't . . . don't tell me that they send you to advise me what to do. What you want me to do? Kill him? Mash up his bicycle? What you want me to do?

Philo Wait! Wait! Wait!

Aldrick No. What the hell happen with everybody? I know Cleothilda put a lotta shit in your head. I know, so don't tell me you don't know what I talking about. Everybody behind me to attack the Indian . . . well, let me tell you something . . .

Philo Me? But I ain't say nothing . . . I come here to . . .

Aldrick No. Let me tell you anyway. You see me here, I is thirty-one years old. Never had a regular job in my life or a wife or nutten. I ain't own house or car or radio or racehorse or stereo. I don't own one thing in this fucking place, except that dragon there, and the dragon ain't even mine. I just make it. It just come out of me like a child who ain't really his father own or his mother own . . . they killing people in this place, Philo. Little girls, they have them whoring. And I is a dragon. And what is a man? What is you or me, Philo? And I here playing a dragon, playing a masquerade every year, and I forget what I playing it for, what I trying to say. I forget, Philo. Is like nobody remember what life is, and who we fighting and what we fighting for . . . everybody rushing me as if they in such a hurry. I want to catch a breath, to try to remember what life is and who is I, and what I doing on this fucking hill. Let the Indian buy his bike. Guy and Cleothilda ain't fooling me. The Indian is a threat to them, he ain't no threat to me.

Philo I didn't come here to talk about the Indian, you know. I come for us to go and take a drink and for you to listen to a new calypso. I don't want to get in no controversy.

Aldrick Get in the controversy, man. Get in. You in it already.

Philo I watching and I listening, that is all . . . (*pauses.*) But, you don't find it funny, this Indian . . . he off by himself, he and his wife. You don't know what going on with them, then sudden so he appear with a brand new bicycle. It strange you know. People don't live so on the hill.

Aldrick How people does live? Cleothilda with she parlour, doing what she like when she like, don't care 'bout nobody; Guy collecting he rent, buying up property and trying to fuck all the little girls on the hill. How we does live? I, grinning and spinning. I can't talk straight to a man, I can't answer a question from a girl; I don't know how to deal with a boy who ain't have no home. They put Fisheye out the band, you know.

Philo They put *Fisheye* out the band?

Aldrick They put Fisheye out the band. Sponsors coming in. They saying they don't want no more bad-Johns. How we does live, Philo? Guy and Cleothilda trying to protect what they own.

Philo What they own? How much they own?

Aldrick I not a arse, you know. I know they don't own the island, but the little they have they frighten the Indian come and give them competition. That must threaten them. The rest of us ain't threatening them at all. All we thinking about is to play a dragon. All we thinking about is to show this city, this island, this world, that we is people, not because we own anything, not because we have things, but because we *is*. We are because we is. You know what I mean.

Philo And you don't see that when the Indian bring a bicycle in this yard, that that is-ness, that is what he threatening? We never crave to have things. Not because things ain't have no value, but because people have more value than things. And that is the life you live. (*With a chuckle.*) We live holding poverty as a possession, not entering the race for things. Look at you. Because the way this world going, if we had to depend on things to make us people, we'll be nothing.

Aldrick You used to sing that in your calypsoes, long, long ago.

Philo (*almost sadly*) I know. (*Silence.*) They pick me this year for the finals of the Calypso King Competition, you know. That is what I really come to tell you.

Aldrick (*stretching out a hand*) Shake my hand. You make it at last. Bravo . . . what calypso you singing?

Philo (*uncomfortable*) Man, you have to sing what the people want to hear.

Aldrick What you singing?

Philo Man, year in year out I singing about how people hungry, how officials ain't doing their duty, and what I get, man? What I get? I want to win the Calypso King Crown, at least, reach the finals this year, one year, so I could say after this whole thing finish, 'I was there'.

Aldrick So you could say what?

Philo So that people could write down my name, man. So that my name could be somewhere.

Aldrick (*with dawning intuition*) Yeh . . . yeh. Well, I suppose is I alone. The dragon alone.

Philo I don't mean that I don't care, or that I give up the battle . . . you understand, man . . . it don't mean that I surrender . . . I is forty-two you know. What we have to choose, Aldrick? What we have to choose? I ain't have no choice, and yet I must choose.

Aldrick Maybe you choose already.

Silence.

Philo Maybe all of us choose already.

Aldrick I don't know what you mean.

Philo Well, the girl, Sylvia, you didn't buy the costume for her . . . all of us have things to face.

Aldrick That is what you singing?

Philo Don't press me, man. Tonight is my big night.

Aldrick Once all of us the whole carnival was rebellion. Stickfighters and black devil and jab jab, and calypsonians too. Now is like all of them gone. And is I alone. Sometimes I does feel to stop, you know.

Philo Stop? To stop playing? You crazy.

Aldrick Really. I does feel to stop.

Philo But you have your costume already.

Aldrick But then as I step outside, Carnival does hit me and I hear the steel band assembling and I see the people, the robbers and the fancy Indians and the people who come to watch and the little fellars venturing to touch a pan. It does hit me, the red and black and gold and green; the colours and the feathers and the wonder on children faces and I does know again. This is warriors going to battle. This is the guts of the people, their blood. This is the self of the people that they screaming out they possess, that they scrimp and save and whore and work and thief to drag out of the hard rockstone and dirt to show the world they is people. I does feel, this is people taller than cathedrals, this is people more beautiful than avenue with trees. And I does feel a tallness and a pride. I does feel my hair rise on my head and I does feel yes, it have something here. I still have a place here and something to say yes to and I could dance the dragon for them.

Philo Don't press me, man. I going in. My big night is tonight.

Philo exits in the direction of **Cleothilda**'s

house. **Cleothilda** is on her verandah. He looks up.

Philo (serious for the first time in his relations with **Cleothilda**) You must put on your radio tonight. I singing on the Calypso King show.

Silence. He stands. **Cleothilda** is thoughtful too. He moves to leave.

Cleothilda Good luck, King Philo.

Philo exits.

Aldrick at work on dragon costume.

Enter **Pariag**.

Pariag (calling) Aldrick.

Aldrick (exasperated at being disturbed) Who is that? (He sees it is **Pariag**.) What you want?

Pariag (timidly) I disturbing you?

Aldrick What it is you want?

Pariag Well, is not nothing much. I . . . I could come back.

Aldrick Okay. Okay. What it is? You here already.

Pariag I was wondering if you could paint a sign on a box for me. I have the words right here. Is for the box to put on my bicycle.

Aldrick (reading from the paper given him by **Pariag**) 'Boya for Best Indian delicacies, Barra and Doubles.' Where you say you want me to paint this? What colours? . . . Look, why you don't come back later. I busy for Carnival.

Pariag (soft, wounded tone at the death of his last desperate hope) Okay.

Sylvia crosses the yard with her costume.

Aldrick resumes his sewing.

Sylvia walks from the direction of **Mr Guy**'s place. In her hands is the material for her costume for Carnival. She reaches in front **Aldrick**'s room. She hesitates for a

moment, as if wanting to keep it secret from
him. But then, tossing her head in the air,
she walks past him.

Aldrick (*sings*)
Me alone me alone
To face this city one man alone
Me alone me alone
I never feel so alone
I never feel so alone

Chorus
Man alone man alone
To face this city one man alone
Man alone man alone
Man shouldn't feel so alone
Hey man you are not alone

Into this life each man did come alone
And so each man shall leave
But ever as we let each body down
Spirits rejoice this ain't no time to
grieve
As we welcome every babe conceived
We struggle on because we do believe
In love
Spirits united in love
Answering your call

Chorus
(*Repeat Chorus*)

Act Two

Carnival Monday morning pre Dawn. In the darkness the scraping sounds of steelbands rolling down the hill. A cock's crow, a baby cries. The hush hush preparations for Carnival behind each closed door. Out of various yards masqueraders appear singly – a bat, robber, Indian, JabJab, sailor, soldier. **Aldrick** *entering his dragon costume. Two small boys with long dresses, masked, sweep the yard with cocoyea brooms.* **Aldrick** *steps out in costume into the street.*

Chorus *taking individual parts.*

Voice One The moment Aldrick step outside, Carnival hit him.

Chorus We hit him!

Voice One Old man Johnson and his three grandchildren as robbers. Prince as a fancy Indian, showing off his headpiece, turning delicately, the breeze rocking him, so the people could see it, so they could say . . .

Voice One Hey, prince! Man, you looking good. Man you looking sweet. You go kill them.

Chorus It hit him!

Voice One The red and black and gold and green, the colours and the feathers and the satin and the people's faces with that look in their eyes, and the smell of cologne and the look of wonder on children's faces as if they alone in the whole world had the real eyes to see the real thing, to see heroes, to see giants, to see gods.

Chorus It hit him.

Voice One 'This is warriors going to battle. This is the self of the people that they scrimp and save and whore and work and thief to drag out of the hard rockstone and dirt to show the world they is people.'

Chorus It hit him.

Voice One 'This is people taller than cathedrals.' With a strong piercing scream he step into the street, his chains rattling, his arms outflung, his head lolling, in a slow, threatening dance of the beast so that the people of the hill turned to him and say:

All Yes! Yes! That is dragon!

Voice One Terry ring the iron, calling the band to attention then.

All One, two, two, three, three, four, pram. Pram! The music burst forth from the steel band

Chorus Yes

All Yes and the women who come to watch

Chorus Yes

All Yes and the little boys waiting to touch a pan

Chorus Yes

All Yes and the Robbers and the Indians and the Clowns, yes; the whole hill began moving down upon Port of Spain.

Chorus (*singing*)
Dance dragon, play mas
Dance dragon, show the world your class
Dance dragon, play mas
This dance could be your last

Aldrick *dances.*

All Look at we dragon.

Chorus *as dragon dances.*

He have fire in his belly and claws on his hands. watch him. Note him well. He is ready to burn down your city. He is ready to tear you apart, limb by limb.

Voice One Oh, he dance; he dance pretty.

Voice Two He dance to say, 'You are beautiful Calvary Hill and John John and Laventille and Shanty Town'. Listen to your steel bands how they playing!

Voice Three Look at we beads and feathers!

Voice One Look at the colours of we costume in the sunshine!

All Look at we colours! Look at we colours! We is people, people; people is we, people!

Chorus Dance dragon, play mas (*etc.*)

The music changes. **Cleothilda** *as queen makes her appearance in her band. The band's masqueraders mingle. They dance.*

The day ending, the band going home slow, tired. People jumping up for the last. In the band, **Cleothilda** *with* **Philo** *with crown on his head, holding her around the waist.* **Fisheye** *with head bandaged,* **Sylvia** *dancing.* **Aldrick** *moving slow, slow, sees* **Sylvia** *dancing with her dizzying aliveness. He reaches out to touch her. She spins away.*

Sylvia No, mister, I have my man. (**Mr Guy** *steps forward and encircles her waist. They move off.*)

Aldrick You have you . . . You have your man? Guy?

He begins to laugh to distance himself from his pain. The band moves on. He is alone. He walks each aching step alone. We see him feel the pain.

The yard. Ash Wednesday morning. **Aldrick** *is in his room.* **Olive** *washing.*

Church organ music.

Aldrick (*holding up broken dragon, the broken bicycle where it used to be parked*) Ash Wednesday morning is the cruellest day of the year on the hill.

Cleothilda *with veil over her face and prayer book in hand, enters the hill from* *early morning Ash Wednesday mass, ashes on her forehead. she is solemn, superior. She goes past* **Olive**.

Olive Good morning, Miss Cleothilda . . . (*and when* **Cleothilda** *doesn't answer*) good morning, Miss Cleothilda.

Cleothilda (*ignoring her, grumbling loudly*) Dog shit all over the place. I don't know why police don't lock up people who, with their own children starving, insist on keeping a band of stray dogs to bring filth and disease in the place. (*She goes to her house.*) And the noise! Good Lord! Carnival ain't well done and they start up again.

Olive This woman, eh! This woman. As soon as Carnival done she gone back to the wretch she really is. (*Looking at* **Aldrick**.) Cleothilda really crazy, yes. Miss Cleothilda really crazy.

Aldrick (*without sympathy*) No, No, Miss Cleothilda not crazy.

Olive (*vexedly*) What you mean, she not crazy? Well, I never hear more. Well, I never hear more. Look, I living here in this yard longer than you and Cleothilda. I know her; I know all of you. You feel because I don't say nothing, I stupid. I ain't 'fraid Cleothilda, I just sorry for her. And as for you, Mr Aldrick, I could tell you things too. Don't think I not seeing you too. What promise you bring to anybody here? What hope you bring to that girl that say she love you. All of you is the same thing. But anyway, I older, I tougher, I have more love in me and prevailing. I will wait on she; I will wait on all of you. I waiting.

She exits.

Aldrick (*chuckling*) Now she vexed with me.

Blackout on one side of stage.

Cleothilda *comes out on her verandah*

watering her plants and singing a hymn.

Forty days and forty nights
Thou was fasting in the wilds

Early morning. **Pariag**'s *smashed bicycle on the ground.*

Dolly (*screaming*) Boya! Boya! Oh God, Boya! The bicycle! The bicycle! It mash up!

The yard come out to watch.

Pariag (*to the whole yard*) You mash it up, eh! Ain't it mash up! What you looking at now? What you looking at the mash up bike that you mash up for? Ain't you satisfy? You satisfy now? You satisfy?

Dolly (*crying*) Boya! Boya! Oh God, Boya!

Pariag It mash up! It mash up! It mash up!

Silence. **Dolly** *exits.* **Pariag** *takes up bike and moves downhill, the bike in his arms like a wounded brother. The yard look at him, they see him for the first time. He walks past* **Fisheye** *and the men at the corner.*

Man at the corner (*seeing* **Pariag** *going by with wounded bike*) Let's touch that Indian for two bob.

Fisheye (*disgusted*) That Indian? You know that Indian? Go on. Get outa here!

Man at the corner (*noting* **Fisheye**'s *mood, apologetic*) I . . . I didn't know he was your friend. Sorry.

Fisheye (*leaning forward and clouting him*) Who the hell say he is my friend.

Lights fade.

Mr Guy *walks up to his house with a hot shirt on.*

Cleothilda (*from inside singing*) All ah we is one in the island . . .

Syvia *and* **Cleothilda** *come out on* **Cleothilda**'s *verandah.* **Sylvia** *in slinky dress clinging to her body. Nails polished.* **Sylvia** *moves down the steps.* **Mr Guy** *stops her. They whisper.* **Mr Guy** *exits.* **Sylvia** *moves on.* **Aldrick** *is on the lookout for her. She moves importantly past him.*

Aldrick I want to talk to you, Sylvia. (*She hesitates.*) Girl, your life is yours. You don't have to spite me. Is your life.

Sylvia I know is my life.

Aldrick I mean is your life to *live*. Is yours *alone*. You don't have to let vexation or revenge rule you. You don't have to prove nothing to me.

Sylvia To *you*? Aldrick, what make you think I even think about you?

She makes to move on.

Aldrick Always in a hurry. Before I say a word to you, you gone. Busy, busy with your foolish importance. I want to talk serious to you. Girl, this is the kinda life you want for yourself? This shit?

Sylvia What kinda life?

Aldrick Following Cleothilda, friending with Guy, fêting your life away, forgetting the beauty that you used to have, getting stupid and vain.

Sylvia You could give me something better? . . . (*Abruptly.*) You want to talk? Talk. I listening.

He hesitates.

You ask me to listen, I stand up. Why you don't talk? What you will tell me? That you begin to make a start on your dragon costume for next year? (*Pause.*) You know what, Aldrick, you don't have nothing to say.

She makes to move away.

Aldrick (*angry*) You know what you

want, Sylvia? You want a good . . .

Sylvia (*turning back*) Well, whatever it is you is one man not going to give it to me.

Aldrick Girl, this is the kinda life you want for yourself? This shit?

Sylvia You could give me something better? . . . Aldrick, you know, I don't know how you even have the brass facedness to talk to me. I don't want to hear what Cleo and Guy doing or where they leading me. Tell me about yourself. Tell me about you. What you doing. And something else: your whole life is the dragon, you ain't have no place for me. You been the dragon so long that the dragon like a prison round you, like shield, and what it shielding you from . . . ?

Aldrick From what?

Sylvia From life, from living. *From feeling*. You forget how to feel, Aldrick.

She makes to move off. **Aldrick** *grabs her.*

Aldrick (*fiercely*) Get a job, settle down, put you in a house, hustle in this town and that will show I care for you? Marry you. That will show I care for you? And we will live poor and humble and everyday nothing ain't enough and everyday we want more and the children bawling and I screaming and you . . . you think that is what I want for you?

Sylvia And so you prefer to remain safe in the bosom of the dragon not venturing out to see what outside?

Aldrick I can't even say, I love you.

Sylvia But, you say it. You just say it.

Aldrick No, I ain't say it yet. I can't say it yet.

Sylvia You feel you will ever be able to say it?

Aldrick And you know why I can't say it yet is because I . . . is because you . . . (*She waits.*) is because . . . yes. (*With anger.*) This place have to change. This place have to change. the whole world have to change. This place have to change.

He grabs her; she waits.

Cleothilda (*from upstairs*) Sylvia!

Sylvia (*to* **Aldrick**) You going to change it?

She tugs away from him.

Lights fade.

Philo *enters with crown and gifts, walks up* **Cleothilda**'s *steps and stands on her verandah. He sings.*

Philo I am the axe man, cutting forests down
I am the axe man, working all over town
If you have a tree to cut I'm the man to call
I never put my axe on a tree
And it didn't break and fall.

Philo *exits.* **Aldrick** *picks up his dragon costume, puts it down. Moves to the corner.*

Chant.

Aldrick (*sings*) Alone alone me alone to face this city alone . . . etc.

Aldrick (*goes to the corner,* **Fisheye** *embraces him*) Hey man, you are not alone.

Police sirens.

Chant: 'Out in the road'.
Out in the road
Come out in the road, warrior
Come out in the road, warrior
Judge and jury go by
You for murder.

Cleothilda *on her verandah.* **Olive** *in doorway.* **Fisheye** *and* **Aldrick** *at corner.*

Cleothilda You don't find our friend change?

Olive Who?

Cleothilda Our friend . . . our dragon friend.

Fisheye We is the last one; the last warriors.

A working man goes down the hill.

Look at him, going to work docile like a lamb and he don't own one damn thing. (*To* **Man**.) Hey! Gimme a dollar!

Man *fumbles in his pocket.*

Olive I find he quiet. But I really can't say how he change. He never do nothing before, except make his dragon costume. And I don't see him doing more nothing now. I really can't say how he change.

Cleothilda I tell you he change man. I only have 60 cents Fisheye, gimme. Long ago he uses to make a joke, laugh, tease somebody. He used to sleep and get up and stretch and yawn and we would know he alive. Now is a different kinda nothing. Now he serious and looking, he thinking and plotting. You think is crazy he going?

Olive I don't know. Though they say when a lively fella gets serious so is to watch him.

Fisheye You can't feel sorry for these people, Aldrick. They is traitors every one of them, to their own self. A man must have guts; a man must have iron.

Aldrick Maybe is their best they doing, man.

Cleothilda I hear he not playing dragon next year.

Olive (*about to exit*) Not playing dragon? He must be going crazy . . .

Fisheye Man, all of us come from this same hill. All of us go through the same hell. How that could be their best? You know what happen to you? You too soft . . . softness will kill you.

Enter **Philo**, *crown on his head, bottle of rum.*

Philo Hey, fellars, how it going?

Aldrick Okay.

Fisheye *is silent.*

Philo I bring a bottle for us to hit. (*Uncorking bottle.*)

Fisheye (*to* **Aldrick**) That fellar is your friend?

Aldrick He is everybody friend.

Fisheye Well, he ain't my friend. Cleothilda and Guy is his friend. (*To* **Philo**.) You is a big shot. It ain't have no big shot here.

Philo (*looking around, thinking it is a joke*) Where the glass? Nobody ain't have a glass? Well, we'll drink from the bottle then. (*To* **Fisheye**.) Look, you break the seal.

Offers bottle to **Fisheye**.

Fisheye I tell you, you ain't have no fucking friend here.

He slaps bottle aside. **Philo** *is struck in the face.*

Philo (*realising it is serious*) I is the same man, not because I win the Calypso Crown mean I change. (*Appealing to* **Aldrick**.) Aldrick, you know me. Is years we is friends. I is still Calvary Hill. No matter what you see me do, you is me and I is you. Listen, fellars, is years I struggle alone, man. Years I just like anybody on this hill, and at last I get a break . . . luck . . . I win the Calypso King Crown. What life for, man? What the struggle for if your friends leave you, if they don't understand? . . . This woman, Cleothilda, been in my blood for years. In my *blood*. I want this woman for my own. Don't ask me why I want she; I just know I want this woman. You know how she treat me, Aldrick? I shame. And nothing I do I could get she out my mind. And then one day, man, one day, I walk up the steps and I say, 'Cleothilda, open the door!' . . . and she open it. She open the door, man.

Aldrick You choose, Philo. You choose.

Philo Choose?

Fisheye You better leave here, Philo. You better go.

Philo (*turning to make another appeal, but thinking better of it*) So is war then?

Fisheye Is war.

Exit **Philo.**

Lights dim on **Fisheye** *and* **Aldrick** *in corner. They are still there as lights up.*

Philo (*on* **Cleothilda***'s balcony, singing*)
Hooligans in Port of Spain
Messing up the place
Last night one of them slap my girl in her face
Next time they see me, they better beware
I have an axe in my hand, a pistol in my waist
When my gun shoot off the police could make their case
Why they so jealous I really don't know
I was their friend not so long ago
Since I start to get farce they grinding their teeth
Like Philo is some kind of meat
The next time they see me they better come straight
I have a dagger in my hand a pistol in my waist
When I protect myself the police could make their case.

Fisheye *and* **Aldrick** *still on corner.*

Sound of police sirens.

Police Move on! Move on! No loitering on this corner. This is the last warning. Next time you going straight inside the van.

Fisheye You see me, one day I going to kill a police.

Blackout.

The corner. **Aldrick** *and other fellars. Sound of police sirens.*

Police (*hailing over megaphone*) This is the police. This is the police. Move on! Move on! No loitering on this corner. This is the last warning. Next time you going straight inside the van. (*Repeat.*)

Aldrick *remains. The other fellows begin to move off. They turn and see* **Fisheye** *dressed all in black, black hat, etc, like a cowboy in a western movie.*

Smalls (*in amazement*) Look Fisheye coming!

They all turn to gaze at **Fisheye** *as* **Fisheye** *crawls slowly steadily towards them. The police sirens grow louder. The hailing over the megaphone continues.*

Fisheye Today we not running. Let them come.

He takes a cigarette from behind his ear, gets a light, draws in smoke . . . He draws from his pocket a pistol, holds it up.

Fisheye (*as the fellows crowd around*) Touch it; touch it. Everybody touch it.

The gun is passed from hand to hand. **Fisheye** *draws bullets from another pocket.*

Here! I have the bullets! I ready to dead this morning. Let them come . . . I want you, Crowley and you, Synco to start a fight.

Synco A fight? For what?

Fisheye When the police come they will come to part the fight. They will come to arrest you.

Aldrick And when they arrest them?

Fisheye When they arrest them? We will see.

Aldrick Well, suppose they don't arrest them.

Fisheye (*holding up the gun*) What happen, you frighten?

Police sirens grow nearer. Sounds of police jeep. Hailing continues over the loud speaker. **Synco** *and* **Crowley** *begin their fight; they hold each other and wrestle each other on the ground. The siren goes, the police hailing stops, the sound jeep stopping, policeman enters with a baton, his gun in holster; sure of himself, he walks towards them.*

Policeman You all deaf? You don't hear we say clear the corner?

Putting a hand on his holster and going to the two fighters, he grabs one of them

Come on! Get up! We going straight to the station. Move!

The combatants rise.

Move on!

Fisheye (*is behind them, posed as a cowboy, pistol in hand*) Nobody ain't moving on. And take your hand off your holster.

Crowley Put up your hand and walk slow inside the van.

The policeman begins to move, **Fisheye** *still standing with gun pointed. Lights go down as* **Fisheye** *and group herd the policeman offstage. Offstage sounds of jeep starting.*

Fisheye (*over the megaphone*) This is General Fisheye of the People's Liberation Army. We are armed and dangerous.

The sound of two bullets shot into the air.

Aldrick (*voice offstage*) This is the People's Liberation Army calling the people of Calvary Hill. Rise up, rise up and take yourselves over. Rise up and take power to be people for your own self; take power, take power.

All Power! Power! Power!

The roar of the vehicle, the buzzing noises of people. Lights down.

Lights up on the yard.

Two weeks later

Olive *is alone washing over the tub.*

Enter **Cleothilda** *and* **Sylvia** *from the city.* **Mr Guy** *following a little way behind.* **Olive** *turns expectantly towards* **Cleothilda** *and* **Sylvia.** **Mr Guy** *makes his way up his steps.*

Cleothilda Five years.

Olive And Fisheye?

Cleothilda Six.

Twin scene with **Aldrick** *and* **Fisheye** *in jail.*

Olive I know something like this was bound to happen to him.

Cleothilda I coulda tell it from since Carnival finish and he refuse to make a start on his new dragon costume.

Olive Leave off making his dragon and gone on the corner and meet Fisheye and five, six strayway young fellars who come with their muscles and their vexation as if they could fight the world.

Mr Guy (*partly up the steps, vexedly, resentful*) Terrorising people with their vexation; acting as if a man who go and do a honest day work for a honest dollar is some kinda traitor.

Cleothilda What they want, Miss Olive? What they want? You could tell me? What they vex for? We could live good good good in this island, all of us, as one.

Guy Shooting bullets in the air; going in the cathedral and blackening the white faces of the white saints . . .

Olive Stick up the police and gone with their jeep like fools into the heart of town.

Cleothilda As if nine men with two guns could turn the world upside down. The thing was a joke.

Olive What I wonder was why the police didn't stop them.

Cleothilda Stop them for what? Let them parade; let them play their big masquerade; let them drive around; let them talk; let them make big speech; let them shoot their guns off in the air. Where they coulda go?

Mr Guy In the end they was glad to surrender.

Sylvia Lots of people was praying for them to win.

Olive Thank God they didn't kill nobody otherwise we would all be in black now . . . (*Thoughtfully.*) So that is why the police didn't stop them. Well, then, what they do it for? What they did expect?

Sylvia The lawyer say it. He say they believed in miracles.

Olive Yes. Like Daniel in the lion den; like the Israelites parting the Red Sea. Yes, we believe in miracles.

Chorus *song.*

Reds (*singing as police herd* **Aldrick** *and* **Fisheye** *into prison cell*)
Why the police didn't stop them . . .
You have to understand
They wanted to show them that they had no plan
They were magicians looking for a miracle

And now that the magic fail they end up in jail
'Cause we believe in miracles
Our life is pure art
We grow up on miracles
It's all we have to start
The authorities knew the men would fail
So they didn't raise a hand
To convince them of their weakness in this crazy revolution
They were magicians looking for a miracle
And when the magic fail, they end up in jail.

Aldrick *and* **Fisheye**
We don't want to build these shanties
We didn't create the slums
Can people decide on their own indignity?
Are people really human?
We were magicians looking for a miracle
And now the magic fail
We end up in jail
We believe in miracles
Our life is pure art
We grew up on miracles
That's all we have to start.

Cleothilda Well is a good thing you didn't get involved with him, eh Sylvia?

Sylvia *says nothing.*

Lights go down on **Sylvia**, **Cleothilda** *and the yard.*

Lights up on prison.

Aldrick You want to know why the police didn't stop us?

Fisheye I really can't say they jail me for nothing. We play a mas, eh? We had them wondering if we would shoot down the town or what. It was great. Even you couldn't play a better dragon.

Aldrick All we did was threaten. You

know we coulda do more than play a mas? I was ready for something bigger.

Fisheye (*perplexed*) More than a mas? You mean after we leave the Square we coulda start shooting?

Aldrick *is silent.*

Or you mean when we went in the Cathedral, we coulda camp right there and wait for the police? (*Still thoughtful.*) You mean we coulda hold those people we find praying in the cathedral sorta like hostages? Nah, man, you can't mean that. Is that what you mean?

Aldrick *is silent.*

You mean we shoulda shoot one of the police?

Aldrick (*with dawning wisdom*) Yes, I suppose it had to be a mas. We didn't have the vision. (*Pause.*) All we wanted to do was to attract attention.

Fisheye (*outraged*) That is all? Since you in prison like you get holy or crazy or something. (*He turns away.*)

Aldrick We have to act for weself.

Fisheye You mean I stick up the police and capture their jeep and parade the town and it wasn't for me? For myself? Man, you beat me.

Aldrick Even with guns in hand, we was looking to somebody else to make the decision. Is like we have a self, but the self is for somebody else.

Aldrick You think I crazy, eh? (*Pause.*) Not full crazy? Sorta crazy, eh?

Fisheye Yes, sorta crazy.

Aldrick We change.

Fisheye Me, I smarter. I know that you have to have real power and if you don't have it you have to learn to survive with them that have it. Now a

man have to learn how to live.

Aldrick Make no peace with slavery, Fisheye. We have survived. We full up the shanty towns, the prisons, brothels, mental asylums. We have to live as people; we have to rise up.

Fisheye But how you rise up with your brothers making peace for a few dollars, and sisters selling their souls. And you have children to school and rent to pay?

Aldrick I don't know . . . (*He thinks.*) We have to rise up.

Fisheye Man, you don't know the things I see. I tired now; I tired now. I just want to get a cigarette to smoke and play a few games of ping pong and let time pass so I could go out into the world again . . . Listen, you know why we play a mas? Why? (*Pause.*) Is because a man alone, that is all he could do. That is all a man alone could do. And I play one of the best mas that ever play in Port of Spain. I see Batman and Ozzie and Barker and Barone. I see all of them. Alone, all a man could do is play a mas.

Aldrick (*appealing*) No, Fisheye. No peace. No peace. No peace.

Lights fade.

Five years later.

Mr Guy *dressed to go abroad, comes out of his apartment.* **Cleothilda** *on her verandah watching.* **Mr Guy** *pauses, looks across at* **Cleothilda**.

Cleothilda (*gleefully*) So when you come back from London we will be eating wedding cake?

Mr Guy You don't find is time. I can't keep on running round. I'm a City Councillor now. With all these functions and conferences I going to, I have to have a wife by my side. You can't go far in politics without a wife.

Cleothilda As I tell you, the best place to buy the wedding dress is in London.

Mr Guy I will depend on you to keep an eye on her for me.

Cleothilda Don't worry. You think I want to see her go away with any of those fellars who come in here with all their grand dreams to change her life. Where they will put her. The last one who come was a revolutionist wanted to carry her with him to live in the bush on top Aripo mountain with a pack of biscuits and a tin of sardines. You can't live so, girl, I tell her, when you could live safe with Mr Guy.

Mr Guy I love that girl.

Cleothilda You love her.

Mr Guy I love that girl, Cleo.

The car horn blows. **Guy** *exits.* **Cleo** *goes inside.*

On **Cleothilda**'s *verandah.*

Philo *knocks.*

Cleothilda Who is it?

Philo Is me, Philo.

Cleothilda Come in, come in. What breeze blow you here. Since you in Diego Martin, I can't see you.

Philo I was passing through, so I drop in to see you. How you?

Cleothilda (*scrutinizing him, she senses something is wrong. She is uncertain*) Still alive, though I don't see my friends as often as I want to. Sit down . . . You get the invitation to the wedding?

Philo I didn't expect it to be Guy. He will destroy her without knowing it. (*Feelingly.*) Because he don't even see the beauty in that woman.

Cleothilda Wait, like you did love her too?

Philo (*confused*) Is just how I see her grow up here in the yard, see the spirit in her, the fire, the speed, the beauty, the promise that make you pull back and want to let her live, to let her grow, let her go.

Cleothilda And Guy don't see all that in her?

Philo Guy? He wouldn't know how to deal with that, to do with her.

Cleothilda Even if he love her?

Philo Love? You believe Guy know what love is?

Cleothilda Well, I telling you just as he tell me and he don't owe me, so I don't see why he should want to lie to me.

Philo So you believe him?

Cleothilda You woulda believe him too if he say it to you the way he say it to me, 'I love that girl'. He will be good for her. He will settle her down.

Philo Settle *her* down.

Cleothilda (*triumphantly*) Yes, tame her, put a ring on her finger. That will stop those young men from coming into the yard on every excuse to watch her, to tempt her . . . And not one of them have anything more than the one thing all men have to offer . . . Anytime now Aldrick will be coming out of prison. Guy not taking no chances. He making sure and put a ring on her finger.

Philo (*affirmatively*) She could go with a ring on her finger too. He can't settle her down.

Cleothilda Not in Diego Martin?

Philo Diego Martin? What you mean not in Diego Martin?

Cleothilda Haii! (*Slapping his leg.*) You mean I didn't tell you that he buying a house in Diego Martin and that is where he carryng her to live?

Philo (*Struggling for certainty*)
Anywhere . . . anywhere on God earth
he carry her, he can't hide her. He
can't stop that spirit in her, not even in
a nunnery.

Cleothilda (*disbelieving*) You don't
know what you saying. Well, you
should know, cause you living Diego
Martin how much years now? I . . .
ain't even offer you a drink. What you
having? (*She senses something is not quite
right with him.*) Philo, what happen?
Tell me. So where you come from?

Philo I was just down at the snackette.
And in the snackette, all these people
gather around me dancing to my
calypsoes, offering me drinks, treating
me as a hero . . . And when I listen to
some of those calypsoes I hear them
dragging down my friends, my
women, my sister, my mother, myself,
and people shaking my hands . . . I am
their big hero. A big hero.

Cleothilda (*with a sense of
resignation*) What you going to do?

Philo Oh, God. And to think I is their
own. I is what come out of their belly.

He looks at the hill, the scene below.

Singing
Just where I am a traitor and betrayer
without memories of self
I want to remember and hold you
and love you . . .

Silence.

Cleothilda You want a drink?

Philo Yes.

*She gives him the drink. She gets closer to
him.*

Cleothilda It chilly tonight, eh. *I know
what happen* (*Triumphantly.*) . . . you
going away and you come to bring a
little present for me before you leave.

Philo Yes, I going away.

Silence.

Cleothilda You want a drink?

Philo *nods.*

Cleothilda And we better go inside, I
feeling a bit chilly out here.

Philo *rises slowly.* **Cleothilda** *stretches out
a hand for him to hold and turns to her
bedroom.*

Cleothilda Come . . . you doing like if
you don't know where my bedroom is.
But with the way the world going even
that wouldn't surprise me.

Three weeks later.

Pariag *now owns the shop at the corner.*
Aldrick *enters. He looks in at shop.
Pauses. Continues.*

Dolly You see Aldrick? You see him?
He stop right in front the shop and
then he walk on.

Pariag I see him. (*Pause.*) . . . I hope
he don't think that because I have
shop now if he come in we can't talk.
Shop don't make a man.

Dolly Why that should worry you?
You don't have to beg them for their
friendship again, or for anything.

Pariag We could talk. People could
talk. It have things for us to talk
about.

Dolly What you going to talk about
with him? Prison?

Pariag You know what worrying
me . . . I see him standing up there
and same time I thinking to call him
and wondering what kinda welcome to
give him. I had a chance to call him in.
I didn't do it. I paused too. Just like
him . . . and moved on.

Dolly Boya, sometimes I don't

understand you. I thought you say you done with Creole people.

The yard.

Sylvia *turns from the standpipe to the tub below the governor plum tree, enduring still in the yard, shelter for the wash tub, pole for the clothesline, bearing still its little green berries that seemed to disappear before they turned the purple of ripeness: and turning still, her body moving in a loose easy unharnessed freedom, dancing to a calypso strummed inside her on a double second pan, a soft, grumbling dancing, the movements printing the outline of her panties against her dress. She lifts her head to the sky and the clouds to see whether she should hang out her washing, and glimpsed out of the corner of her eyes, this figure, this male, blue and dark colours coming softly past the fence of woodslats and stubs of hibiscus.*

Sylvia Oh gosh! Is Aldrick!

Aldrick How you?

Sylvia I say you dead.

Aldrick I come to see you.

Sylvia I get old, eh?

Aldrick You can't get old.

Sylvia You spend a long time in prison for that stupidness. Five years. It didn't do nothing for nobody. The government started to fix the streets up here, and they give some fellars work on a project, then they stop. Why you all do that?

Aldrick It just happen.

Sylvia Some people was glad though.

Aldrick They was glad?

Sylvia I was there. I went to listen to hear what it was all about, but I didn't understand one thing. You didn't see me? I was right to the front, on the pavement. I hear you talking. I didn't know you coulda talk so. Everybody

was surprised you coulda talk so.

Aldrick I wanted to say I love you . . . I wanted to shout it for everybody to hear.

Sylvia Why didn't you do it? 'Fraid?

Aldrick Yes. But I ain't afraid now.

Sylvia You see your old room gone. Two fellars lived there before I move in.

Aldrick I ain't frightened now.

Sylvia And Pariag . . . you remember the Indian fellar with the thin wife . . . he gone from the yard. The shop at the corner is his own now. Miss Cleothilda still here as the rock of ages. She gone to town today, but she should be coming back just now. She sure will be surprised to see you. And I guess that you know that your friend, Philo, is a big star now. He live in Diego Martin, singing calypso all over the world, going to America and England. He is a big shot. Now and again he does come here and look for Cleo.

Pariag You know is how he come so sudden, so outa the blue. If I wasn't as surprised to see him . . . if I myself wasn't so sure that he was going to come in. I could call him in . . . unless, maybe I was frighten.

Dolly But they don't have any power to insult you again, Boya, you don't owe them nothing. I don't see whether if you call him or he call you, why that shoulda worry you.

Pariag I wish we was luckier, all of us; us and Aldrick and Fisheye and the yard and the hill. I wish we was luckier with each other . . . I wish . . . I wish I was just beginning now, just coming into the yard for the first time. I wish I had come with me, my own spirit and soul and grief and love and say, 'Look me! Look me!' I wish I did walk with a flute or a sitar, and walk right in there in the middle of the steel band yard where they was making new drums, new sounds, a new music from rubbish tins and bits of steel and oil drums, bending the iron over fire, chiselling out new notes. New notes. I wish I would go in there where they was making their life anew in fire, with chisel and hammer and sit down with my sitar on my knee and say, 'Fellas, this is me, Pariag from New Lands. They woulda see me. They woulda see me. You know they never see me.

Dolly Boya, they see you. Everybody see you. With the shop and everything, everybody see you.

Pariag They never really see me.

Dolly But you here . . . with the shop . . . they must see you.

Pariag You right . . . Yes, (*Thoughtful.*) you know what is the hard part?

Dolly What is the hard part?

Pariag They see one part of me – the shop part – and they take that to be the whole me. (**Pariag** *and* **Dolly** *hanging out clothes on* **Sylvia**'s *line*.) You think it will rain?

Aldrick You ever think about leaving this place, leaving here?

Sylvia And now I living by myself. I have this room you used to live in; I fix it up . . . and Ma in hospital. I have to go to see her this evening.

Aldrick You know . . . you know I didn't know nothing about life before . . . life was only my dragon long ago.

Sylvia And the little boy, Basil, the boy who used to come by you to make the dragon costume . . . if you see how tall the little boy get. He is a recruit now in the Police Force . . . And I playing mas this year.

Aldrick You playing mas? What you playing. (*He smiles.*) A slave girl!

Sylvia I playing a lady. A lady in waiting. Next year I might play the queen. You know what mas the band playing? Devils.

Aldrick (*excited*) Devils? People playing devil on the Hill again?

Sylvia Two thousand strong.

Excited at this hope.

Aldrick Two thousand devil coming down this Hill, going into Port of Spain?

Sylvia Not real devil, you know. Not terrible like the dragon you used to play. Fancy devil. With lamé and satin and silk. Pretty devil. I have my costume already. You want to see it?

Aldrick Pretty devil. With silk and satin? Oh God, girl!

Sylvia People come from all about to play with us now.

Aldrick Now I know I ain't just a dragon. Funny, eh? Years. And now I know I is more than just to play a masquerade once a year for two days, to live for two days. I ready to face the whole of life now. It have life for us to live, girl . . . life.

Sylvia Why you come back here for?

Aldrick To see you. I come back to see you. You didn't tell me about Guy. What about him?

Sylvia Come inside out the sun . . . you want a drink? All I have is rum and orange juice.

Aldrick Rum and a little orange juice . . . you have a nice place here.

Sylvia I comfortable here. I have everything I want.

Aldrick You didn't tell me about Guy.

Sylvia What you want to know?

Pariag They take the part of me that they see, that . . .

Dolly That they want to see.

Pariag What?

Dolly The shop part.

Pariag That is the part that I show them . . . I wanted to show them me; but, only a part I show them. *What you show is what you is, Dolly.*

Dolly (*protective, anxious, authoritative*) You is more, Boya. More than what you show them. I is more than what I show you, not so?

Pariag *is quiet.*

You not vex I say that?

Pariag I not vex. I glad you say that; you right. Everybody is more than what they show. That is why we have to live. But how you make someone know you, who know you too long and don't know you at all . . . (*Pause.*) When you expose your whole self to them?

Dolly I see now . . . you should talk to Aldrick in truth.

Pariag (*tenderly*) *We* have to start to live, Dolly, you and me.

Dolly (*tears choking her with astonishment and respect*) *Me* and you?

Pariag You looking at me like how you look when I tell you you going to have to live in Port of Spain. Hmm! Port of Spain, Port of Spain.

They exit into shop.

Pariag Yes, I wish he did stop to talk to me.

Freeze.

Lights fade.

Cleothilda *enters.*

Cleothilda Sylvia, if you know how things dear in Port of Spain. I went to buy sequins for my jacket, and if you know what price they selling them . . . hey! You have visitors . . . hi! Is you!

Sylvia Aldrick just drop in. We just this minute sit down here.

Cleothilda Well, if you have visitors, I better go. You could see me any time.

Sylvia No. Come in.

Cleothilda No. I will stay too long. Let me go and put down these things . . . well . . . shake my hand. Is a long time. You looking well. Jail agree with you . . . and, you know, last night . . . yes, it was last night . . . I dream you. I didn't tell you, Sylvia? I dream how you come here with a rope in your hands and was pulling down the shop, my shop; but you didn't have to pull it down. It gone to the dogs already. I find it so funny that you should want to pull down my shop. But you don't have to pull it down, Aldrick, it pull down already. Sylvia ain't tell you the Indian boy, Pariag, buy the shop at the corner . . . well, he buy it. I ain't vex with him. I ain't vex at all. I ain't jealous. He young, and is a free country, so if he come to this town, to this hill, and put up a shop for people to buy from him, I is the last one to say anything ill. The only reason I mention it at all is because last night I dream how you come with this long, long rope and tie the shop and try to pull it down, and I want you to know that it pull down already and I tired. I really tired, you know. I find things ain't have no value these days, and the little value they have they losing faster than babies borning on this hill. This place going to the dogs. Long ago when you and Philo was living here, it had decent people on this hill – poor, but decent. Now is the last crumbs and dust of people here, doing anything for a dollar. They racketeering, they robbing, they shooting. No! They ain't using knife again. Is like since Fisheye pick up that gun and stick up the police and kidnap their jeep, guns sprouting all over town. Prayer is all remain. Prayer. I don't know what woulda been my condition if I didn't used to pray. Battoo's Funeral Home woulda long carried me away. And, with Sylvia going away from here in a month or two, I can't imagine what I would do . . . she ain't tell you? You ain't tell him, Sylvia? I don't want to tell him your business, you know, though when you give out the invitations everybody will know. You shame? You shouldn't be shame, you know. Guy is a City Councillor now. He is a man treat you good from the beginning: TV, radio, fridge, stereo, dress, show. He old, is true. Everybody have to get old . . . people say I old too . . . you don't have to love him now. Love will come, and if it never come, at least you will be comfortable; for one thing you know about him is he will take care of you which is more than you could say for these young fellars buzzing around behind you. The boy, Raymond, good looking but where he going to put you? Now and again he make a pair of sandals for one of his friends. He ain't working nowhere. How you going to live so? You will him 'bout Raymond? You know 'bout Raymond? You ain't tell him 'bout Raymond?

Sylvia We hardly start to talk anything.

Cleothilda Well, I better shut my big mouth and go. I will see you later. But the reason I saying all this is so he will know he can't come here just so, breeze in here after five years in prison and tantalize your brain. What you could do for her, Aldrick? I

talking plain. Tell me what you could give her.

Exits.

Sylvia I was going to tell you . . . is time for me to settle down, make something of my life, have children. I ain't getting younger, you know. And I tired with these fellars I offer myself to. I tired listening to them talk and can't see nothing.

Aldrick So you getting married to Guy?

Sylvia Yes . . . you want another drink?

Aldrick No thank you.

Sylvia (*suddenly challenging*) What you could give me?

Aldrick Yourself.

Sylvia You know, you change.

Pause. He sips the drink.

What you come here for? Eh? What?

Aldrick I'm sorry.

Sylvia Where you going to go?

Aldrick I'll get a place somewhere. I'll do something. I could paint . . . a sign painter. (*He chuckles.*)

Sylvia What signs you will paint?

Aldrick New signs. (*Pause.*) You know I don't regret nothing.

Sylvia You have money?

Aldrick Because I was a good dragon when I was a dragon, the best in Port of Spain, in Trinidad, in the world.

Sylvia You have money?

Aldrick I was the best dragon in the whole world.

Sylvia You know you crazy. You think you going to go and live and not pay rent like long ago. Things change, you know . . . (*She goes inside and returns with twenty dollar bill.*) Take this. Don't look at me, take it. You could at least buy cigarettes. Take it. Don't say anything. Just take it . . . and go. I is nearly a married woman. And don't come back.

Aldrick Keep well . . . keep well, eh. You's a real princess, girl.

Sylvia Goodbye! Goodbye!

Aldrick . . . And all this polish and glitter is not you. You is a queen, girl, and this room, pretty as it is, is not you, is not your end. And you young still, and you don't have to hide yourself underneath no polish and in no room. You don't want nobody to take care of you, to hide you, to imprison you. You want to be a self that is free, girl; to grow, girl; to be, to be yourself, girl.

Sylvia Aldrick, goodbye!

Aldrick You's a queen, girl.

Sylvia Goodbye! Shake my hand.

Aldrick *walks with her into the yard, still holding her hand.*

Cleothilda (*from her verandah*) We'll send you an invitation.

Aldrick (*affirmatively*) I don't regret nothing. (*Loudly for* **Cleothilda**'s *benefit.*)

Cleothilda (*stridently. She feels she's losing* **Sylvia**.) We'll have the steel band playing, roti, rum, bacchanal. We going to have a fête big as Carnival.

Aldrick For I was a good dragon when I was a dragon, the best in this city, this island, this world. I was the best dragon in the whole fucking world. I just feel I would like to sit down with the fellars, with Fisheye and Philo, with everybody who went through those days with me and tell them we was good, we was the best.

(*To* **Sylvia**.) Come, let's go again.

Guy *appears with suitcases, boxes of presents and flowers.* **Sylvia** *stands between him and* **Aldrick**. *She looks in both directions not knowing which to choose.*

Chorus begins song 'Dance Dragon'.

Let's go again.

A Rock in Water

Winsome Pinnock was born in Islington in 1961 and obtained a joint-honours degree in English and Drama from Goldsmith's College, London in 1982. Over the next four years she worked as a marketing assistant for a unit trust organisation and then as a sales support supervisor, before deciding to write full-time. In September 1986 her first play **A Hero's Welcome** was presented in a rehearsed reading at the Royal Court, Theatre Upstairs, London and in the following year her second play **The Wind of Change** was performed at the Half Moon Theatre, London and toured thereafter. In 1988 **Leave Taking** was produced at Liverpool Playhouse Studio and, later in the year, **Picture Palace**, a play commissioned by the Women's Theatre Group was toured nationally. In 1988 Winsome's first television script, an episode of **South of the Border**, was transmitted. A revised version of **A Hero's Welcome** was produced by the Women's Playhouse Trust at the Royal Court Theatre Upstairs in 1989.

Author's Preface

When Elyse Dodgson approached me with a view to commissioning a play about Claudia Jones for the Royal Court Young People's Theatre, I jumped at the chance. Claudia Jones was such an intriguing woman: credited with having started the Notting Hill Carnivals, she also ran one of the first black presses virtually singlehandedly. Yet when she died in 1964 she was alone and by the 1980's had been forgotten, even by the community she had served tirelessly for most of her life.

With the 14 actors who had responded to a mail-out, we held twice-weekly evening workshops. Some people had never acted before but everyone had something interesting to contribute. These sessions were a period of creative exploration during which we looked at the events that would have influenced Claudia.

And then I was packed off to write. One of my more terrifying experiences. While exploring the facts we had somehow managed to avoid looking at Claudia's character in any real detail. So, armed with a cassette recorder and a few memorised questions, I set out to interview people who had known her. This made my task all the more difficult because each interviewee carried their own select memories and I gained no real sense of the flesh and blood woman until I spoke to actress Corinne Skinner-Carter. Corinne had so many anecdotes, so many fond memories, all recounted with tremendous love. Claudia must have made a great friend. Most importantly, the woman Corinne conjured up was *real*: a heroine who never forgot her roots, a fearless campaigner who gave up an ambition for 'political stardom' in order to work at grass roots level – comforting, encouraging and fighting on behalf of a people who could so easily have given up the struggle in those turbulent days of the mid-50's. But they didn't give up. And the play is as much about them as about Claudia. They're still fighting and so, in a way, is she.

Winsome Pinnock

A Rock in Water was premièred at the Royal Court Theatre Upstairs, London on 12 January 1989, with the following cast:

Claudia Jones	Lunga Yeni
Claudia Jones *as a girl*	Eveline Okonfo
Elizabeth Gurley-Flynn/ Evicted Tenant	Angela Bell
Ben/Donald Hinds	Junior Blanche
Mother *Mrs Cumberbatch, Claudia's mother* **Mrs Cochrane**	Heather Durrant
Ned	David Edwards
Stella/Prison Officer	Avril Evans
Ben's daughter *aged four*	Marcelle Grant
Factory Foreman/Mr Paulsen	Luke Mariner
Carole	Yetunde Otuwehinmi
Messenger Boy/Ahmed	Marcus Powell
Claudia's lawyer	Mary Richards
Alice/Dina	Jenneba Sie Jalloh
Charles/Cumberbatch/Mackenzie	Godfrey Walters
Mary/Red	Paris Yaw

All other parts played by members of the company.

Choir: Geoffrey Aymer, Ninia Benjamin, Alison Brushfield, Tessa Forbes, Debbie Lawomie, Clare Plater, Eveline Okonfo, Marcus Powell, Mary Richards, Mark Spillane, Sandra Tavernier.

Directed by Elyse Dodgson
Designed by Anabel Temple
Lighting by Rick Fisher
Musical Director Mark Holness

Act One

Scene One

Claudia *and her mother stand on a street corner in Brooklyn, USA, 1927.*

Mother Look, Claudia.

Claudia What?

Mother Can you see it?

Claudia No.

Mother You're not looking. Over there.

She gazes up for a moment.

Claudia My eyes keep closing.

Mother Try to keep awake for me.

Claudia I'm trying mama.

Mother Would you rather go home?

Claudia I want to stay with you.

Mother I'm so sorry baby.

Claudia Let's both go home.

Mother I need a job.

Claudia You got a job.

Mother It's not enough.

Claudia Even with daddy working?

Mother Even with daddy working.

Pause. She gazes upwards.

My, isn't that beautiful? Think, Claudia, we fret, we toil, we die and the sun still rises. Even in Brooklyn. Your sisters need new clothes.

Claudia Can I have new clothes?

Mother You'll grow into your sisters'.

Claudia Why don't we go back to Trinidad?

Mother I thought you'd forgotten it.

Claudia I think about it sometimes.

Mother Do you want to go back?

Claudia Not always. It was better there, there were good places to play. Let's go home.

Mother Look, Claudia, see how big it is now?

Claudia It's scary.

Mother It's only the sun.

Claudia Ben gave me a seed weeks ago but it never grew.

Mother Knowing that child, it was probably just a stone that looked like a seed.

Claudia That Ben. Wait till I get him.

Mother You mustn't fight, Claudia, it isn't nice. You could get hurt. Besides, it's not good. You want to be good?

Claudia Sometimes. But a lot of the time I just feel like fighting, Mom. Ben gets me mad. He calls me names. I know I'm old enough to know better. Dad says . . .

Mother You're so pretty.

Claudia Am I?

Mother You're so beautiful. My girl.

Mother *hugs* **Claudia** *very tight.*

Claudia (*quizzical*) Mom?

Mother I'm so proud of you.

Claudia You're pretty too.

Mother Washed out, tired looking. I wish I had someone to wash my clothes.

Claudia I could do it.

Mother You'll see, when we get a job, how clean those women are, how soft their hands are.

Claudia You're soft at the sides. I like to put my head on your lap, like a pillow.

Mother What woman doesn't wish her own daughter could live like a princess?

Claudia I don't want to be a princess.

Mother You'll grow up and marry Ben.

Claudia Never, never, never. The women that come out of the Apollo don't look married.

Mother Are you still hanging around outside that theatre?

Claudia Will my legs grow long enough?

Mother What'm I going to do with you?

Claudia I want to dance, Mom, and sing. It's all I want, I don't want anything else.

Mother Calm down Claudia. Get excited you'll make yourself ill.

Claudia I haven't had an attack for months.

Mother You must take care of yourself. I won't always be here.

Claudia You always say that. If I did everything you said, I'd never do anything.

Mother As if you ever listen to a word I say.

Claudia I do and I try, but I'm going to be a dancer at the Apollo. Oh, it's like there's something bursting in me, if I don't get up sometimes or run around or shout out I feel like I'll explode.

Mother Claudia.

Claudia Like any minute I'll be able to fly.

Mother Stop it Claudia. I can't bear to listen to your nonsense. That's rubbish about flying and long legs. You've got to grow up fast. I won't always . . .

Claudia I know.

Mother I been waiting on other people since I was much younger than you are now. My head was never full of such nonsese.

Claudia I'm going to be an actress and you can't stop me.

Mother The sooner you get used to washing some white woman's clothes . . .

Claudia Stop it, Mom.

Mother . . . the better. Because it's what you're going to be doing for the rest of your life. Even if you pass those wretched exams.

Claudia No.

Buries her head in her hands.

Mother Claudia, Mom didn't mean it.

Claudia Then why did you say it?

Mother Feelin' mean and pinched in, wishing we were back home in bed.

Claudia I don't like you.

Mother You're old enough to understand.

Claudia You never say these things in front of Daddy.

Mother He spoils you.

Claudia You're a jealous old woman, he said.

Mother He was only joking.

Claudia He watches me dance and listens to my speeches. He claps. You never do.

Mother Because I know better. Oh, my girl, life is tough. You got to fight and fight and fight until you die.

Claudia You said I mustn't.

Mother You'll learn. You know I only say these things for your own good.

You know how much you mean to me.

Pause.

(*Puts her arm around* **Claudia**) Friends?

Claudia (*pulling away*) No.

Two women enter. **Mary** *and* **Stella.**

Mary My poor bones, get me a seat girl.

Stella *gets her mother a box to sit on.*

Mary I'm getting too old to be standing on street corners waiting for work.

Stella *starts to sing.* **Stella**'s *song should be almost choreographed – curt, jerky movements in time with song.*

Mary Do you have to start up with the singing as soon as we stop somewhere? (*To* **Mother**.) She thinks some impresario in a big limozeen is gonna cruise past some day and discover her in the street. She's read one too many stories in Movie Magazines about starlets being discovered while working over some machine in a sweat shop. I've told her that only happens in the magazines. But I just let her be. There's no telling them these days. 'Course employers like her 'cos she always singing round the house, cheers them up 'cos they lead such tiring lives. She's like a breath of fresh air. That your daughter?

Claudia No.

Mother Claudia.

Mary You shouldn't frown so. Time you're my age, face'll be a bag of wrinkles. Pretty girl like you. Isn't she too young to be working?

Mary She's got to get used to it.

Claudia I won't.

Mary This one swung from the breast while I scrubbed the stairs of some Alison's house. (*Laughs.*) Come to think

of it, perhaps that's what started it. I had to sing in order to get through.

Mother Don't you mind?

Mary Long as she keeps singing I know she's all right. It's when she stops I'll start worrying. And she's company for me. She don't set foot outside the house.

Mother Why not?

Mary She gets scared. Don't want to leave her mammy's side.

Claudia I'm going to be an actress when I grow up.

Mother Claudia, don't dig your heels into the ground like that, you'll ruin them.

Mary And they cost a pretty penny. (*Talking down to her.*) Policeman'll come along and take you away for digging up the road. Put you behind bars. Lock you up. Now you wouldn't like that, would you?

Claudia Don't care.

Mother She's not usually so rude.

Mary It's a long hot morning. The women sleep late round here. You'd think we'd got a bite by now.

Mother You're not from round here?

Mary From down south.

Mother Things are very different here.

Mary Girl, I feel like I've escaped from a prison. This is like a holiday.

Mother How long have you been here?

Mary Two weeks. I've always looked on the bright side of things. I'd be happy anywhere.

Claudia (*as she digs her heels in the ground*) I'll. Never. Clean. Some. White. Woman's. Dirt.

Mary Listen to her. Miss Do-It-My-Way. I like cleaning white women's houses. Especially when they're not in them.

Mary and **Mother** *laugh conspiratorially.*

Mary You do that too?

Mother All the time.

Mary I once got caught.

Mother My dear.

Mary I was so ashamed. I was wearing her best hat and gloves. And Stella had put on one of her long silk skirts. She looked divine. We got booted out right there and then. She wouldn't even pay us for the day's work. For wear and tear she said.

Mother Oh my. To get caught.

Mary It hasn't hurt us. We go on doing the same old thing. We don't care. Do we Stell!

A white **Woman** *enters. Atmosphere changes. Where the two women were relaxed, they're now tense and nervous. The white* **Woman** *stops in front of* **Stella.** **Claudia** *watches closely.*

Woman What's your name?

Mary Stella.

Woman Doesn't she speak?

Mary Sings mostly. I'm her mother. We work together.

woman Do you cook?

Mary And sew and polish. No domestic work is beyond my experience, ma'am.

woman I'm rather particular about how things should be done.

Mary Quite right too.

Woman I'll pay you 45 cents an hour.

Mary Thank you ma'am. Come along Stella.

Mary and **Stella** *exit.*

Claudia I'm going home.

Mother Claudia, I've told you.

Claudia I'm going.

Mother Listen to me.

Claudia Don't touch me. I hate you.

Pause. Mood changes.

Mother Go on, go home.

Claudia *hangs around for a while, kicking her heels. She doesn't know what to say, then she runs off. Her* **Mother** *reaches into a bag she has and takes out some darning. She darns furiously. She pricks her finger and puts it in her mouth.*

Scene Two

A street in Harlem, later the same day. **Ben** *and* **Claudia** *are on stage.* **Claudia** *shields something in her hands. She won't let* **Ben** *see it.*

Ben I'm going to play in the park with the boys.

Claudia Go on then.

Ben *doesn't move.*

Ben Coming?

Claudia No.

Ben Bet it's just a pigeon with a broken wing.

Claudia Is not.

Ben Who wants to see anyway?

Claudia Then go away.

Ben I got a secret in my pocket. I'll show it to you if . . .

Claudia Go and play with the boys.

Ben I'll even listen to a speech if you've got one.

Claudia I haven't.

Ben Don't you want to be an actress any more?

Claudia 'Course I do.

Ben Then why . . .

Claudia Don't bother me, Ben. All I can think about right now is this poor creature, I'm gonna take care of it, till it gets better, then I'm gonna throw it up in the air and watch it fly off into the sky.

Ben It is a pigeon.

Claudia A chick.

Ben Let's see.

After some hesitation, **Claudia,** *cupping her hands, shows bird to* **Ben**. *He laughs.*

Where'd you find it?

Claudia I'm gonna make a little nest for it, give it a new home. Make it safe so no one can harm it.

Ben I'll help.

Claudia You mustn't tell anybody else.

Ben A secret. Oh my, wait till I tell Jonas. That I've got a secret.

Claudia Maybe I'll teach it tricks.

Ben You said you was gonna let it go.

Claudia I am. One day.

Ben Can I hold it?

Claudia *sighs then places the bird in* **Ben's** *hands. He giggles.*

Ben It tickles. There was a pigeon squashed flat like a pancake in the road. It's been there three days.

Claudia Why don't you scrape it up?

Ben Daddy says the government should do it. That's why we pay taxes.

Claudia Your daddy's stupid.

Ben Is not.

Claudia You're both stupid. And you wanting to be a driver when you grow up.

Ben I am gonna be a driver.

Claudia How?

Ben Same way you're going to be an actress.

Claudia I ain't dumb.

Ben You are.

Claudia Then that makes you super dumb because you bottom of the class.

Ben Am not.

Claudia Teacher said you was dunce.

Ben And you're too big, black and ugly to be a dancer.

Claudia Give me back my bird.

Ben No.

A battle of wills commences during which **Claudia** *tries to force* **Ben's** *hand.*

Ben You're hurting.

Claudia Give it back to me.

Ben *wriggles away from* **Claudia** *and drops the bird. They both stand and stare.*

Ben I'm sorry Claudia.

Pause.

If you hadn't . . . I'll find you another one.

Claudia Maybe you could give it the kiss of life.

Ben (*shaking his head*) We better bury it.

Claudia I wanted something for myself.

Ben Let's take it to the park.

Claudia *stoops to pick it up.*

Ben Let me.

Ben *picks up the dead bird and wraps it in tissue then puts it in his pocket.*

When I'm a driver I'll drive you all round New York for free.

Claudia Could we go outside New York?

Ben We could drive all over the world.

Claudia When I'm at the Apollo I'll get you free tickets.

Ben I'll wait at the stage door for you in my car.

Claudia Because I'll be too tired to walk home after all that dancing.

Ben The car's going to be sky blue.

They exit.

Scene Three

A garment factory, Manhatten. Later the same day. Women stream into factory and clock their cards. Exaggerated sound of machines. After clocking in the women set their machines and get down to work. They talk as they do this. Each woman carries out her business without even thinking about it.

Woman 1 I'm glad you told her. I wouldn't want to see you get into trouble.

Woman 2 I felt so bad. I did want to help her out. But I couldn't face being caught.

Woman 3 Management catch you doing something like that and your name is dirt. No more work. Might as well be dead.

Woman 2 I know how hard things are for her . . .

Woman 3 Aren't they for all of us?

Woman 6 Not for me, I feel free as a bird.

Woman 7 You would.

Red Life is to be lived.

Woman 7 They all say that before they settle down. Wait till you've had a few kids.

Woman 5 Red'll never settle down.

Red You tell her.

Woman 4 What's so wrong with settling down?

Woman 1 Some people don't know when it's time to stop playing the field. I think it's about time she grew up.

Red Since when has having kids meant you'd grown up? You're just a baby.

Woman 4 Am not. (*Proud.*) I'm a married woman.

Red Sorry. I forgot. Anyone seen Cumberbatch?

Woman 2 She's late. As usual.

Red She promised she'd attend a meeting with me last night.

Woman 1 The woman works two jobs and you expect her to go to your stupid union meetings?

Red Done wonders for me. Unfettered my mind, removed the blinkers.

Woman 7 Long as I'm being paid for it, I'd rather stay blind.

Red Where's her card?

Woman 2 *gives* **Red** *card. She clocks in for* **Mother**.

Woman 1 You'll look a fool if she reports in sick.

Red I'll say I made a mistake and punched the wrong card won't I? For god's sake what're you all so afraid of?

Foreman *enters and talks in a loud booming voice.*

Foreman Hello ladies. Welcome to Hell.

Woman 5 Does that answer your question? The very devil. All he needs is a pitchfork.

Foreman Come on ladies, you're dragging your heels. There's enough work to keep us all going non stop for months.

Red Well, isn't that nice?

Foreman I want to see you all sweating today. (*To* **Red**.) Especially you.

Red My every pore has started secreting at the very thought of it.

Foreman Well, I'd best not disappoint you had I? I'll go and get you some work.

Foreman *exits.*

Red (*shouting after him*) Slave driver!

Woman 3 Ssh!

Red He can't hear me. He thinks we're animals. Every time I open my mouth all he can hear is a donkey braying.

Woman 5 How's the baby?

Woman 4 I don't know why he's so healthy.

Red The boy's a born Commie. It's a well-known fact that Commies thrive in the direst circumstances.

Woman 7 They bloat on their own self importance.

Red Anger keeps you alive.

Woman 7 Super Commie lives on air.

Red That's right, comrade. Got a match?

Woman 3 We're not allowed to smoke.

Woman Who's to see me?

Woman 3 The wolf'll be back any minute.

Red I'll put it out when he does, then.

Woman 7 Long as you go down alone.

Red I wouldn't dream of taking you with me.

Woman 8 It's enough just struggling to keep a job.

Mother *enters carrying a shopping bag.*

Woman 2 You're late.

Mother I'm half asleep.

Woman 1 Where have you been?

Mother Did someone clock in for me?

Red Sure did.

Mother (*relieved*) Dear. I owe you. (*Goes to her machine and quickly prepares it.*) Has the wolf been in?

Woman 1 Didn't even notice you weren't here.

Mother The woman wouldn't let me go. Scrub the stairs, mop the kitchen floor, polish the silverware. Didn't even pay me.

Red Not again. What do I keep telling you, Cumberbatch?

Woman 2 No one could take advantage of me like that.

Mother She gave me some of her old clothes, though. Save me buying any. Might be a nice dress in there for me.

Woman (*turning over clothes*) Rags. Make yourself something better outta the remnants from this place.

Foreman *enters.*

Foreman I won't tell yous again. This is not the annual conference meeting of the negro women's institute. Hi Cumberbatch. Late again? She thought I hadn't noticed. I see everything. Even your thoughts. So be careful. Once more this week and I'll dock your pay. Now get on with your work.

You make me sick all a yous.

Foreman *exits. Women get back to work mumbling.*

Woman 4 Do you ever dream of flying?

Women are all working their machines. **Mother** *yawns.*

Red Take it easy if you're tired. I'll help you out. Here. (*Takes up some of* **Mother**'*s work.*) I've got a lot of energy today.

Mother Thank you.

They exchange smiles. **Mother** *yawns then puts her head down on the table.*

Red Hypnotic isn't it? The wheel turning round?

Mother (*weary*) Yes.

Red Like the wheel of life turning ever onward. My mother had a spinning wheel. Sometimes, as she spun she'd tell me stories, other times she'd just hum to herself. As I watched the loom I'd get drowsier and drowsier. My mother always looked serene on the loom, like she was spinning all her troubles away. That would be nice, wouldn't it? That's right, Cumberbatch, you take a little nap.

Mother I can't.

Red I'll call you if the wolf comes back.

Mother I . . .

Woman 5 Hey, Red, seeing as you're playing good samaritan, wanna help me out with this batch?

Red Go back to sleep Carter.

Woman 5 Wouldn't I just love to. Look at Cumberbatch. Falling asleep on the job. It's not fair.

Red Such is life honey.

Messenger *boy enters and gives a long, low wolf whistle. He carries a pile of material and spools.*

Woman 9 Was that whistle for me?

Messenger All a yous. You's all beautiful.

Woman 4 Who do you love sugar?

Messenger No one but you.

Woman 4 That's my baby.

Woman 2 Sing us a song.

Messenger What do you want?

Woman 1 Call me baby, baby.

Red Do you know the Internationale? Or perhaps (*Looking down at* **Mother**.) Lullaby of Broadway.

Messenger How about this?

He sings. As the song comes to an end **Foreman** *enters.*

Foreman How cute. Love songs at dawn and a bunch of women with nothing on their minds but bedtime.

Red (*trying to shield* **Mother**) We love you too comrade.

Foreman No wonder productivity's low. We gots to shape up, work hard and pick up. It's in your own best interests. Factory closes say bye-bye to your livelihoods.

Red And hello to President's wallet. Did you know he finances the dole out of his own pockets?

Foreman Very funny, Red.

Woman 5 If I could dress like the First Lady.

Woman 3 Three inch sparklers and a four foot tulle.

Red Twinkle twinkle little star.

Foreman Forget about the First Lady, you's got your own problems. We got an extra order.

Red Now ain't that nice. And in our own best interests too. Rest quietly Johnny you can eat tonight, after all.

Foreman Yes, despite your best endeavours to screw things up we still get orders from people. But this is a very special order. A big firm. Plenty money. We've got to impress them. If you get this order processed quickly and efficiently, by that I mean on time, then you's'll get a bonus at Christmas.

Woman 4 (*sings*) Christmas is so far away. Tra la la la la la.

Foreman So you're all working late tonight.

Red Can we take this to the union?

Foreman Which union?

Red C'mon, don't mess around. You know very well what I'm talking about.

Foreman I don't want no trouble, Red.

Woman 4 Neither do we.

Woman 2 Who said I wanted to join the union anyway?

Woman 1 That ain't no place for black women. I've heard some things I tell you.

Foreman That's my girls. Just think Christmas Bonus and you'll fly through that material.

Red I'm not giving up, Miller.

Foreman You can do what you like. In your own time. I'm certainly not going to waste mine. How does the saying go?

All Time is money and money is time.

Foreman Is Cumberbatch sleeping or is she studying that piece of material for boll weevel? What am I, a babysitter? Lily-livered softies all a as yous. Don't know the meaning of hard work. Could tell you stories if I thought you could handle it. Somebody wake her up and tell her the good news. I got work to do.

Foreman *exits.*

Woman 4 It's going to be a long night for some of us.

Woman 2 Someone wake up Cumberbatch.

Red (*sings*) Hush little baby don't say a word.

Woman 3 Talk about a heavy sleeper.

Woman 3 C'mon Cumberbatch you're not the only one got to catch up on their beauty sleep.

Woman 2 She's exhausted, aren't we all?

Woman 5 Know what I'd like for Christmas? One day to myself. Just one day. Is that too much to ask?

Woman 1 Throw some cold water over her, that should do the trick.

Woman 5 Some of us got enough self discipline to at least keep our eyes open till the wolf has gone back to his lair.

Woman 1 (*shouting and shaking* **Mother** *roughly*) C'mon Cumberbatch, rise and shine.

Woman 2 Don't do that. You might hurt her.

Woman 1 Why not? It's more trouble for her otherwise.

Woman 2 I ain't never seen a sleep that deep.

Woman 1 Ain't even set her machine right.

Red (*troubled*) No, she hasn't. C'mon Cumberbatch, wake up for your old friend Red.

By now all the other women are standing round watching in silence.

Woman 5 You don't think . . .

Red 'Course not.

Red *takes* **Mother**'s *hand. She lets go of her hand. It just drops limply. They all stand, shocked, looking at each other and then at* **Mother**, *frightened but saying nothing.*

Scene Four

A shed in a tenement block in Harlem. Night time. **Claudia** *is curled into a tight ball on the ground. Her father, Charles, enters; a rather weary looking man who's yet got a little bit of fight left in him.*

Charles Claudia?

Charles *approaches* **Claudia** *and stands and watches her. At first he can't bring himself to touch her, then he lifts her up. Her face is wet.*

Too cold for a little girl like you. You'll catch something. Take you inside, make you something nice and hot to drink, put you to bed. Warm, snug and safe. My best girl.

Claudia *pulls away from her father then curls herself up tight again. Then she arches her head back and cries out with a child's confused anger and pain.*

Claudia Why did she have to die?

Charles (*at a loss as to what to say*) Because God wanted her.

Claudia No. I'm not a child. Don't tell me lies like a child.

Charles (*gently*) Let's go inside, shall we?

Claudia Get the hell off me.

Charles This isn't my little Claudia speaking, where's my little Claudia?

Claudia She's dead, little Claudia is dead.

Charles This is just the pain of the moment. It won't always be this bad, I promise. Come Claudia, you should try to get some sleep.

Claudia She keeps staring at me. She never closes her eyes or blinks. Tell her to go away.

Charles I'll sit at the end of your bed and every time you see her you need only look up and I'll be right beside you.

Claudia *sobs. Her father comforts her by rocking her gently.*

Claudia It's not fair.

Charles These things happen, they have to.

Claudia They killed my mommy.

Charles Who did?

Claudia Somebody.

Charles Haven't you been praying, Claudia, it would help.

Claudia I pray. To keep myself from hating.

Charles Hate? You're too small for such a big word. Hatred serves no purpose. Don't let me hear you talking of hating again, Claudia. Now anger . . .

Pause.

Shall we go inside?

Claudia *nods.*

Claudia Dad.

Charles Yes?

Claudia (*hard*) I'm never gonna die.

Scene Five

Inside the head of the Statue of Liberty. **Claudia** *and* **Ben**, *both 18, enter. They* *stagger and pant.* **Ben** *carries a large paper package.*

Ben Where shall I put it?

Claudia Anywhere.

Ben *gets out a hip flask and takes a swig.*

Ben Claudia, now we're alone.

Claudia Unless we want to be caught we'd better get a move on, don't you think?

Ben You're a coward at heart, aren't you?

Claudia I never said that I was brave.

Ben It's my last day before I go away to the army.

Claudia It's very good of you to spend it working for the cause.

Ben That's not what I meant.

Claudia I know.

Claudia *sits on her heels sorting through leaflets.* **Ben** *watches her then leans forward and kisses her forehead.*

Claudia Ben.

Ben Claudia, talk to me, please.

Claudia What're you after? One last fling before you set off? Find someone else, I'm busy.

Ben I want you to come with me.

Claudia (*shocked*) What? (*Pretending to busy herself with leaflets.*) Don't be ridiculous.

Ben I'm serious. Why not? Hey?

Claudia I can't leave my work.

Ben Stop pretending to be grown up. The Scotsboro boys'll hang whether you drop a few leaflets from the top of the Statue of Liberty or not.

Claudia Least I'll have tried to do something.

Ben I see. So, it doesn't matter what effect the action has, just so long as you get to feel you've done your bit, so that you can feel self-righteous.

Claudia I'm beginning to see how different we are. You're a conformist.

Ben And you . . .?

Claudia Believe we can change things.

Ben If we work really hard for them. The American Dream. You're a conformist too. Besides, how do you choose which action you take? Every issue has so many sides.

Claudia You follow your conscience.

Ben But how do you know it's right?

Claudia You don't. You just have to trust your instincts. We know instinctively what's right and wrong. This is silly Ben.

Ben How can you know? How do you know that those boys didn't rape those two poor white-trash country girls?

Claudia I suppose, the same way I knew you didn't steal any money from that house your mother was working in.

Ben That was different.

Claudia Why? Because they only had to look in your face to see that you're a different kind of black boy? That could have been you on that train, it could be you behind bars.

Ben But it isn't.

Claudia I'd fight just as hard for you. Harder.

Ben It isn't me. I'm here.

Carole *enters, panting, followed by the rest of the 'gang'.*

Carole I'm dead.

Claudia No progress without struggle, comrade.

Carole *takes a swig from flask.*

Carole Ecstasy. It's not what I expected.

Ben It is a little small.

Claudia We're here on business, not to take up residence.

Carole Maybe it's because I'm just a poor unsophisticated girl from the Bronx, but I had expected it to be a little more . . . dazzling.

Ben Our lady has a full heart and a small empty head.

Carole Mom used to take us to look at her some weekends. We'd just look up and listen to momma's stories about daredevil feats of escape. It sounded exciting. Don't you think she looked just a touch angry as we approached the island?

Claudia You're not getting cold feet on me, are you Carole?

Carole She didn't seem at all pleased to see us. It wouldn't have surprised me if she stepped down from her pedestal and set our ferry alight.

Claudia She ought to be proud of us.

Rest of the gang enter.

Boy 1 Where's the leaflets?

Claudia Don't worry. I have them. Are you sure it'll work?

Girl 2 'Course it will. The impact it makes on landing should force it to burst open.

Boy 2 Then the wind'll scatter them.

Ben What if there's no wind?

Girl 3 There's always a wind stupid.

Carole (*looking out through a small window*) Would you just look at that.

Girl 4 So huge.

Claudia Doesn't capitalism make an ugly skyline?

Boy 3 I think it looks rather beautiful.

Carole Doesn't it do something to you just looking at it?

Claudia Then don't look. (*Moves away from window.*) How shall we do this?

Ben Claudia takes this all so seriously.

Carole We all do.

Ben Other people find time to go to dances, to have fun. Not Claudia. Ever since your Commie tutor told her she had a natural instinct for leadership she's been in a world of her own.

Claudia I wouldn't call editing the Young Communist newspaper a world of my own, comrade.

Ben No? Please stop calling me comrade. I'm not one of your pretentious Commie gang. I knew you when you had scabby knees. I don't understand what's happened to you. Why're you all so anti everything?

Girl 1 Because we use our brains. If we didn't think then I'm sure we'd be as pro as you are.

Girl 2 It's like you've been brainwashed.

Ben I think you're all very childish.

They all groan.

Boy 1 You're just out of high school yourself. Coming on like old father time.

Ben I think what you're doing is reckless and ineffective, to think that you can change the world with a few sensational leaflets, which people are just going to tread into the ground anyway. You'd do anything she told you wouldn't you Carole?

Carole I do have a mind of my own.

Ben Why do you all hate America so? I love that skyline, love capitalism, I love the lady with the lamp. Yes, I love America.

Boy 2 He loves the lady with the lamp.

Carole Poor Ben, he finds solace in the idea of a safe harbour, a fairytale land far from the pain of the real world. You're going to be so disappointed when you grow up comrade.

Ben Shut up Carole.

Claudia (*teasing him*) Give me your tired, your poor . . . (*The others join in.*) Your huddled masses yearning to breathe free.

Ben You've changed.

Claudia So have you.

Ben I can't remember the last time I saw you laugh.

Claudia I laugh all the time, but right now I'm busy.

Ben Too busy for your old friends.

Claudia You're here.

Ben When we could be on a beach somewhere or strolling in a park.

Claudia Holding hands and discreetly averting our eyes from the struggle around us?

Others . . . The wretched refuse of your teeming shore. Send these the homeless, tempest toss't to me . . .

Ben You could come with me. We could both work hard to make up the money we'd need. It wouldn't be easy but it'd be . . .

Claudia What?

Ben A life.

Others I lift my lamp beside the golden door.

Claudia I can't.

Ben You don't want to?

Claudia (*shakes her head*) I can't.

Ben OK. (*Quietly.*) 'Bye Claudia.

Ben *goes.* **Claudia** *stands looking after him.* **Carole** *goes over to her.*

Carole You've had lots of arguments. He'll be back.

Claudia Not this time.

Carole Then good riddance.

Boy 3 Come on, there's people on the way up.

Girl 2 Who's gonna throw them?

Carole Me and Claudia.

Girl 4 That's not fair.

Carole It was our idea.

Girl 3 Well, I think we should take a vote on it.

Boy 1 That'd be more democratic.

Claudia I don't care who throws the stupid things as long as they get thrown.

Carole Come on Claudia, cheer up. He's just one bloke.

Girl 1 Plenty more shrimps where he came from.

Boy 2 Who're you calling a shrimp?

Claudia He was my good friend. Now I've lost him.

Carole There'll be other friends. Besides, I'm still here. Are we going to throw this thing or not? Come on, let's do it together. After three. One. Two. Three . . .

Scene Six

Living room of the Cumberbatch's flat, Harlem. **Claudia** *sits on sofa draped in a towel.* **Paulsen** *enters carrying two mugs. He gives one to* **Claudia**.

Paulsen Dry?

Claudia Not very.

Paulsen I hope you don't catch cold.

Claudia I'm strong as an ox.

Paulsen Your father tells me you suffer from asthma.

Claudia Not often.

Paulsen The years I've known your family and I'd never have guessed, you looking so healthy. Sugar?

Claudia One. It's very kind of you to come and babysit.

Paulsen It was the least I could do. Your father and I have been friends for many years. He won't be pleased.

Claudia You should have seen their faces. So vicious.

Paulsen I suppose you have to see it from their point of view: when a way of life, a good, a steady way of life is under siege, people start to panic. They feel they got to root out the cause of the problem.

Claudia Or turn the hose on it.

Paulsen Drink your tea. (*Pause.*) Your father and me got here round about the same time.

Claudia He often talks about it.

Paulsen I couldn't speak a word of English. He helped me to get a job at his factory, taught me the phrases I'd need to get through the day.

Claudia You don't owe my father anything.

Paulsen The immigrant depends on the kindness of strangers. You half expect to get spat in the face and kicked like a dog, but the other half of you dreams of living like a king and gaining instant acceptance. But that's something you got to work for. You have to prove you belong. You know, it hadn't even occurred to me that no one would understand a word I said. How's that for innocence? Them first few years were not easy, I tell you. I was like a sponge, just watching, absorbing, like a chameleon. I wanted a deep understanding of the American mind. From then on it was plain sailing, a simple matter of getting rid of everything I had been up to then. It's not easy, takes a special kind of temperament, but you know what the hardest thing was? Learning to think in English.

Claudia Daddy says that you were a good student.

Paulsen I began to act like an American, speak like an American, but I still thought like a foreigner. I had to work very hard at it.

Claudia And now that metamorphosis is complete?

Paulsen Even now I sometimes find myself slipping back into the old ways.

Claudia That must be very frightening for you.

Paulsen It's a useful reminder of what I escaped from and how lucky I am to be here. I dread to think what I'd be doing if I hadn't left. What would you be doing now if you'd stayed in – where was it? – Trinidad.

Claudia (*shrugs*) Working in the fields, maybe something not too different to what I'm doing here.

Paulsen It's that uncertainty that keeps me going.

Claudia Most of us have a great instinct for survival. I'm sure I would have survived wherever I grew up.

Paulsen Because you're a very strong, purposeful woman. Not everyone is like you. Take my daughters. I married them off as soon as I could. Why? Because I didn't know how they'd fare out here if they tried to go it alone.

Claudia As long as they wanted it too.

Paulsen I always wanted them to be like you. It woulda been a weight off my mind knowing they could look after themselves.

Claudia You think I can look after myself?

Paulsen Claudia, do you ever stop to think about your father?

Claudia You know I do, all the time.

Paulsen It can't be easy for him to watch you ruining your life.

Claudia I'm not.

Paulsen These things weigh on a man's heart.

Claudia My father leaves me to live the life I chose.

Paulsen I'm sure he does. All I'm saying is he won't allow you to see the grief deep down inside. (*Suddenly.*) Now isn't that a thing?

Claudia What?

Paulsen An image just flashed across my mind just this moment. Now fancy that. I'm starting to see visions now, is it? In my mind's eye I had an image of a little negro girl holding up some sort of prize she's won at school.

Claudia That's unfair emotional blackmail.

Paulsen I remember that so well, the whole block was proud of you. What was it for now?

Claudia Good citizenship.

Paulsen That's right. Now ain't that a thing.

Claudia Isn't it?

Paulsen Tell me, Claudia, do you still love America?

Claudia Of course I do.

Paulsen Then why do you do the things that you do?

Claudia Because I love America.

Paulsen Claudia Cumberbatch.

Claudia Jones.

Paulsen I forgot. You even change your name to suit your party.

Claudia It was a matter of practicality, not politics. Cumberbatch doesn't fit the space allocated for my column.

Paulsen I'd have thought, you being such a high up member that they'd have given you more space.

Claudia We all have to compromise.

Paulsen My sentiments exactly.

Pause.

You must understand. People like your father and myself are very vulnerable. That's why it's so important for us to fit in. Why, I remember when my papers came through. I jumped for joy. Literally. Sarah and the girls thought I must have gone mad. But it meant so much to me, you see. I felt safe, like a baby all wrapped up in cotton wool. It was all written down. It couldn't be erased. I couldn't be erased. At last I felt that I belonged.

Claudia What are you trying to tell me Mr Paulsen?

Paulsen These are dangerous times, Claudia. Only last week the woman upstairs' son was taken away by the police.

Claudia She must be distraught. I'll have to go and see her.

Paulsen She made the phone call that incriminated him. Her own son.

Claudia Some people are very patriotic.

Paulsen Not even I could be so loyal. Please don't do anything to hurt either yourself or your father. Promise me. I sometimes look on you as one of my own. I would be as upset as your own father if anything were to happen to you. Why, I would . . .

Carole *and* **Charles** *enter.*

Carole Claudia, you're here. We've just come from the station.

Claudia They had to let me go. I've done nothing wrong.

Charles To have to set foot in one of those places. A place for common criminals.

Claudia They haven't charged me daddy.

Charles Not this time.

Carole We'd better get you out of those wet clothes.

Claudia I'm all right.

Carole I can hear your teeth chattering from here.

Charles What would your mother have thought? We had it hard, Claudia, but we never got into trouble with the law, we always stuck to the rules.

Paulsen Charles, I better go back upstairs. She gives me such a hard time for being late. I'll never hear the end of it. Yes. (*Exits.*)

Claudia Walked around on tiptoes, trod on nobody's toes. I can't do that.

Charles Because you're so much better than everyone else.

Claudia Of course not.

Charles Then why must you always be right?

Claudia I'm not that arrogant, father, I don't know any answers but I have to do what I think is right. If my mother had been free, she might still be here. At least her life would have been worth something more.

Charles She was everything to me.

Claudia And to me.

Charles She worried about you more than any of the others. She saw through you. I was too blind, too wrapped up in dreams.

Claudia I love you both.

Charles Had I been more realistic things would have been different. I should have been harder on you.

Claudia Poor daddy, I'll make you a nice hot drink.

Charles You don't go to church any more.

Claudia I haven't had the time.

Charles Is that the truth?

Claudia (*looks down embarrassed*) I'm not sure I can bring myself to attend those services.

Charles Because you think that you can play God, take charge, manage the world on your own. All your grand schemes and plans will come to nothing until you realise that only one man has the power to change things.

Claudia Your God is a bigot, he hates blacks, jews and women.

Carole Claudia please.

Claudia If he can change things then why doesn't he? Why should some of us have to die struggling to live? I'll never accept that this is the way things are meant to be, that I have no power.

Charles You're just one woman.

Claudia And I'll fight your God to the death.

Pause.

I'm sorry. I lost control.

Charles Humility was never one of your strengths, Claudia.

Claudia I'm only human. Your God, if he exists, made me imperfect.

Charles *starts to go.*

Claudia Don't go, daddy.

Charles I'm sure you can manage things quite well on your own. You always do. I'm going to bed. I'm very tired.

Charles *exits.*

Claudia He hates me.

Carole He's very proud of you. He just gets frightened for you.

Claudia You don't think I should give this up do you?

Carole Of course not. (*Putting an arm round* **Claudia**.) You like to have me traipsing around behind you don't you? Even when we were children playing pretend you were the boss and I your secretary.

Claudia What would I do without your friendship.

Carole Someone's got to keep you in line.

They smile.

Carole Oh Claudia, always this need to be the centre of attention and to do the right thing at same time.

Claudia Is that how you see me?

Carole How do you see yourself? As Joan of Arc no doubt. Just as long as you don't end up being barbecued at the stake.

Claudia I've a meeting to go to.

Carole You've always got a meeting to go to. Claudia, why not stop being the all powerful Lady-with-the-Lamp-Liberationist just for one evening and let me take care of you.

Scene Seven

The Cumberbatch's flat very late at night. **Claudia**, *older, is sitting up, reading a letter that she's just written.*

Claudia (*reading*) Dear Ben. A great cloud hovers over us and we live with the constant fear of arrest. Every mother is afraid of her own children, every child of their own mother and father. Daddy won't open the door to anyone and has warned me to do the same. This is virtually impossible as I am always inviting members of the community to call on me whenever they need to. Most accept the invitation and daddy is exasperated by the endless stream of people asking for help with their immigration papers, people wanting me to sign petitions, start petitions. He says I'll exhaust myself but doesn't understand that if I stop moving I feel that the ground will shift beneath me, opening up to swallow me into a bottomless pit. (*Pause.*) Despite yourself I'm sure that you would be proud of me. I have turned into quite a woman (even if I say so myself), an able leader. You should see me in the debates. Fearless. Or so they all believe. (*Pause. She puts letter down.*) Won't post it anyway.

A knock is heard at the front door. **Claudia** *jumps up and goes to door.*

Claudia Who is it?

Voice A friend of a friend.

Claudia What?

Voice Asked me to give you a message.

Claudia Which friend?

Voice I have it right here. Just one moment. (*Long pause.*)

Claudia Hello?

Voice I'm still here. Won't you let me in?

Claudia Who are you?

Voice Please open the door. I'm in big trouble. You won't send me away will you?

Claudia What sort of trouble?

Voice I'm not guilty. I was walking, is all. Along the street. They can't arrest you for walking the street. This is a free country.

Claudia Mr Paulsen?

Voice That is you Claudia?

Claudia Yes.

Voice Claudia Jones?

Claudia (*exasperated*) Yes.

Voice Open the door.

Claudia Tell me who you are.

Silence.

Voice I'm in trouble. There's a child.

Claudia With you?

Voice I left her in one of the sheds. can you hear her?

Claudia No.

Voice She thinks I've forgotten her. Stay there.

Claudia Hello.

No reply.

Light change we move straight into the next scene.

Scene Eight

Inside a New York police van. **Alice** *lies with her head in* **Claudia**'s *lap.* **Claudia** *has her arm around her.*

Alice Tell me another story.

Claudia Are you still frightened?

Alice Are you?

Claudia A little.

Alice Me too.

Claudia You shouldn't be shy of admitting your fear.

Alice Do you always?

Claudia (*smiles*) No.

Alice Go on.

Claudia (*telling a story*) They came to my house and the homes of other working-class leaders early in the morning. They arrested seriously ailing and sick people. They refused to allow the men to shave.

Man 1 I haven't fed Willy.

Woman 1 Who cares about Willy? I haven't fed that rabble – my family – their breakfast.

Woman 2 My hair still in curlers. What will the neighbours say? You know how they can talk.

Woman 3 It's all right for you. I'm the one suffers. My teeth are floating in a glass mug on the bedside table, grinning at an empty room.

Man 2 He'll starve to death. I can't bear it.

Claudia They drove through the early morning even as the German fascists drove through the streets, while children trotted to school and early wagons delivered milk for families who can afford to pay the high prices these days.

Man 1 Right now Willy and myself would have been taking our early morning stroll.

Man 2 Shut up can't you? I am trying to get some sleep. It's bad enough without yous chuntering on.

Woman 3 See, I am reduced to nothing. Not even the clothes on my back belong to me. A woman with no papers might as well not exist.

Man 2 Like a madhouse.

Woman 3 No clothes, no money. No teeth. Such is the suffering of my life.

Man 2 Besides, what're yous afraid of? See me, I'm going to stroll into wherever they're taking us and I'm going to demand to see the man in charge. I'll put my case forward. Polite but firm. Man to man. He'll listen. I'm white, free, single and over 21. They can't harm me.

Alice Go on.

Claudia One heard people who drove by near us, talk about ordinary things, never suspecting that next to them was an example of the denial of free speech and thought. That even now an almost imperceptible shift in the atmosphere had changed the lives of a few forever.

Alice I don't like this story.

Man 2 After all, I'm an American. I can't remember even being alive before America.

Alice How does it end?

Claudia I don't know.

Alice Make it up.

Claudia I can't.

Woman 3 They should at least have let me wash before I came out. I still have the work sweat on me.

Woman 1 Thinks she's the only one works shifts. Do you hear me complaining?

Alice Maybe I can think of an ending if I try really hard.

Claudia Try to get some sleep. You'll be exhausted otherwise.

Alice In here. It's so cramped.

Man 1 This is preposterous. Who ever heard of a lawyer being arrested for no reason whatsoever, other than that someone didn't like the look of his face.

Man 2 A lawyer?

Man 1 Well, a lawyer's clerk.

Man 2 Then you'll come with me. You'll put my case before him. Tell him I'm innocent. I can prove it. All my life I've lived clean. Simple. A simple man. An American.

Alice Where are they taking us?

Claudia Ellis Island.

Woman 2 *laughs*.

Alice What's so funny? Why's she laughing at me?

Woman 2 Ellis Island.

Alice If I fall asleep you'll wake me up, won't you? Don't forget me. You're the only one I trust.

Woman 2 You arrived by boat. They stamped your papers. Registered you. They did their job efficiently. Like machines. Still, I suppose, it becomes routine when you've been doing it for so long. They didn't so much as look you in the eye. Not a flicker of human recognition. A cold welcome but a welcome nonetheless. After all one had arrived. What more could one desire? Now they're imprisoning us on the very island we sought sanctuary from.

Woman 1 Shut up can't you? Who cares what it used to be. Now it's just another prison.

Man 1 Detention centre.

Woman 1 A prison by any other name.

Alice What have I done wrong?

Claudia Nothing.

Alice I must have.

Woman 2 Good thing you left your teeth at home.

Woman 3 If I had them in I'd bite your arm off.

Woman 2 Charming.

Claudia Think like that and they'll have won. You've done nothing wrong. Understand? Remember that.

Man 1 It's like a never ending ride into hell.

Man 2 Shut up I said.

Woman 2 Least it'll be warm without us having to worry about the cost.

Woman They call these places open prisons 'cos they realise that everybody knows that outside is even worse. They can leave the gates wide open 'cos nobody wants to go outside.

Man 2 You will speak up for me won't you?

Man 1 I told you. I'm not a lawyer.

Alice Once a man I worked for lost some money. I didn't take it, but I felt as if I had. He didn't even accuse me. Sometimes silence is enough, isn't it? He walked around the house silently. Sometimes he just stood and watched me, as if he were waiting for me to put it back.

Claudia We are not guilty.

Van stops.

Woman 2 Have we arrived?

Woman 1 (*sarcastic*) No, they're gonna let us have a little wander round just to stretch our legs, and relieve ourselves. Of course we've arrived.

Man 2 right, here's my chance. You stick beside me. I don't want to lose you. You're my one chance.

Man 1 somebody please tell him that I am not a lawyer.

Alice Do we have to go outside now?

Claudia Why, don't you want to?

Alice No. I don't want to go out there.

Claudia Your fear is an illusion. You've nothing to be afraid of. Seeing how brave you are. It's them who'll be afraid.

Alice Aren't you afraid?

Claudia Like I said, there's nothing to fear. And look, I'm holding your hand.

Scene Nine

Claudia Homing pigeons gather aimlessly in the large yard on an island which lies in New York's great harbour. Occasionally, a homing pigeon flies in from the bay dotted with whitecaps and the pigeons scatter.

They gather as a solid mass and, with a loud grace, flap their wings and fly away . . . over the massed brownstone buildings with numerous windows. The windows of all the buildings are wired with criss-cross, light, iron bars. Around the huge yard, barbed wire way beyond the height of a man towers and outdoor lights, as on a baseball diamond, are spaced with regular frequency.

The Statue of Liberty lies on the left of this shore . . . And well it does – for this woman, with liberty's torch, still stands proudly aloft her earthly home . . . and literally stands with her back to Ellis Island.

Scene Ten

Common room in Alderson prison, West Virginia. **Prison Officer** *stands guard while the women in the centre of the room surround a large birthday cake.*

Woman 1 (*thumps radio*) Damn thing's busted.

Prison Officer Easy Peters.

Woman 1 Can't have a party without music.

Woman 2 We could make our own. I'll sing for you.

Woman 1 No thanks. I've heard you singing in the shower.

Woman 2 Of course it's busted, the way you keep thumping it.

Elizabeth (*to* **Claudia**) It's not often that you're lost for words.

Claudia I'm astounded.

Woman 3 Thinks she's a scientific genius, huh, Claudia?

Woman 2 Bear with us Claudia, you'll have music on your birthday if it kills us.

Prison Officer Keep the noise down in here, else there won't be no free time, no party, no nothing.

Woman 2 And she shall have music wherever she goes.

Alice Cut the cake Claudia.

Claudia I don't want to spoil it.

Woman We made it so's it could be eaten, not stared at.

Alice I love birthday cake.

Woman 3 We'll have a cake fight.

Prison Officer *coughs and then folds her arms.*

Woman 3 Well, perhaps not.

Alice Go on, Claudia.

Claudia *cuts the cake. They all cheer.*

Women Speech! Speech!

Claudia As Elizabeth says, I'm lost for words.

Woman 3 You'll find some. You always do.

Claudia (*clears her throat*) Today, on this, my birthday, I think of my mother. My mother, a machine worker in a garment factory, died when she was just the same age I am today. I think I began then to develop an understanding of the sufferings of my people and my class and to look for a way to end them. I am flattered that you should think me worthy of this celebration and look forward to the day when we can celebrate our freedom without (*Looks at* **Prison Officer**.) the fear of persecution.

Woman 2 Sounds good to me. I now declare this party officially underway. Who wants to dance?

The women get up and dance to radio music. With the other women gone **Elizabeth** *and* **Claudia** *are glad to be alone together for a moment and take each others' hands.*

Elizabeth We don't see enough of each other. How are you?

Claudia I ache all over.

Elizabeth Me too.

Claudia A pain like toothache that reaches right down deep in my bones and, yet, isn't physical.

Elizabeth It won't be long. We just have to hold on to what we believe in. They can't win.

Claudia It seems that we can't either.

Elizabeth This can only make us stronger.

Woman 1 Are you two talking your politics again?

Elizabeth Just talking.

Woman 1 Because today's supposed to be a holiday. You do take holidays don't you?

Woman 2 Come and dance.

Alice Dance with me Claudia.

Claudia I think I'll sit this one out. Every year my birthday recovery rate gets a little slower. I didn't used to mind the fact that I'd clocked up yet another year. You dance, enjoy yourselves. I'll sit here quietly with my friend Elizabeth.

The women continue to dance. **Claudia** *and* **Elizabeth** *sit on the ground and continue cutting up the cake and pouring lemonade into cups.*

Claudia *nibbles at a piece of cake.*

Claudia Tastes good. (*Lowers her head.*)

Elizabeth I get depressed on birthdays too.

Claudia Just a little tired.

Elizabeth I've noticed that when you're not talking to the women, whenever I catch you on your own you always seem so lonely.

Claudia I've been writing about this place.

Elizabeth Always working.

Claudia You're just as bad.

Elizabeth I admire your energy and commitment.

Claudia The great Elizabeth Gurley-Flynn envies me?

Elizabeth Your people should be proud of you.

Claudia And yours?

A slight pause.

You know, I can't tell you how grateful I am to be here.

Elizabeth Grateful?

Claudia With these women. They're like my sisters. It all feels so real.

Elizabeth And don't you think your work before was real?

Claudia Yes, but just a little like a game I was playing. Like I was trying on different masks, personas and not quite comfortable in any one of them.

Elizabeth And you're comfortable here?

Claudia I'm not sure that comfortable is the right word, but I belong with people. (*Pointed.*) Yours and mine.

Elizabeth I'm sorry.

Pause.

Claudia (*hugging her knees*) I wonder what my life would have been had I married, had children and lived quietly on the outskirts.

Elizabeth Could you?

Claudia I don't know. (*Slight pause.*) Then I look at you and the longing disappears. You look like one of those lady pioneers who carved a way through the Wild West.

Elizabeth Tough and ready for anything. That's not a bad epitaph.

Claudia Pioneers don't die. (*Ironic.*) Their spirits live forever.

The women come back.

Have you tired of dancing?

Woman 2 We can't find the music we like.

Elizabeth Sounded all right to me.

Woman 3 Because you're an old fogey.

Alice It's just like a real party.

Woman 3 It is a real party stupid.

Alice I never knew they had parties in prison.

Elizabeth (*handing out cups*) It sounds like someone should make a toast.

Woman 1 Alice wrote a speech didn't you?

Alice I never wrote it down.

Woman 3 Because she can't write.

Alice It's in my head.

Woman 1 Go on then, kid, spit it out.

Alice I just wanted to say that I know being in prison's not very nice and everything, but meeting you two, being on the island with Claudia, then coming here . . . it's well, it's . . . I know I'm just a simple girl.

Woman 3 Simple's not the word.

Alice They said that Communists were bad at home. I never met one before, never even knew what it meant, but now I feel . . . different.

Woman 2 I think the kid's trying to say you've had a good effect on her.

The women laugh, **Alice** *is embarrassed.*

Alice Julie wrote a song.

Julie It's not much, just a stupid little thing.

Claudia Now I'm embarrassed.

Woman 1 Come on, let's sing.

Women get into a line and sing 'Birthday Song'. When they've finished **Claudia** *and* **Elizabeth** *clap.*

Woman 3 Good isn't it?

Claudia I want to cry.

Woman 3 And just think, two months ago she was fiddling the welfare. I think it can safely be said that Alderson is an institution for rehabilitation.

Woman 2 *thumps her playfully. The other women laugh.*

Prison Officer Cells!

Woman 1 Wondered why she was being so quiet.

Woman 3 She was saving up to say the magic words just when we were beginning to enjoy ourselves.

Woman 2 It's not fair we've got a whole hour yet.

Prison Officer When I say it's time. It's time. Now move.

Woman 3 One thing I won't be able to stand when I get outside is the jangle a door keys. I'll have to find a place you don't need to lock up.

Prison Officer Move.

They start to move out slowly, reluctantly. As she passes **Woman 1** *holds a piece of the cake under* **Prison Officer***'s nose.*

Woman 1 Birthday cake?

Prison Officer *doesn't reply.*

Woman 1 I don't think she likes birthday cake.

Woman 3 (*as they go*) Prison officers have to watch their figures.

Alice Happy birthday Claudia.

The women are all off stage but we can hear them singing the 'Birthday Song' in the background. **Elizabeth** *takes* **Claudia***'s hand.*

Elizabeth We'll talk when we can.

Claudia *is left alone onstage with* **Prison Officer***.*

Prison Officer I'm not as easily taken in as these girls. Most of them have very little education and are very easily impressed.

Claudia I think you underestimate them. They don't give their trust lightly.

Prison Officer I don't doubt it, all I'm

saying is just remember who you are
and where you are.

Claudia With you around to remind
me, how can I forget?

Claudia *leaves*.

Act Two

Scene Eleven

Piggery in Alderson prison. Sound of pigs grunting. **Claudia** *has just finished mucking out. She's filthy. She moves quite slowly because she's been quite ill. A* **Prison Officer**, *an impassive black woman in her thirties, stands watching* **Claudia** *with her arms folded.*

Claudia I smell like a pig, (*Touches her side.*) feel like a pig. Do I look like one?

Prison Officer *makes no reply.* **Claudia** *honks like a pig gently.*

Claudia I think that's it for today, don't you?

No reply from **Prison Officer**.

Claudia Seeing as we've both been relegated to the piggery we might as well make the most of it.

Prison Officer This is just one in a string of duties I have to perform.

Claudia Don't get me wrong. I've grown fond of pigs. I even have a favourite, though I admit that makes me feel a little guilty. Roberta. Of course, you wouldn't know who Roberta was would you, them being just numbers to you? She's the black sow with the one white patch on her snout. The poor thing hasn't been at all well just lately. I'm very worried about her. She has respiratory problems and her feet are none too good either. However, despite my requests, they won't let her have the medication she so needs. Listen officer, you wouldn't consider having a word with the governor, would you, and telling her that . . .

Prison Officer Don't think I can't see through you number 11711.

Claudia There's nothing to see through.

Prison Officer I'm sick of your poses.

Claudia I gave up acting long ago.

Prison Officer The martyr . . . languishing in jail suffering, you would have them all believe, from an illness exacerbated by your menial surroundings; the victim . . . hounded by an unsympathetic government. What you seem to forget is that you're a common criminal, just like all the other criminals you surround yourself with.

Claudia Some of these women have committed murder.

Prison Officer Crimes of passion.

Claudia I salute your philanthropy, but wasn't mine a crime of passion?

Prison Officer As always you *romanticize* yourself.

Claudia And which particular grudge of yours are we re-enacting today?

Prison Officer You're supposed to show respect to an officer.

Claudia Why is it that you never look me in the eye?

Prison Officer Get on with your work.

Claudia Are you afraid that having so much in common we might just find that we like each other?

Prison Officer We have nothing in common.

Claudia Except for the fact that we both happen to be negro, that we're both female . . .

Prison Officer And that's all.

Claudia And that we've both been imprisoned partly because of those two factors.

Prison Officer I chose to work here.

Claudia Really? You gained a college degree . . .

Prison Officer How did you know that?

Claudia And chose to work among our porcine friends? I must say that's very noble of you.

Prison Officer You have been incarcerated for a heinous crime. I will not stain myself.

Claudia You already have. (*Indicates.*) The hem of your skirt.

Prison Officer *hesitantly looks down. Sees nothing.*

Prison Officer I'm warning you.

Claudia At the back.

Prison Officer *doesn't trust* **Claudia** *but looks behind herself anyway.*

Prison Officer (*brushing her skirt with her gloves hand*) Damned filthy animals.

Claudia I don't know. I've found working amongst the pigs most beneficial. I suppose this is how one gains humility. It's no accident that the prodigal son had to eat swill and live in pig shit before he was allowed the delicious ecstasy of fatted calf.

Prison Officer *can't reach behind to remove the stain properly.*

Claudia Here, let me help you.

Claudia *wipes at skirt with a cloth.*

Prison Officer (*not quite sure, now that she's let down her guard a little, of how to act*) Thank you (*Slight pause.*) Better tidy those things away and get washed up. It's almost dinner time.

Claudia (*tidying things away*) You didn't go to college to work as a prison officer in a piggery.

Prison Officer I wanted to teach.

After months of looking for an opening, I decided to take the best that was on offer, just to keep the wolves at bay. I'm still looking for a post.

Claudia Life does strange things to our dreams, doesn't it?

Prison Officer I'll get a teaching post. It's just a matter of time. Then I'll save up and buy a car and take Daniel, that's my little boy,

Claudia You have a child?

Prison Officer for drives on Sunday afternoons.

Claudia Imagine that. I never saw you as a mother.

Prison Officer It would be good to feel human again. What?

Claudia I just said that from the evidence I've seen in this piggery you must be a wonderful mother.

Prison Officer That's enough 11711.

Claudia Uh huh I blew it. And just as we were beginning to get on so well.

Prison Officer I said that that was enough.

Claudia Do the other officers still refuse to eat with you?

Prison Officer I will not discuss official matters with a prisoner.

Claudia If they do, you should do something about it.

Prison Officer Like what?

Claudia Stand up to them. You have a right to.

Prison Officer Life means so little to you so called revolutionaries that you can afford to abuse it. It's what you call courage. She was a brave woman they'll say when they look back, but a woman like me has to take life seriously. I have a child who depends on me, he needs to be fed and clothed. I can't afford to be brave.

Claudia I don't know that you're not more courageous than me, after all.

Prison Officer I take what I'm given.

Claudia A little longer on the swill and pig shit and who knows what might happen?

Prison Officer With all your fighting you've won yourself a very strange freedom.

Claudia Even so, within a few months I'll be out of here, free and you'll still be snuggling up to the pigs with yet another black inmate to keep you company.

Prison Officer What makes you so sure that even when you're out of here that you'll be free? They'll deport you.

Claudia My lawyer has appealed.

Prison Officer Why should the United States government listen to the squeals of a traitor.

Claudia He's a very good lawyer.

Prison Officer I wouldn't bet money on your chance of freedom.

Claudia I have a charmed life. I usually get what I wish for.

Prison Officer I think your luck's running out.

Claudia Do you? We'll see. But for now I'll enjoy my time with the pigs.

Scene Twelve

A waiting room in the prison. Visiting time. **Claudia**'s *father,* **Carole** *and her lawyer are waiting.* **Claudia** *is led in by* **Prison Officer***. She can barely walk. She embraces* **Charles** *and* **Carole***.*

Claudia You put up with all this for me.

Charles You're an uncut diamond, but each time I see you you seem to shine. And I'm getting used to this place.

Carole The hotel has become a second home.

Claudia Any news?

Lawyer Letters of support from all over the world, from students in Germany to the Jamaica Federation of Trade Unions. The list is endless.

Claudia I'm very grateful for their support but I'm talking about real news, the appeal . . .

Charles Be strong, my girl.

Lawyer . . . Has fallen on deaf ears.

Claudia *turns away from them. After a pause to let the news sink in she turns round again.*

Claudia So I'm to be deported?

Charles My dear, you've been strong up to now.

Claudia How can I be strong when these people are putting nails in my coffin.

Carole There's nothing any of us can do now. We've gone up every blind alley, exhausted every avenue. There's nothing left.

Claudia A new home. I can't even remember what it was like. So I'm to go back to Trinidad.

Lawyer Not exactly. The Trinidadian government are reluctant . . .

Claudia They don't want me either? Why?

Lawyer I haven't had a proper answer yet.

Carole But it's something to the effect

that you weren't a communist when you left Trinidad.

Claudia I was nine years old!

Carole America made you a communist, so America has to deal with you.

Claudia Well I'll be . . . (*Laughs.*) It does have its funny side. So Trinidad rejects its prodigal daughter?

Lawyer I'm afraid so. But England has agreed to accept you.

Claudia Of course. Because Trinidad belongs to England and so, therefore, do I.

Lawyer At least there you'll be able to get the medication and hospital treatment that you need.

Charles My girl doesn't look at all well.

Claudia Are you sure that this decision is irrevocable, isn't there something else that we can do?

Lawyer Nothing whatsoever.

Claudia I feel like an orphan. I'm too old for such a big change in my life.

Carole What about us? How will we live without you?

Claudia In a few months you'll have forgotten who I was.

Charles How can you speak like that.

Claudia I might as well be dead.

Charles Claudia.

Claudia I know poppa, you want me to be brave. Your brave girl. And I will be when the time comes. But for now, please indulge me this once, I'm scared as hell.

Scene Thirteen

Inside cabin on the Queen Elizabeth ship, New York harbour. We can hear sounds of crowd that has gathered outside to see **Claudia** *off.* **Claudia** *sits putting finishing touches to her toilette.* **Carole** *enters.*

Carole Such a crowd. Of course, they're impatient for you. I've said it's because you're ill. You're father's just made a speech and the crowd have gone crazy. Have you taken a pill?

Claudia I don't need a pill. What did he say?

Carole Not very much. He couldn't.

Claudia Look after him for me.

Carole He said that wherever you go, he's sure you'll do your best.

Claudia It's all he's ever wanted of me. So they're having quite a party out there?

Carole Listen to them. Someone in the crowd asked me to give you this (*Hands her a posy.*) and there's someone waiting to see you outside. One of your ardent fans, no doubt. He wouldn't take no for an answer.

Claudia Good looking?

Carole Not bad.

Claudia Then what are you waiting for? Show the man in. No, wait. Do I look all right?

Carole Well, there's a great black smudge under your eye and your hair's gone frizzy with all the seat mist.

Claudia Where?

Carole I was joking. You can be so vain.

Claudia A healthy respect for the way one looks is all.

A cheer goes up outside.

Claudia They're talking about me as though I were dead.

Carole If they didn't laugh they'd cry.

Claudia You'd think they'd be happy to see the back of me.

Carole How much more love can you take?

Claudia Is that love?

Carole Close enough.

Claudia I suppose I'd better face them. They'll be expecting a speech. I hope I don't dry up.

Carole Since when have words ever failed you?

Claudia (*wistful*) It's a beautiful crisp morning.

Carole Somebody up there likes you.

Claudia How can I live without the lady and her lamp?

Carole You sentimental fool.

Claudia How can I be British? They don't have tea do they? They take tea and play croquet on their well-kept lawns. They don't talk to each other directly but pass telepathic messages which, if you don't understand, makes you an outcast. I've been a loudmouth American too long to suddenly become British.

Carole Britain's a tiny island.

Claudia Which drags half the world behind it on a leash.

Carole You could cause quite a stir in Britain. It'll be like a fresh start.

Claudia I'm too old for fresh starts. There aren't any new leaves left in my copy book.

Carole Shall I send in your fan?

Claudia Does he have a name?

Carole *has gone. She re-enters with* **Ben**
who holds a baby.

Ben Hullo Claudia.

Claudia It's been a long time.

Carole I'll wait outside.

Carole *goes.*

Ben I had to say goodbye.

Claudia I thought you already had, a long time ago.

Ben I thought you hadn't heard me.

Claudia I heard.

Pause.

Claudia Is she asleep?

Ben Hold her.

Ben *gives* **Claudia** *the baby.* **Claudia** *is entranced by the wonder of the child.*

Claudia So tiny. Tiny hands, feet. So warm.

Ben She likes you. See how she's smiling. (*To baby.*) This is Claudia Jones, the woman I told you about, isn't she beautiful?

Claudia (*in another world*) This is it. This is what we're working for.

Another cheer goes up outside.

Ben (*taking baby from* **Claudia**, *who reluctantly gives it up*) I don't want to keep you from your public. But I just wanted . . . I don't know what I wanted.

Claudia I understand.

Ben Good luck, Claudia.

Claudia Good to see you.

Ben *goes.* **Carole** *re-enters.*

Carole Old boyfriend? Nice. (*Noticing* **Claudia**.) Did he upset you, Claudia?

Claudia I'm so afraid.

Pause while **Carole** *holds* **Claudia** *and*

rocks her gently like a baby. After a while
Claudia *stands.*

Carole You don't have to go outside
until you're ready.

Claudia (*takes out a handkerchief and
wipes her eyes*) They've come all this
way.

Carole If you're sure you're up to it.

Claudia No progress without struggle,
comrade. Besides, the show must go
on mustn't it?

Claudia *smooths down her clothes, braces
herself and exits. Sound of cheers from
crowd.*

Scene Fourteen

*Southampton Docks, England, December
1955. Early morning. A man and woman,*
Ned *and* **Dina**, *stand waiting for a ship to
come in.* **Dina** *is wearing too many layers,
but even so has to hug herself and shivers
with the cold.*

Dina I like to be by the sea. It
reminds me how small we are.

Ned Just a rock in water really.

Dina And ports. All that coming and
going. This is where you met me.

Ned Her boat will be a little grander
than yours was. She's on the Queen
Elizabeth.

Dina Remember Ned?

Ned You don't forget a day like that.

Dina What thoughts went through
your mind?

Ned (*uncomfortable*) I don't know. I
can't remember.

Dina Try. Go on. Tell me.

Ned (*shrugs, then*) Has she changed;
gained weight, lost weight. Have I

changed? Will she like it? Have we
done the right thing?

Dina You felt all that?

Ned And you?

Dina (*remembering*) Maybe his head's
been turned by those English women.
I miss my mamma. Fear. Have we
done the right thing?

Ned You not disappointed?

Dina No.

Dina *and* **Ned** *hug.* **Ahmed** *enters.*

Ahmed Now, now you two. There's a
time and a place for that sort of thing.

Dina We were just thinking back.

Ahmed It looks like it. I've checked
the times, she should be here any
minute.

Ahmed *ties and unties his shoelaces.*

Dina Must you do that?

Ahmed It's late.

Ned Have some patience, man. (*To*
Dina.) He can't wait to meet her, look
at him, like a puppy dog straining at
the leash.

Dina I don't know what all the fuss is
about. If all I had to do to make
myself a heroine was to be thrown into
jail . . .

Ahmed You don't understand, her
achievements are outstanding. Here,
we have no one like her.

Dina . . . They would be singing my
praises in Trafalgar Square tomorrow.

Ahmed A woman too.

Dina Why should you think that so
unusual? Women have been quietly
achieving great things through the
centuries, only most of us don't ask for
anything in return, but choose to
remain in the background.

Ahmed What can be achieved in the world by remaining quietly in the background? You know nothing of politics.

Dina And if it's going to make me look as old and unattractive as you do, I don't want to know.

Ned Little Dina's getting angry.

Dina And why did you marry me? Precisely because I had nothing to do with your wretched party. I get enough talk talk talk from my friends in the party, you said. And when you look at it, just what exactly are they saying? Nothing of any real importance.

Ahmed You said that?

Ned Not exactly that.

Dina Yes you did. There's an absurdity in things, he said and all attempts to give one's life meaning and dignity are in the end hopeless.

Ahmed You're becoming a cynic in your old age, Ned.

Dina He is getting on. Twenty-seven years old.

Ned Practically middle-aged.

Ahmed You're not thinking of leaving the party are you?

Ned Of course not . . .

Dina Why they should call it a party is beyond me. No one ever sings or dances or laughs.

Ned . . . It's my life.

Dina You do drink a lot though.

Ned When have I ever had the money to buy alcohol?

Dina Rolls home drunk in the middle of the night smelling of rum and expecting me to be up to serve dinner and clear up after him. He's ruined countless meals.

Ahmed No one said it would be easy being the wife of a revolutionary.

Ned Dina wouldn't be happy if she wasn't nagging me.

Dina I can't for the life of me see how you're ever going to achieve this blessed revolution when you spend most of your time boozing in your so-called meetings.

Ahmed You see, Dina, every revolution needs a ground plan. The formulation of ideas takes a long time.

Dina I intend to sleep through your revolution. Will it be noisy?

Ned It won't be that kind of revolution.

Dina And wake up when they've locked you all safely away in an institution somewhere in the country.

Ahmed Your wife is quite a little spitfire, really, isn't she?

Ned It's the main reason I married her.

Dina I'll bet your Claudia Jones isn't forever throwing away spoilt dinners.

Ned She isn't married.

Dina It doesn't surprise me. The few women there are in your party are unmarriageable.

Ahmed I never think of them as women, funny.

Ned Now that you mention it . . .

Dina I'll bet she's one of these serious women who's always got her nose stuck in a book and never changes her clothes or presses her hair. I'll bet she wears sensible shoes, lives on pistachio nuts, has squinty eyes, a double chin and knock knees.

Ahmed I've seen pictures of her.

Dina You can't tell anything from a picture.

Ned I want to see the American Amazon for myself.

Dina *shivers.*

Are you still cold, poppet?

Dina I'll never get used to this.

Ned My little precious won't even set foot outside the house.

Ahmed Why not? What are you frightened of?

Ned Everything: the fog, the snow, the people.

Dina I simply think that this isn't the kind of country where one should stay outside for any length of time. You could get frozen stiff if you stood still for too long. It's an indoor kind of country.

Ned When we've achieved the new world you won't be frightened of anything.

Dina People stare at you.

Ahmed You could try staring back at them.

Dina As though they can't believe their eyes, as though they're waiting for something strange to pop out of you, a tail or something. They make me sick.

Ahmed You shouldn't talk like that. After all, they are our comrades.

Dina You sound like a priest: we're all brothers under the skin. They don't seem to share your views.

Ned Because they have no conscience. They have to be made aware. Now you understand why we have to make plans.

Ahmed It's an uphill struggle, comrade.

Dina That's your answer to everything. In my view those people are just pig ignorant.

Ahmed You should give her the paper to read.

Dina I have. Or tried to.

Ahmed And?

Dina It might as well have been written in Chinese.

Ahmed So how's work?

Dina Thank you for indulging the little woman's ignorance and switching to a subject that she understands.

Ned She hasn't worked since we married.

Dina It's just a matter of finding the right opening. and someone who'll take me on to do something other than cleaning.

Ned And my Dina so clever.

Dina What with Ned studying and everything, I can't believe how well we actually manage.

Sounds of ships horn.

Ned Here she comes.

Ahmed She'll see us here won't she?

Ned Surely she'll miss us. How will she know it's us?

Ahmed I've seen pictures of her.

Dina So many people. Look at them.

Ahmed There she is.

Ned Where?

Ahmed No, that's not her. What if she missed the boat?

Ned They'd have sent a telegram.

Dina At least they don't look as desperate for escape as we were.

Pause as they all look out in anticipation.

After a while they relax.

That appears to be the last. Looks as though she's given us the slip.

Ned We ought to check. We may have got the time wrong.

Dina Perhaps she changed her mind and decided to go somewhere else. I wouldn't blame her.

Ned I'll go and check.

Before **Ned** *can exit* **Claudia** *enters walking backwards and shouting to somebody offstage. She wears a party hat and has a paper Christmas decoration round her neck.*

Claudia Then we'll have to beg to differ. I'll give you a call when I'm settled. I'd be only too happy to win another argument with you.

Claudia *turns round and is startled to find the trio staring at her. They're all a little embarrassed.*

Claudia Is this my welcoming committee?

Ned There's a press conference arranged for later.

Claudia *removes the hat and takes off the decoration.*

Claudia New Year celebrations. (*Slight pause.*) So, this is England. Not much of it to see, is there?

Ahmed It isn't always this foggy.

Claudia No?

Ahmed (*holding out his hand*) Miss Jones, we are so proud to have you with us, the work you've done in America. We feel humbled to receive . . .

Claudia Does he always talk like that?

Dina If you let him.

Claudia You must be Ahmed.

Ahmed That's right.

Claudia I read your paper on the ship. It was very interesting. I think I might have a few suggestions for you.

Ahmed I'd be very grateful for your comments.

Claudia I'd like to get involved: you know, I've worked on newspapers since I was a very young girl.

Ahmed I'd feel humbled to have you work for us.

Claudia (*to* **Dina**) And you must be my secretary.

Dina I don't – er. Ned.

Ned Dina is my wife.

Claudia A husband and wife team? It sometimes works very well. (*Takes deep breath in, as if testing the air.*) Not bad. No worse than New York anyhow. Perhaps even a little fresher. Where am I to stay?

Ned With us for a while, until we can find somewhere more suitable.

Claudia All I need is somewhere clean and that isn't too cold. Well, what are we waiting for, let's go. Do you know any good restaurants round here? I'm starving.

Ahmed Restaurants?

Dina We live on tea and digestive biscuits.

Claudia It's not every day that Claudia Jones lands on your shores. Doesn't that warrant a celebration?

Ned (*to* **Ahmed**) There is that Italian place.

Ahmed I have a little cash flow problem.

Ned We'll have to pool what we have. Oh dear, I hope she isn't going to prove too expensive. (*To* **Claudia**.)

There's a little Italian place not far from here.

Claudia That sounds marvellous. We'll have a good meal, a chat, then after I've rested up we'll get right down to work. (*Linking* **Dina**'s *arm*.) I want you to tell me about everything from the political scene to the best place to get my hair pressed.

Dina I don't know too much about the first subject, but Carmen England is a wonderful hairdresser.

Claudia *turns to the men.*

Claudia Bring my suitcase would you? There should be a trunk somewhere. Perhaps you could find it for me.

Claudia *and* **Dina** *exit. The men stand and stare at each other bemused, shrug then drag suitcase off.*

Scene Fifteen

Offices of West Indian Gazette, London 1959. Four black women are in the office alone. **Mrs Cochrane** *covers her face with her hands and the other women lead her to a chair.*

First Woman Where is everybody?

Second Woman Gone to lunch, no doubt.

Third Woman Death in the streets and Claudia Jones stuffs her face.

First Woman A woman must eat. (*Softly to* **Mrs Cochrane**.) Sit.

They sit **Mrs Cochrane** *down.*

First Woman (*in* **Mrs Cochrane**'s *ear*) You're as stiff as a board. Relax.

Third Woman I'm stifled. Somebody open a window.

Second Woman (*sighs*) Exhausted.

First Woman Sit.

Second Woman You're the oldest. You sit.

First Woman Not so old that I can't stand on my own two feet.

Third Woman An old battle axe.

First Woman A little respect for the elderly, if you don't mind.

Second Woman (*at window*) It's stuck.

First Woman Leave it.

Third Woman I can't breathe. Where the hell are they? There should be people here.

First Woman We can wait.

Second Woman You're so philosophical. I want to . . .

First Woman What?

Second Woman I don't know. Tear things up.

First Woman What would that achieve?

Second Woman (*shrugs, then*) A sense of release?

First Woman Claudia will know what to do.

Second Woman She's not a miracle worker, not Jesus Christ.

First Woman She'll know what to say, who to say it to.

Third Woman I doubt that even she can breathe life into the dead.

Second Woman Ssh!

Third Woman Sorry. (*Of* **Mrs Cochrane**.) Is she all right? She isn't going to be sick?

Second Woman Why doesn't she say something?

First Woman Shock.

Donald *enters followed by* **Irishwoman**.

Donald All I can do is apologize for having kept you waiting.

Irishwoman And me about to be thrown out onto the streets.

Donald I'm sure it won't come to that. (*Turning to other women.*) And I suppose you want to see Claudia Jones as well hmmm? What is it? Immigration papers, union matters or simply wanting her to sign her name to a reference?

First Woman Watch your tongue Donald. Remember I know you from back home, since before you fancied yourself a part-time journalist, since before you was a bus conductor, before you could write or even speak.

Donald Beg pardon Miss Bea. I'm new at this job and it's been one of those days.

Irishwoman You can tell he's inexperienced can't you, from the way he talks.

Donald People don't want to waste their time talking to me when they come to see Claudia. I get all the flak.

Irishwoman You see, young man, this is my situation. Yesterday the landlord left a note on my door saying that if I didn't get out of his house by four o'clock today . . .

Second Woman Can you open a window?

Donald It is hot. You can feel the heat rising up out of the ground to the soles of your feet. This window gets a little stiff but . . . (*Pulls it open.*) There.

Irishwoman He'd enter my room and throw my things out onto the street himself.

Donald Oh dear. I don't quite know how to help you. Miss Jones shouldn't be too long.

Irishwoman I can't be waiting all day, can I? Why, my heart's in my mouth even now just at the thought of the man going through all my private papers. Not that he hasn't already done so. What a thought. That someone can come into your room and look at your life. They could come in while you were asleep couldn't they? Imagine that, while you were sleeping they could come in and . . . I don't like to think of it.

Donald I only wish I could help you myself.

Irishwoman Why can't you?

Donald What could I do?

Irishwoman You could go there with me and confront him.

Donald I'm no fighter.

Irishwoman You're a man aren't you?

Donald Don't be hasty. After all, you do have until four.

Irishwoman He's after moving someone else in.

Ahmed *enters.*

Donald (*relieved at the diversion*) Ahmed, how are you?

Ahmed Where's Claudia?

Donald Talking to the bank manager. As you can see we've been overrun. And a deadline to meet.

Ahmed I'll wait.

Irishwoman As long as he takes his turn in the queue. I'm first and these women are after me.

Ahmed How's life on the buses?

Donald It's a living.

Ahmed I wasn't knocking it. I think you're very courageous.

Donald I wouldn't go that far.

Ahmed What is it they're calling you? Oh yes, Conductor Calypso, on account of the writing.

Donald But I don't write songs.

Ahmed I know. Aren't people cruel?

Claudia *enters followed by* **Dina**.

Claudia That's what the man said.

Dina And you didn't even shout at him? I would have. How dare he?

Dina Ned's been trying to get him to come round for ages, but he's too good for us now.

Claudia Let me sort these ladies out then we'll have a lovely chat. Donald get Ahmed some tea.

Ahmed I haven't come here to indulge in pleasant teatime chitchat.

Dina What do you want Ahmed?

Ahmed Give me back my paper.

Dina I thought we'd resolved this ages ago.

Claudia I acquired the title lock, stock and barrel, it's legal.

Ahmed That paper was my life. I won't stand back and watch you destroy it.

Donald Sit down man, calm yourself.

Ahmed Take your hands off me, Mr Bus Conductor. I won't be manhandled by a fool. Look at you. You're all fools if you believe that this (*Holds up paper.*) is to be our deliverance. (*To* **Claudia**.) You've found yourself a snug little niche here, haven't you? They all think you're a saint but I see through you. In order to appear superior you surround yourself with ignorant amateurs. Because you have no true ability yourself, you consort with artists and intellectuals, basking in the elevated status their acquaintance confers on

you. (*To others.*) She's nothing but a cheap social climber who's using your paper to ensure her immortality.

Irishwoman I can't understand a word he's saying.

Ahmed Look at how she reduces everything to the level of triviality.

Claudia You think ordinary people's lives trivial? At least two hundred years violence course through my veins; my grandmother died poor and beaten as did my mother; the US government held its fist to my face and beat me with it, leaving me for dead. Yet I'm still here. Alive. Why would I be afraid of you?

Pause. **Mrs Cochrane** *rises.*

Mrs Cochrane There's too much noise. Too much. Noise outside in the streets and inside. Here. In our hearts. Today my son was killed. Murdered. In the street. For what? Who could hate him who knew him? Silence. No more. My son. Killed. And I don't know why. Everything is noise, confusion, pain ringing out loud like bells. And here, now, we kill each other with words. Which is worse? Will there never be peace? Who will give me silence, calm, and who will tell me the meaning of my son's death?

Scene Sixteen

Claudia *and* **Mrs Cochrane** *on Hampstead Heath. A month later. Very early morning. We can just hear the birds starting to sing.* **Mrs Cochrane** *delivers her lines without any emotion.*

Mrs Cochrane I'm scared.

Claudia I'm here.

Mrs Cochrane So cold.

Claudia The first step is always the

hardest. The next should be easier.

Mrs Cochrane I don't like outside.

Claudia In the wide open you feel free.

Mrs Cochrane I prefer inside.

Claudia How can you be cold in all those clothes?

Mrs Cochrane I want to wrap myself up so no one can see me.

Claudia Is that what you're afraid of? That someone will see us? No one comes out onto the heath this early. We have it all to ourselves. We'll catch the sunrise. Listen.

Mrs Cochrane What is it?

Claudia Birds. How lovely. I never seem to have time just to reflect these days. It's very important to be able to do that, don't you think?

Mrs Cochrane Inside is a hot drink and blankets.

Claudia Can't hide yourself away forever.

Mrs Cochrane But outside I get this terrible sensation of falling.

Claudia That's because you haven't been out for so long.

Mrs Cochrane Right down through the ground. Being swallowed up.

Claudia You can't live like this. Life goes on. If you want me to, I'll help in any way I can to get you back among the living.

Mrs Cochrane Am I dead?

Claudia I'm confusing you.

Mrs Cochrane I must be. And yet it's better this way. Why would you take this little bit of pleasure away from me?

Claudia Surely you're not happy living like this.

Mrs Cochrane Inside is cold as an ice box. I don't want to feel anything anymore.

Claudia It's what makes us human.

Mrs Cochrane You want me to live out here with those people?

Claudia We help each other.

Mrs Cochrane But you don't understand.

Claudia We're meant to live in communities.

Mrs Cochrane Surely you don't, you can't want me to . . .

Claudia Your doctor said that after a few little jaunts like this you'll soon recover.

Mrs Cochrane They killed my son.

Claudia Mrs Cochrane, please help me to help you.

Mrs Cochrane As if he wasn't already dying, gradually drifting away from me. (*Very cold.*) I hate them.

Claudia That's a very big word, hate. A dark, ugly word. Anger now . . .

Mrs Cochrane I have no reason to like white people.

Claudia You mustn't let hate take you over.

Mrs Cochrane Did I ever know what love was?

Claudia I'll help you to remember. Hate will kill you, and you don't really want to die.

Mrs Cochrane (*weakly*) No.

Claudia Then let me help you to live.

Mrs Cochrane *becomes confused. She sways a little.*

Mrs Cochrane I'm falling.

Claudia *grabs her and holds her tight as she sobs in her arms.*

Scene Seventeen

A few months later. The Carnival. Some guests dance together, some mill around, talking, eating and drinking. **Claudia** *is surrounded by a group of people who talk and joke with her.* **Ned** *and* **Dina** *are a little apart from the others, arguing, although* **Dina** *tries to hide the fact by smiling at passers by and waving over to* **Claudia** *every now and then.*

Ned Look at her, she looks more like a star than the people she's invited to entertain us.

Dina She does look glamorous, doesn't she?

Ned Funny how everything has to be centred around her.

Dina She organized it, didn't she? You're in a strange mood today.

Ned This is a party, isn't it? Well, this is my party mood. (*Gulps from his cup.*)

Dina You're drinking too much.

Ned And you're beginning to sound like old bossy boots.

Dina You flatter me.

Ned Really think you're somebody don't you? (*Bitter.*) Claudia Jones's secretary.

Dina So that's it. It was all right when I sat at your feet listening to your speeches without understanding a word you were saying. What are you afraid of? That now I do understand I'll be able to see that there was nothing in it but complex sentence structures?

Ned You know nothing of politics.

Dina Oh but I do. It's about my life. About my choice, my freedom.

Ned Thank you Claudia Jones.

Dina Don't spoil things, Ned. You're making me unhappy.

Ned My heart bleeds for you, little miss secretary.

Dina You should be proud of me.

Ned Oh but I am, my little sycophant.

Dina *starts to move away.*

Where are you going?

Dina To enjoy myself. I'm not going to stay and listen to your rubbish. You can get drunk and depressed on your own.

Dina *moves away to join* **Claudia**, **Donald** *and* **Mackenzie.**

Ned (*raising his glass after her*) Happy carnival.

As they talk **Donald** *makes notes in a notebook.*

Claudia Is Ned drunk?

Dina He's sulking.

Claudia What about? I can't stand men who sulk.

Dina (*to* **Donald**) What the hell are you doing?

Donald Claudia asked me to write up the event for the gazette.

Dina You could be a little more discreet.

Claudia Oh dear, poor Donald, frantically scribbling away as usual. His notes will be full of my rantings and Dina's complaints about stale rotis. Have a drink, Donald, you deserve one.

Donald I enjoy taking notes.

Dina We have noticed.

Mackenzie As long as it keeps him off the streets.

Claudia Donald doesn't need to be kept off the streets, he's a very good boy.

Mackenzie I meant that it keeps him from having to sweep them.

Dina Nothing wrong with sweeping the streets.

Mackenzie Have you ever tried talking to one of those men? All they can think about is how to get from one end of the street to the other in the quickest possible time and with the least possible aggravation. Nothing else matters.

Donald I'm a bus conductor.

Mackenzie And they're just as bad, I tell you. Always playing around making paper chains and ringing bells. You don't by any chance, happen to drive the number 36?

Claudia He sells tickets.

Mackenzie Because as I was getting off the number 36 the other day the damn driver started driving off when I only had one foot on the damn pavement. Can you imagine? And me an old man. Blasted tear me in two.

Claudia Do you think it's safe to talk to Ned yet?

Dina I'd wait until the sulk had well and truly receded. I know what his anger's like.

Claudia Mr Mackenzie, may I take this opportunity to thank you for your help. You've been a valuable committee member.

Mackenzie So what? Party finish? I can go home now?

Claudia I'd rather you stayed and enjoyed yourself.

Mackenzie And you know I never sit on a committee for anything in me life.

Claudia I hope you enjoyed it.

Mackenzie Every minute. A old man like me is grateful for these little diversions. One thing, though, I don't like the noise. And all the jump jump. These young people don't know what the hell them doing, just fling themself about an' never mind the consequence. I could show you how to dance. (*Moves a little in time to the music then starts to totter.*) But I'm a tired old man. I'm going home.

Claudia Please stay.

Mackenzie I'm a man love him yard. I could pinch a few pattie?

Dina As much as you want.

Mackenzie (*putting food in paper napkins*) Most kind. Anyway, is the least you could do, after a man a my years come from so far.

Mackenzie exits.

Dina Another of your uncut diamonds. Where did you find him?

Claudia In the bagwash.

Dina How romantic. You chatted him up as you both watched your smalls revolve in the superwash.

*Their attention is diverted to **Ned** who is the centre of a rumpus with some other guests.*

Ned How dare you refuse to serve me. If I want a drink I'll have it.

*One of the guests takes **Ned**'s arm and seems to be mollifying him.*

Dina Oh Ned.

Dina *leaves them and goes over to **Ned**. She takes him off into a corner. Other guests lose interest in the incident and* *concentrate on enjoying themselves again.*

Donald Miss Jones?

Claudia (*who has been engrossed in watching the incident*) Will you never call me just plain Claudia? You take politeness to extremes.

Donald Miss Jones, this might not be the right time, but I need your advice on something.

Claudia Fire away.

Donald You may think this silly, me being just a bus conductor and everything.

Claudia A very talented one. I spotted that almost as soon as we were introduced.

Donald I'm very grateful for your indulgence. I mean, where else would I have been employed as a journalist?

Claudia Their loss. You're one of the best cub reporters I've ever worked with.

Donald It means a lot to me, working here for the gazette.

Claudia Me too.

Donald Not the least because of working with you. You never laugh at me. No matter how stupid my ideas.

Claudia Why should I?

Donald As you know, I've never been to university or anything, but I feel I could do it: I want to write a book.

Claudia A novel?

Donald I'm not up to that. No. I simply want to record the facts. Of our experience, you understand. I feel that we should leave behind some mark.

Claudia Lest we forget.

Donald Yes. I haven't your stamina. I can't attend meetings every day. I'm

not the speaker that you are. Yet I too feel the need to do something. This is all I *can* do.

Claudia And it's wonderful.

Donald You don't think me silly?

Claudia I'm very proud of you.

Donald A year ago I wouldn't have even dared think about it.

Dina Don't be stupid Ned.

Ned (*shrugging out of* **Dina**'s *grasp*) Leave me. I've got something to say to her.

Ned *has gone over to* **Claudia**.

Claudia Enjoying yourself Ned?

Ned Steel bands, beauty contests for coloured girls, pick your carnival queen. Leave your troubles at the door, and while you're at it leave your brain there too. Dance all night, comrade, dance as though tonight is the last night you'll ever experience. We don't want you to think, 'cos thinking is painful and our job is to wipe out pain.

Claudia It's a gesture of peace, that's all.

Ned Ahmed was right. We don't need gestures, we need action: protection groups patrolling the streets so that people can go out without the fear of walking into a beating, lobbies, protests.

Claudia And I agree with you, but, as always, my duty is to the people. We've been wounded. It's time we began to heal. Why shouldn't we enjoy ourselves? Can't we be proud of what we came out of? It's hard enough to stay alive without punishing yourself trying to forget who you are. Try to see this carnival as a tribute, a way of drawing us together. So what if we leave the pain behind for one night?

It'll still be there in the morning. We won't erase it, but we might begin to come to terms with it. It's been a tough year, we've all worked hard organizing, campaigning, attending meetings. We'll have our carnival because we deserve it. (*Crowd applauds.*)

Ned Well, I hope you enjoy it.

Ned *exits.*

Claudia Why this constant battle for control?

Dina I'd better go after him. It's awful when he gets like this.

Claudia Don't go Dina.

Dina I have to.

Claudia I need your support here tonight.

Dina My husband needs me.

Claudia No wonder I never married.

Dina I'm not you.

Claudia And you never will be if you keep shuffling along after your husband as if you had no will of your own.

Dina (*firm*) I'm not you. (*Slight pause.*) And neither do I want to be.

Dina *exits. Pause.* **Claudia** *takes up glass, drinks.*

Claudia Oh dear. All alone.

Donald I'm still here.

Claudia Old faithful. With me to the end.

Donald I've been thinking about my book.

Claudia Not now, Donald.

Donald I'm sorry.

Claudia No, I'm sorry. (*Sighs.*) Yes?

Scene Eighteen

A hospital room, London, 1964. **Dina** *sits by* **Claudia**'s *bedside, grapes in her lap.* **Claudia** *is trying to get out of bed.*

Dina Will you get back into bed or will I have to force you?

Claudia Try it.

Dina That's not fair. You're taller than me, Claudia.

Claudia's *much too weak to get up anyway. She falls back into bed.*

Claudia I'm needed at the office and they want me to stay in bed.

Dina I brought the papers you asked for.

Dina *hands* **Claudia** *a file which* **Claudia** *quickly looks over.*

Claudia My paper's dying.

Claudia *reaches under her pillow and hands* **Dina** *some sheets of paper.*

Claudia A list of things to do, people to call.

Dina Don't you ever relax?

Claudia What does that mean? To relax. To empty the brain, to cease striving for the things you believe in, an excuse to stop feeling for a moment.

Dina A temporary respite from the daily toil in order to gather strength for the next onslaught.

Claudia Relaxation is for people who've had enough of living. I'm not half done.

Dina You old fox.

Dina *takes* **Claudia**'s *hand.*

What's going on in this hospital? Such a fuss I had to get in here. Flashbulbs popping, policemen running around. It's not because of you, is it?

Claudia Some sort of scandal. A politician tried to cut his wrists.

Dina *That* scandal?

Claudia Yes, *that* scandal. What with all the noise last night I didn't get a wink of sleep. By the early hours I was half wishing that he'd succeeded.

Dina It's quite exciting.

Claudia I'll let you know of any further developments.

Dina (*voice falters*) To be caught up in it. (**Dina** *looks down, biting her lip*.)

Claudia You're biting your lip, Dina, is there something on your mind?

Dina Can't I hide anything from you?

Claudia No.

Dina It isn't easy. (*Blurts.*) Ned's leaving the Gazette.

Claudia I see.

Dina He's had nothing else on his mind for the past week. It's been like living with a mad man.

Claudia He's lucky to have you.

Dina Not that I've been much use. You know me and politics.

Claudia Poor Ned.

Dina Are you angry?

Claudia Ned has my respect. That doesn't change. You're not leaving are you?

Dina (*shakes her head*) It won't be easy with Ned and everything. I suppose it's time I stopped taking the easy way out.

Claudia What a time to be ill.

Pause.

How long is it since I first arrived in England?

Dina Almost nine years.

Claudia It hardly seems like two. What have I done with the years? Tell Ned to come and see me.

Dina I'm sure he will. This rift between you has saddened him too.

Claudia What have I achieved in nine years?

Dina I remember that day going to meet you. Cold. Foggy. Ned and Ahmed were like two schoolboys. I thought you'd have two heads.

Claudia Imagine me. I didn't know what to expect. I was terrified.

Dina Were you? It didn't show. You couldn't have achieved more.

Claudia No?

Dina What have I achieved?

Claudia Ned. The baby.

Dina *takes* **Claudia**'s *hand as they smile.*

Claudia Will you book some tickets for me? I want to take a holiday.

Dina About time too. I'm always saying. Where do you want to go?

Claudia Russia and China.

Dina That sounds like reconnaissance, not a holiday.

Claudia Now feels like the right time.

Dina What about the paper? How can you afford to go away? The paper won't last two weeks without you.

Claudia You and Donald will be able to manage. You've had the best teacher.

Dina I'm not going to change your mind am I?

Claudia No.

Dina You look so sad today.

Claudia Everything's dying. My father, Elizabeth, and now my paper.

Dina Perhaps we should take one of those companies up on their offer.

Claudia If the paper is important enough to the people then they'll support it.

Dina You're always right.

Claudia Not always.

Dina I'd be lost without you.

Claudia You'd blossom, I'm sure, without old bossy boots carping on. (**Claudia** *tries to get up.*) It's no good, Dina. I'm no good at lying in bed all day. I feel like a corpse.

Dina Claudia, please.

Claudia, *using what little strength there is in her body gets out of bed. She's very shaky on her feet and has to steady herself by resting a hand on the bed. She looks awful.*

Claudia There. You see. And just in time for the pub. I believe it's your round. Make mine a double scotch.

Scene Nineteen

West Indian Gazette office, January 1965. **Donald** *enters. He goes to* **Claudia**'s *'desk' and looks at items on it. He clears up some papers, flicks through others and throws them away. He sits and stares into space listlessly.* **Dina** *appears, stands in doorway.*

Dina She here yet?

Donald (*as if caught unawares*) No.

Dina Good. (*Enters carrying a cake tin.*) I made her a cake. Sort of a welcome back. I hope she likes it. Oh Donald I'm sorry. (*Hugs him and kisses his cheek.*) Happy new year. Have a good Christmas?

Donald It was . . . it was all right.

Dina I don't know. My values must be all wrong or something. Because I only

like the hectic days surrounding it. Coffee?

Donald No thank you.

Dina Are you all right?

Donald Fine.

Dina She'll be late. Of course she'll have to make a grand entrance. Walk in here looking rested and disgustingly healthy. She sent me a New Year card from China. Did you get one?

Donald Yes.

Dina It seems as though they treated her like royalty. You think she'll have brought us back a present? Not that I'm expecting one. I'm so excited. I couldn't wait to get in this morning, ran all the way here.

Donald Dina, I have to tell you. Claudia's been back for a week.

Dina A week? Why hasn't she come to see me?

Pause.

Donald She died on Christmas Eve.

Dina (*disbelief*) That's not funny.

Donald It isn't a joke.

Dina *lowers her head and starts to cry. After a while she looks up.*

Dina How?

Donald Her heart.

Dina Stupid. I told her to look after herself.

Donald There was no one with her when it happened. If there was, then perhaps . . .

Dina That's absurd. How could she have died alone?

Donald The funeral's on.

Dina She was always there when you needed her, how come there was no one around when *she* was needy?

Donald *embraces* **Dina**. *They comfort each other. After a while* **Dina** *breaks away, wipes her eyes.*

Dina What do we do now?

Donald Carry on.

Dina I don't think I can.

Donald She wouldn't want us to give up. She'll expect us to make sure the next issue goes out on time.

Dina Yes.

Dina *picks up a copy of the West Indian Gazette and looks at it. Suddenly she crumples it up into a ball and lets it fall to the ground.*

Dina I'm sorry. I can't.

Dina *exits. After a pause* **Donald** *gets up, picks up the paper that* **Dina** *let fall. Straightens it out. He puts it down, picks up a notebook and pen and starts to write.*

Scene Twenty

Claudia *and her* **Mother** *standing on street corner in Brooklyn, USA, 1927. It's early morning.*

Mother Are you asleep?

Claudia I'm wide awake.

Mother Because if you go to sleep you'll miss it.

Claudia I've seen it many times before.

Mother I never tire of watching the sun rise.

Claudia Why?

Mother (*smiles*) Because it's free. And, no matter how tough this day gets, there's always the promise of the sun rising afresh tomorrow.

Claudia Doesn't he get bored going through the same routine every single morning? I would.

Mother That's because you're a (*Tickles* **Claudia**.) twitchy little girl.

Claudia (*laughing*). Stop.

Mother Here she comes.

Claudia I'm getting sleepy.

Mother (*gently*) Claudia, Claudia.

Claudia (*sleepy*) When I grow up I'm going to be a dancer at the Apollo. I'm going to wear a stringy skirt with spangles on it. And have diamonds in my pressed hair.

Mother Isn't that beautiful?

Claudia (*sleepy*) And people will come to see me from all over the world and after I've danced for them they'll say isn't she the best? And even if they never set foot in the Apollo ever again, they'd always remember me. They'd always . . . (*She yawns and falls asleep.*)

Mother So beautiful.

Blood Sweat and Fears

Maria Oshodi was born in South London in 1964. Her plays include **The 'S' Bend** (Longman, 1986), chosen for the Young Writers' Festival at the Royal Court Theatre, 1984; produced by the Cockpit Youth Theatre, 1985 and chosen for the first International Festival of Young Playwrights, Interplay '85 held in Sydney, Australia. **From Choices to Chocolate** had readings at the Royal Court Studio and Riverside Studios, London in 1986 and a workshop production at Riverside Studios in 1987. She is currently writing a play about childcare **Here Comes A Candle** for the Inner City Theatre Company for their production in 1989, as well as three short plays for schools. She is a script tutor for Paddington Arts.

Author's Preface

In 1986 I received a phone call from one of the staff at the Sickle Cell Centre in Lambeth. I was asked if I would be interested in writing a play about the Sickle Cell Anaemia blood condition, and initially I was reluctant. I was embroiled in medical problems of my own and was not interested in writing anything at that time. However, I told the centre to give me time to think about it and I would let them know if I had any ideas. A couple of months later I had contacted the centre to ask them if they could introduce me to any young Sickle Cell Anaemia sufferers. I had become curious, not only about the manifestations of the disease, but more so about if and how its victims perceived themselves as disabled people. Then the Arts Council commissioned me to write the play, exploring the agonising tensions surrounding invisible disability.

In writing the play, I felt a huge responsibility to the Sickle Cell Anaemia sufferers, I had interviewed for my research. I wanted to accurately present the trauma of the disease, but also to show some of the social implications. The Star Trek Cafe seemed the ideal setting to do this. I hoped a fast-food store would act as a suitable metaphor for our increasingly competitive society's sometimes dismissive, or superficial, attitude to disability. It is no surprise that in an environment such as this, containing people with similar attitudes to the macho Curtis, disabled people like Ben experience a polarisation in their emotions: should they reveal or conceal their condition? Yet there are times when certain aspects of ourselves, which we may prefer to keep hidden, have to be confronted and come to terms with in order that we can grow as individuals and in our relationships. In the play it is the persistence of Ashley that encourages Ben in the understanding of this fact.

My obligations in writing this play were too many. Not only to the centre in Lambeth, and the patients connected there, but also to myself. I had to try to incorporate in the work the many permutations of Sickle Cell Anaemia, from complex medical terminology to crass reactions to the disease. Also, I felt the need to provide good, strong main characters for young black actors. I sincerely hope I have achieved this in **Blood Sweat and Fears**.

Maria Oshodi

Blood Sweat and Fears was premièred by Harmony Theatre at Battersea Arts Centre, London in May, 1988 and toured in England, with the following cast:

Ben Stranelle	Steven Woodcock
Ashely *his girlfriend*	Yvonne French
Curtis Sinclair **Kid***	Clinton Blake
Tessa Stranelle *Ben's mother*	Winsome Pinnock
Chris Hayse **Doctor***	Nicholas Bell
Peggy **Medical student** **Nurse***	Claire Vousden

*These characters can be played by one actor.

Directed by David Sulkin
Lighting by Ace McCarron

The play is set in 1987, in London.

Act One

Scene One

The stage is in darkness. A loud echoing voice is heard: 'Space the final frontier'.

Then the droning of the 'Star Trek' theme is audible, as well as kitchen noises offstage.

Three silhouetted figures, two boys and a girl, are busy serving from behind a counter. Their darkened shapes come up to take orders, and then rush left and right to pick up the packaged food, and then to waiting customers. The three, though they seem pleasant, have an irritability somewhere in their voices, which grows steadily.

First Boy (*coming to counter*) Can I help you sir?

Girl (*calling as she rushes off*) One Captain Kirk Quarter Pounder!

First Boy (*rushing off*) One Transporter Shake, and two Spock regulars.

Second Boy (*at counter*) £3.45. Thank you. Have a cosmic day sir. Yes, next?

Girl (*returning to counter*) Thank you, and beam in here again soon.

Second Boy (*rushing off*) Energize juice, and one Uhura Special.

Girl (*rushing off*) Two Clingon Burgers with cheese, and two Vulcan pies!

First Boy (*returning to counter*) Thank you, and have a cosmic day. Next order please.

Second Boy (*rushing off*) Trekian Chicken, Spock regular and a Warp Factor One Coke! No ice!

First Boy (*rushing off*) Enterprise fries, and two Transporter Shakes.

Girl (*returning*) £1.67. Thank you, and have a cosmic day.

First Boy (*returning*) Your Enterprise fries and shake.

Girl (*rushing off*) Uhura special and double Clingon Burger.

First Boy (*rushing off*) Vulcan pie, and two Trekian Chickens!

Second Boy (*returning*) £1.45. Thank you, and have a cosmic day.

Girl (*returning*) Your order. £1.98, and have a cosmic day.

First Boy 90p please, and have a cosmic day.

Girl And I hope you have a cosmic day.

Second Boy And have a cosmic day.

First and Second Boys Hope you have a cosmic day!

All (*now more aggressive than irritable*) Yes. Have a cosmic day!

A high pitched signal sounds, and lights go out on the backdrop. Lights up on stage centre. It is the downstairs rest bay of the restaurant. There are lockers, table, chairs and a potted plant. To the right there are sounds of the boys and girl coming downstairs for their break.

First Boy, *black, in his late teens. He is* **Ben**. *He is wearing the uniform of the restaurant. Black narrow tight trousers, and a bright red long sleeved T-shirt with black band round the neck line and cuffs and a gold V symbol on the left breast. He is also wearing a white cardboard hat. He is followed by the* **Girl**, **Ashely**, *who is wearing a similar uniform, but she has a shortish black skirt.* **Ashely** *is black, and about the same age as* **Ben**.

Ashely It was delicious.

Ben (*going off the other way to get a padded waistcoat jacket*) Disgusting!

Ashely (*shouting to him*) You're too critical.

Ben (*off*) I can't help it. When it's something as important as that. I can't help it.

Ashely If your standard gets too high, you'll never be satisfied.

Ben (*coming on, jacket in hand*) If you want to know what a proper soufflé is, I'll make you one. When you off next?

Ashely Two days.

Ben (*thinking*) Yeah. That's OK. Then, then.

Ashely (*kissing him. Lunch box in hand*) Then, then.

Ben And I'll try something special for the main meal as well, but there's a condition.

Ashely I was planning on staying anyway.

Ben No . . . there's got to be wine.

Ashely Oh, all right. What one shall I get?

Curtis *comes in. He's black, and the same age as the others, and wearing a similar uniform. He's carrying a tray heavy with cafe products.*

Curtis Uh-hu, come on, now now, none of that. I don't wanna be put off me food.

Ben Easy Curtis. Wha's up?

Ashely (*opening her lunch box*) He's just vexed 'cos Chantelle keeps prowling past the windows upstairs.

Ben So?

Curtis (*biting into a hamburger*) I don't wanna see her.

Ashely The girl's keen to see you though, isn't she?

Curtis She sniffed me out on the common when I was training on Sunday.

Ashely I wonder why she's bothering so much Curtis?

Curtis She keeps saying she wants to tell me something, but I was too seriously shagged after my physical jerks and running through formations to stand up, let alone talk, so I told the girl to move, and don't bother me.

Ashely (*sings*) 'Hey girl, don't bother me.' I wonder what it is she wants to tell you, don't you Curtis?

Curtis Probably moaning, why won't I take her to see Luther Vandross. (*Kisses his teeth.*) Rubbish!

Ashely If you say so Curtis.

Curtis Yeah, that is what I'm sayin'. Safe.

Ben (*looking in* **Ashely**'s *lunch box*) More Bugs Bunny food again Ashely?

Ashely Actually, I haven't got one leaf in here today, it's just cheese and date.

Curtis Nastiness.

Ashely (*to* **Ben**) There's probably more processed bunny food in that additive saturated pile of junk he's eating.

Curtis How can you say that? Don't talk rubbish girl. There's no additives, or such things in this. You done the kitchen, you know what's gone in it.

Ben *gets up to look at the notice board by the pay-phone.*

Ashely OK. Not that burger, but what about that. (*Pointing at one of the boxes on the tray.*) You don't know what goes into that do you? It's just brought here ready made and chucked in the vat. A fiver, half the ingredients in that you can't even pronounce, let alone have heard of.

Curtis (*picking up a box*) No ingredients. No fiver, chill.

Ashely They can't fit all those chemical names, monosodium whatever, on there that's why, and they wouldn't dare either, it'd scare everyone off. Well, any intelligent person.

Curtis Well, I'll tell you somethin'. All that brown dry stuff in there (*points in the box.*) scares me off! Look at it! It's distressed! Everything's brown and dry! Brown dry bread. Brown dry, what is it? . . . a biscuit? And look, look at that! Even the apple's brown and dry!

Ashely This is a kiwi fruit Curtis.

Curtis (*sniggering*) Oh!

Ben (*feigning shock, looking at the notice board*) Oh my God! We're way down on our prime objective targets this week folks.

Ashely Oh, dear dear dear. What are we going to do?

Ben (*sitting down*) Battersea are still five points ahead of us.

Curtis Well, we'll have to tighten our belts, pull our socks up, and work our balls off even more.

Ashely Captain Hayse is probably drowning in a cold sweat over his desk, trying to figure out how he's going to get us to do just that.

Curtis That man is extra. When I went training down the common on Sunday, I drive past this place, right, and I see in my rear view mirror, some geezer crawling all over the roof. So I turn up the side road, and come round the front again and I see it was Hayse. I beeped, right, and he waved, an' dis is 'im, 'I'm just checking security!' Nar man, the brother's distressed. Sunday's his only day off, and he can't keep away from this place. Jesus!

All laugh.

Ashely The man is so sad.

Ben You nar.

Ashely And he hates me so much.

Ben Ever since that filter powder thing 'in it?

Ashely Yeah.

Curtis What?

Ben You nar. When Ash told him that filter powder stuff we use to clean the vats out, is out of order.

Ashely The training video shows we should wear masks when we use it.

Ben And Big H said he'd get us some.

Ashely But he never, of course.

Ben So Ashely rang the inspector at head office and he come down on Hayse. That really shamed him up.

Ashely (*to* **Curtis**) Can't you tell, Hayse is cool with me?

Ben And he don't rate me much either.

Curtis That's 'cos you're a slack ragamuffin, boy. If you're gonna be a skiver, you shouldn't be a silly arse as well, and let him catch ya, like he's gonna do any minute now.

Ashely Yeah Ben, you're meant to be on freezer duty now, cleaning it out.

Ben Laters, laters.

Curtis (*kissing his teeth*) Laters, laters. That's your theme tune bushman.

Ben Yeah, well, working five nights a week in this manic place on top of college is just untold pressure, you nar Curtis.

Curtis Why don't you just sack it then, nar what I mean.

Ben I can't, yet.

Curtis Why not?

Ben Reasons.

Curtis Like what?

Ashely Rent arrears.

Ben Shut up Ashely.

Ashely Just 'cos you're in a bit of debt since we went to Paris. So what?

Ben Don't have to broadcast it. (*To Curtis.*) Anyway Curt, what's happened to your great escape plan?

Ashely Yeah Curtis, you're always chatting about leaving.

Curtis (*stretching*) I am leaving. Just pay off the last for me motor and I'm out 'a here. Safe.

Ashely Yeah, the money's the only good thing to come out of this place. Not that I see too much of that stuff after going to all of your restaurants.

Ben You don't have to pay your way all the time. I said I would.

Ashely If you did we couldn't afford to go so much, and I like going.

Ben Yeah, you mean you like going and telling me how bad all the food is we're eating, and how it's mashing up our hearts.

Ashely Well, that's the thrill of it, knowing it's bad and still doing it.

Curtis You've got some distressed idea of what a thrill is girl!

Ashely Anyway Ben, it's not that I don't take precautions after. Look, my brown dry apple! (*She bites into it.*)

Curtis But then you come to work in this disease centre and help poison the rest of the public. Right? That makes serious sense.

Ashely Don't cuss me, Curtis, for working here! It's up to everyone to decide for themselves, right? I don't

go around trying to convert people unless they show some sign of repentance, and the people who come in here ain't exactly showing them signs is it?

Curtis Why don't you go and work where they are showing them then?

Ashely Well I will when I've done my massage course. I wanna be involved with people again, like when I worked at the Health Club.

Ben When you gonna do it then?

Ashely When I've prepared myself for the gross life of a student, reading cold general facts out of cold text books, and having no money.

Curtis Oh, so all this fitness thing's rubbish. You're into the money like the rest of us.

Ashely *tuts and looks away.*

Ben If I was you Ashely I'd keep away from this 'Shit-stew' massage thing, whatever it is. It sounds a bit dodgy, nar what I mean?

Ashely Shiatsu!

Ben Why don't you do physiotherapy or something? At least everyone's heard of that.

Ashely Ah, shut up Ben, I do what I wanna do. I'm not gonna make plans and fit myself into them like you do, and like that diary you've got, where everything's charted out. Where you're gonna be in X amounts of months.

Curtis *is pretending to snore through this, then . . .*

Curtis When I grow up and I'm eighteen years, five and a half months old, I plan to be serving up Spock burgers at the Star Trek Cafe.

Ashely What's the point in living like that? You might as well do something when you feel for it.

Curtis She's right Benny boy! You should leave plenty of room for them unseen things to happen.

Ben Na. (*Shaking his head.*)

Curtis (*getting dramatic*) Like when the coach of the Miami Dolphins just happens to be cruising in a DC10 over Clapham Common when I'm training and spots me out of the window and shouts, 'Pilot! Halt this craft!'

Ben Curtis, you're really out of order, man.

Ashely Nar, I'm not talking about rubbish like that.

Curtis He'll see me calling the plays for the South London Centurians, and he'll say, 'Who's that stinging QB? I wanna know!'

Ben What's a QB?

Ashely Quite boring.

Curtis Quarter back, girl. General of the offensive unit. (*Shouts.*) 444.

Ben 444.

Curtis Blue 32.

Ben Blue 32.

Curtis Red 29.

Ben Red 29.

Ashely Two fat ladies, 88.

Curtis You lot are fools, man! You don't know what it's like. (*He tosses a cardboard box from the tray into the air.*) Break the plain of that line, and score those touch downs. Sweet. (*Now he begins to use the box as a football.*) Centre snaps the ball back through his legs to QB.

Ben Curtis, quieten down will ya.

Curtis QB tosses ball back to running back. (*To* **Ben** *and* **Ashely**.) That's a pass, flip pass, or hand off into the stomach, see? Then the ball swings out, flying like a bird, through the air to a wide receiver. Pitch out, Joe Montana style. The man's a hero. Flair passes like Dan Marino can only do. First down and ten. See him go. Third down and seven. He's coming home, and go for it. Break the plain of that line. Hit it and touch down!

Hayse *the manager of the restaurant has come in carrying a small watering can. He is white and in his early 30's and wearing a blue shirt, black tie, and trousers and standing inches away from the box that* **Curtis** *has slammed down.*

Hayse Are you feeling quite well, Curtis?

Curtis (*screwing up the box*) Yeah. Yeah.

Ashely So sad.

Hayse (*seeing* **Ben**) I can't believe this! Ben, what the hell are you doing here? You're meant to be cleaning out the freezer room. You had your break an hour ago. Get in there will you. I'm sick and tired of finding you sitting about. Sometimes I get the impression your whole heart isn't in this job. You haven't got anywhere near your personal target high for this week. No wonder that this branch is doing so abysmally in the ratings.

Ben Sorry Captain.

Hayse You'd better just buck your ideas up, and get on with the work in the freezer. You might just make up some of those lost points. You're going to remain at band one if you don't pull your socks up. Curtis pulled his socks up, and look he's on his second band already, aren't you Curtis.

Curtis Yes Captain.

Hayse This crew has got to pull more tightly together to make a more homogeneous unit. The sign that my crew has thrown itself, body and soul, into their work and this branch, will only be evident when we reach that top position in the ratings.

Ben *exits*.

Hayse And that number one spot is even more important now. I've just had news through from head office that whichever branch holds that top spot in the ratings in January, will be the branch privileged to send one of its crew members to New York, to represent London in the fifth International Fast Food Festival that is being held at Amalgamated Hamburger University.

Ashely (*unenthusiastic*) Great.

Curtis Triff.

Hayse Your powers of deception are convincing. If I didn't know my crew better, I'd swear you were showing a marked lack of interest.

Curtis (*alert*) 'Old on, 'old on, 'old on. What did you say again?

Hayse You weren't listening?

Curtis Just checking to see if I've got it right Captain. There's a chance one of us can get sent free to New York for this Festival thing in January?

Hayse Good, you were taking it in.

Curtis Carry on, carry on.

Hayse (*nervous laugh*) Well there are two initiative schemes that the omnipotent powers at head office have issued, and that I think can be used to better our position in the ratings. One is a new comment slip that the customers will be encouraged to fill out and this will request comments on such things as food, service and individual crew members etc. That will help me to see who, out of my crew, are sub-standard, and I will thus act accordingly. Now, the second thing is a sales gimmick. From Monday the 12th

of this month, models of the Starship will be given away free with every Kirk Quarter Pounder sold, with cheese, that is. When ten of these Starships have been collected by a customer, and brought back to the store, they will be given a free Quarter Pounder, without cheese that is. But first they must recite the item's full title, and total ingredients which are . . .? Come on. Come on.

Curtis
Ashely } (*bored, and in unison*) A Captain Kirk Quarter Pounder, includes a bonus bun, bumper burger, choicest cheese, heavenly ham, salad, relish and chilli sauce.

Hayse Excellent! And what does the Captain expect from his crew?

Curtis
Ashely } Service with a smile.

Hayse Well I hope your enthusiasm will be as adept as your memory.

Curtis It will, Captain, it will.

Hayse Good, good. (*High pitched signal.* **Hayse** *laughs, and claps his hands.*) Right Ashely, it's back to the Bridge for you isn't it? And Curtis, litter patrol outside. (*He goes to leave.*) Come on, come on. Get your skates on. (**Hayse** *goes to the potted plant, and waters it from the small watering can he is holding.* **Ben** *comes in.*) Finished Ben? Well you're on swab duty, aren't you. Get a move on. (*He goes.*)

Ben (*going to table*) God, I'm freezing. That room's a killer Any coffee left Curtis? (*He takes a drink. He is shivering. He sits down.*)

Ashely God, that man! He took five minutes off our break to talk all that rubbish to us. He should've said that in a staff meeting, not taken it off our time. We have little of it, as it is.

Curtis (*quickly*) Ah, shut up woman! He can take the whole damn break if he's gonna tell me news like that. You know what January in America means, don't you? Course you do. The Superbowl, that's right! (*Going to get a broom.*) If big H ain't messin', it could be TWA to the USA, hey! (*He goes.*)

Ashely (*sulkily*) What's wrong with you?

Ben Nothin'.

Ashely It's 'cos I mentioned the rent isn't it.

Ben Nar, that's forgotten. I'm just cold, nar what I mean? These stupid jackets are useless against that room you nar. What you on now?

Ashely (*sighing*) Bridge. Ah God, this bloody place is so horrible! What am I doing here? I think it's right what you said Ben, I should get myself together. I dunno what I'm waiting for. There's nothing stimulating gonna happen round here, unless I want to go to the fifth International Star Trek Fast Food Festival, convention, whatever. (*Pause.*) Ben, I'm gonna leave. I'm going to college.

Ben (*distracted*) Right!

Ashely Oh Jesus, you could sound more enthused. You're the one who's . . .

Ben Ashely, it's good. I'm glad. OK?

Ashely (*going*) Right, OK. Fair enough. See you later.

When **Ashely** *has gone* **Ben** *sighs, and feels the lower part of his left arm carefully and instinctively. He gets up, goes to get a bottle of pills. He takes some.* **Curtis** *runs on with a broom in his hand.*

Curtis (*slapping* **Ben** *on the back*) Easy Benny boy! Popping pills again? But the question is 'Can he handle it?' (*He runs off.*)

Ben (*choking, calling after* **Curtis**) It's a headache. It's a headache. (*He feels his arm again. Looks at the bottle still in his hand.*) Course I can. (*He takes two more pills.*) No panic, just the usual. Bear it out. Give the stuff time to work on it. Keep cool. Keep cool. (*He goes to clean the table, using only one hand to do it. Then, to the audience.*) The freezer is a place I know, for a fact, does not agree with me. Then again, that ain't no unique thing. Who does it agree with? I mean, what mug wants to spend his time cleaning out a room ten below zero, mm? Not this one I'm tellin' ya. But there are the times when it can't be bunked and you reap the consequences, as they say. (*Sighs.*) All that food in the freezer, packed on the shelves, makes me think of how Hayse wants us lot to be identical and false. Upstairs on the Bridge we might be, nar what I mean? But down here we warm up to reality again and become normal. Have a laugh. No one takes it seriously, 'cos it ain't real, except for the money. That's real enough. Now if I was working in a proper kitchen, I'd take the whole thing serious, nar messin', but I'm biding my time for that. Everything's worked out. I ain't waiting for it to drop out of the sky like Curtis's DC10. I can't afford to leave any gaps waiting for things like that to happen. I've been working on things since I come to London from Bushey, que Curtis's stupid joke 'Bushman'! And in the meantime, I put up with these poxy jobs. This ain't the first one I've had. (*Sits down, tired. Feels the top of his arm, concentrating. Laughs. Rubs his hand across his eyes.*) It'll get to it. Give it a chance. As my old boss used to say 'Prenty patience Ben, prenty patience.' I used to say to him, 'Mr Ho Wung, you said you'd show me how to make the sweet and sour this week' and he'd give me the usual, 'Prenty patience Ben, prenty patience.' I'd cuss him for wasting my time, and then he'd scream at me in Chinese, as if I could understand his lyrics guy. That Mr Ho Wung was no fool though. He used to take advantage of me 'cos he knew it was my first job and I needed the experience in the kitchen. Jesus the things he made me do! Washing the woks, washing the floors, day in, day out, and the worst thing! (*He slaps the wet cloth on the table.*) Getting that damned duck! Dis is 'im, 'Ah, Ben, I'm very grad you come in earry today. I want you to get my duck, and I want you back here in prenty time for me to cook it, or your wages cut.' So, I'd go on the tube, most of the time getting lost 'cos I wasn't used to it then. Somehow find my way to Oxford Circus, get off, walk into Soho and go to this little Chinese restaurant where I bought Mr Ho Wung his four dead ducks. Then I'd come out of the restaurant and stuff the ducks inside my jacket, two on each side, and zip it up, right up to the neck. I'd walk through the crowds to the tube station, quick. I thought if I slowed down, people might notice this rough smell, and think it was me. I'd get on the tube next. That was double wicked! I had to sit in this packed out carriage and I had my arms folded over my bulging chest, and looking round like I never knew where the smell was coming from either. All I could hear was, sniff, sniff. Sniff, sniff. I thought it was better to join in, or I might look suspicious, nar what I mean? And then after all that shame up, he never taught me how to cook that sweet and sour, or the Peking duck. The only thing he taught me before he closed the Red Dragon, and went home to Shanghi, was how to work the rice steamer, and get a seat on the tube. Nar man, that place was untold misery, and a waste of time for me. The best chef I ever knew, my uncle Andre, missed out on telling me about

bosses like Mr Ho Wung, but there again, he couldn't tell me everything.

Curtis (*coming in*) Yo bushman! Easy. Wha's 'appening? Scivin' it again are ya?

Ben Nar, nar.

Curtis (*leaning over **Ben**'s shoulder*) Look, I've found us the real business. I've just been chatting up these two stingin' birds outside. They just come out of Chelsea Girl.

Ben Yeah?

Curtis One's a real slapper; her mate's a bit of a rough dog though. What you doin' tonight Ben?

Ben Well, I was thinking, em . . .

Curtis I thought we could take them out, up the Studio.

Ben Yeah?

Curtis Or down Cinderella's.

Ben Yeah?

Curtis Chill out over a drinking session.

Ben Couple of cans of Red Stripe yeah?

Curtis Tennants mate, Tennants.

Ben Right.

Curtis Barcardi and Coke for the birds. They look that type. (*He looks at a piece of paper in his hand.*) Yeah, thought as much. One's Tracey, and one's Sharon. They give me their numbers. Sweet.

Ben But Curtis, aren't you forgetting one thing?

Curtis What?

Ben Ashely.

Curtis (*kissing his teeth*) God. The girl's deadstock. Deadstock man! You've been going out with her for nearly six months bushman. Sack her! Put her back on the market. Listen, it's time you stepped out of line a bit more Benny boy!

Ben Yeah, but Curtis, it's a bit out of order innit? And anyway, what about Chantelle?

Curtis Chantelle! I gave her notice a long time back.

Ben Yeah, but Curtis, she ain't taking much notice, is it?

Hayse *comes in with watering can.*

Hayse Ben! What are you doing?

Ben *moves to take out sack and cloth.*

Hayse Leave that. I want you two to unload. Delivery's just come and you two look as if you can manage. I'd get Michael down from the bridge, but I'm short enough as it is. (*Laughs.*) Anyway Ali and Sam managed it on their own yesterday, and you two ought to be made of better stuff. Let's see if you can beat their time. (*He takes out a stopwatch. Waits for the second hand to get to zero.*) Right. Go! (*He steps back to watch them work.*) And remember, perseverance means points, and points mean pounds! (*He watches them begin unloading. Waters plant and leaves.*)

Curtis (*running from one side to another with boxes of Star Trek Cafe products*) But it's still cookery, innit, in effect? That is what it is, the bottom line, safe.

Ben (*following* **Curtis**) Yeah, I know, but there's a lot more to it Curtis. There's so many different parts you nar. Really technical. It's an art, a craft, a science, all in one.

Curtis 'And we're glad to have with us today, helping us to unload the delivery at the Star Trek Cafe, none other than Professor Ragamuffin with an MA in Combined Cake Technology.' (*Laughs.*) Aye, Ben.

Catch. (**Curtis** *chucks* **Ben** *a box which falls to the floor.* **Curtis** *laughs.*) Come on. Get busy.

Ben (*gathering up the dropped box*) Nar, serious though Curtis, I mean, what is the thing that will always be around as long as people are around? Something that always needs to be done, and something that all classes, races, ages, and sexes want, and need? Food, innit?

Curtis Yeah, but come on bushman, icing cakes? Leave it out.

Ben But that's only one part of it. My uncle said to me 'Get into it, 'cos it's a trade that'll always be in demand.'

Curtis Yeah I suppose so.

Ben And you don't just go in the kitchen and start cooking, you know. It's just like being an engineer, or something like that. You go to college and get your training and exams.

Curtis That sort 'a life's just distress. Any mug can do that. There ain't no adventure in that. No excitement. Move yourself Ben, come on! You're slackin' man. Use both hands. Get hold of the box proper!

Ben But it's a challenge for some people Curtis.

Curtis I don't see that as no challenge, not a real challenge. Come on, come on, get busy! Use both hands! Both hands!

Ben What d'you call a real challenge then Curtis?

Curtis Something that just comes at you slam out 'a nowhere, and you get on its case before it has a chance to get away. Move the damn box Ben!

Ben Or can it be something that comes at you, slam out of nowhere, and you try and duck it, taking the chance yourself to get away?

Curtis (*shouting*) Pick it up! Pick it up!

Ben (*shouting back in anger and frustration. Holding his arm*) I can't! I told you, I've got a headache.

Curtis What there? (*Pointing at **Ben**'s arm.*)

Hayse (*coming in*) Finished?

Ben (*going*) I have.

Blackout.

Scene Two

Ben's room. Sofa with telephone on one arm. **Ben**, miserable under a quilt, holding the receiver and talking into the phone. There is a continuous high-pitched sound in the air.

Ben I'm sick. Sorry, another time. Yeah, when I'm feeling better. The 'flu, yeah, that's it. No don't, you might catch it. Sorry about the meal Ash. I'll ring you soon. Bye. (*He puts the receiver down, and sinks back on the sofa. He reaches for some pain killers in a bottle on the floor. The bottle is empty.*) Shit! (*Chucks the bottle across the room. He tries to relax by sinking into the sound. He closes his eyes. He opens them again to look for cigarettes. Opens the box and takes one out.*) One. (*He lights up and exhales a long column of smoke, and sighs.*) And why not one tablet as well. Aye? Not much to ask for is it? Oh yeah, I remember. I gave up asking for little favours like that a long time ago, didn't I. When I found out asking was like shouting down a well. You just get your own voice coming back at you again and again, till in the end it's you asking yourself for what you want, not anyone else. So it was a slip of the tongue that I asked for one more tablet. I'm sorry, right. It's my fault. I was a sucker to forget them. I take the blame. (*Pause.*) There again, it's not too hard to see why I weren't prepared for this is it? In one whole year it's just been a little ache in one or two places for one or two days. An aching that the pain killers could beat, or at least bruise up a bit. I thought it was all drying up. Gone back to where it come from. Jesus, don't say it's revving up to bulldoze its way back in again. Like last time. It really rocked the house then. (*The sound increases. **Ben**'s voice can only just be heard.*) You can't come in. You're banned. You ain't gonna turn up the volume on this pain and let your speakers blast me out so I'll howl like a dog. Get out! (*The sound quietens down to its previous level. **Ben** rolls up more in the quilt.*) I'm so tired, tired, tired. If only I could sleep through all this.

*Lights change. A **Woman Teacher** stands by the sofa.*

Teacher Down in the medical room again Ben? A pain? Where? Well, here, I'll put a bandage on it, but that's all I can do . . .

Tessa comes and stands by the sofa.

Tessa Ben, you filthy child! Eight years old and you're still doing it. Yes I will smack you till you grow up and learn what the bed is for and what the toilet is for.

*A **School Kid** comes and stands by the sofa.*

Kid (*pointing*) Urrr, what's that? Ben's got the lurgies!

Tessa We'll go and see the Doctor. You might be allergic to something.

Doctor comes and stands by the sofa. He is wearing a white coat.

Doctor (*as he comes*) Just a juvenile case of eczema. Lots of children get it at his age. Nothing to worry about. I'll give you an ointment.

Teacher Kick, kick, kick! That's right! Let's have those legs moving. (*Blows a whistle*.) Now class 4H I want you to get out quietly and stand round the pool till I say you can go and get changed. Yes, I know it's cold.

Tessa Doctor, he hasn't been well at all. Tired, headaches, pains and now all these swellings.

Doctor Mild case of gout. I'll prescribe you this, and come back if there's any more trouble, but there shouldn't be.

Kid I don't want Ben on my side Miss, he's useless.

Teacher If you want to play football Ben, you must try harder. Saying you're tired is no excuse. Now let's see you do the sportsfield twice with the others.

Doctor Ben Adrian Stranelle, due to the undeniable concrete evidence of this blood test I find you guilty of possessing the blood group SS.

Tessa SS?

Doctor He has sickle cell anaemia.

Tessa What's that?

Doctor (*embarrassed, shrugging it off*) Well, you may well ask. I'm not too well acquainted with the condition myself, but I think I'd be right in assuming all his previous problems can be related to this new find.

Kid Urrr, a disease! Vane-ites, vane-ites. I'm stayin' away from you.

Tessa But I'm a strong, healthy woman. Never a day's illness in my life. How can I have a child like this? And how can he have got it from me?

Teacher Now children, we must remember to treat Ben kindly. Some things he can't manage, can you Ben? Would you like to tell the other children about it? No? OK then, I will.

Ben will be allowed to leave the class at any time when he feels he needs his tablets that help his pain.

Tessa No, I'm not going back to work son. It's difficult to keep a job. I never know when you're going to be sick.

Kid It's not fair Miss! How come Ben can stay in 'cos it's raining? And he never has to do PE. (*Pause*.) Oh yeah, I forgot. (*Grudgingly*.) Yeah, sorry Ben.

Tessa I write and tell your father everything and all he can reply is 'Keep going, you're a good woman, and tell my Ben I'll be sending him something soon.' Nothing ever comes. Now look at this. (*She read a letter*.) 'I had a blood test done in 1961, and the Doctors didn't say there was anything wrong then.' The stupid man doesn't understand that back home they don't look for such things as this in the test.

Teacher Have you thought of sending him to a special school? One that can deal with his handicap?

Tessa But there's nothing wrong with his brain. He's normal.

Doctor It's very unfortunate, but there's no cure for this particular blood condition. We can only prescribe penicillin, folic acid and some strong pain killers. I'm afraid he'll just have to live with the irregularities his disease presents. Some of the time he'll be perfectly normal and on other occasions he'll be like this, *but* if he drinks about six pints of water every day, keeps warm and generally looks after his health, then attacks should be few and far between.

Tessa Yes, Uncle Andre has got it as well. When he comes to stay you'll have a lot to talk about.

Kid Sorry I never invited you to my party on Saturday Ben, but Gary said you might not be able to go to parties.

All the people go as the lights change. **Ben** *rolls over and turns on a cassette tape-recorder. It plays 'Summer Time' by Sam Cook at a low volume.*

Ben I met Ashely this summer. I hadn't had much to do with anyone before I went to work in the cafe, especially girls. I just felt that they knew, even though I was trying to hide it, and they kept away, 'cos they could tell something wasn't right. Funny Curtis never seemed to see anything. He's my first real mate, innit? He tried to get Ashely when she started at the cafe. I felt I never had a hope in hell against all his chat, but I dunno, she didn't seem to be impressed with all that. One break, I was just sitting there telling her about my college, just for something to say, like, and going on about some escallopes I'd tried, and she just goes 'I wouldn't mind trying them. I ain't had them before.' Curtis says I should go with a challenge. He doesn't know what he's talking about . . . but anyway . . . I went with that one. I still can't believe we're together. Ashely don't seem to sense anything's out of order, and even if she did . . . (*Sighs.*) . . . Well, I dunno.

Knocking at the door. **Ben** *turns off the tape.*

Who is it?

Ashely Night nurse for Fanny Craddock.

Ben Ashely, I really don't think you should come in here. It's full of germs.

Ashely I've already got a cold. We can share each other's misery. (*She knocks.*) Come on then, open this door.

Ben Ashely, please. I'm all right. Thanks for coming, but I . . .

Ashely Look, I'm freezing out here. I didn't come all this way to go home again.

Ben *gets up and opens the door.*

Ashely (*in coat and gloves*) If you hadn't opened that door, I would've thought you were doing something illegal in here with Curtis. You're eyes aren't glazed, so I've cleared you of that one. (*She takes off her coat.*) Now lay back down. I'm here to look after you.

Ben (*getting on the sofa*) You're just wasting your time. I'm all right.

Ashely You don't look all right, and how d'you expect to be all right living in this freezing hovel? (*Picks bread off floor.*) Off dry bread? (*Picks up bottle of pills.*) And what's this?

Ben Pain killers. I've got a headache. Ash look, why don't you just . . .

Ashely I haven't seen these before. DF118. Where does it hurt? (*Going to massage him.*) If I find the right muscle, I can usually . . .

Ben Get off me will ya! (*Pushes her away.*)

Ashely Okay, okay!

Ben Sorry.

Ashely Well, if you're that bad, you should see a Doctor. Have you?

Ben Nar. It'll pass.

Ashely How exactly are you feeling then?

Ben It's just flu.

Ashely Vitamin C. That's what you need. Fights infection. I've taken tons today. I'll get you some.

Ben If you want.

Ashely And inhale over a bowl of steam.

Ben Oh God, Ashely, I just want to be left alone.

Ashely Have you eaten?

Ben Yes. No.

Ashely I'll make you some soup.

Ben No. Please go.

Ashely I'm going to look after you.

Ben You can't.

Ashely Why? Who else've you got?

Ben No one. But there's nothing you can do. I'm tellin' ya.

Ashely How d'you know?

Ben Because I know. Please Ash, leave me alone. Just for today.

Ashely But listen, I don't like the idea of you being here all on your own, sick. If you won't let me do anything, then at least have the Doctor round. I'll call him for you.

Ben No. I'll go and see him sometime on my own.

Ashely Why, when he can come here? I can get him.

Ben No. Please don't.

Ashely What's wrong.

Ben Nothing. There's nothing he can do.

Ashely Why are you so sure Ben? Is it the flu? (*Silence.*) Ben?

Ben (*quietly*) No.

Ashely What is it then?

Ben I'm just ill.

Ashely Ill with what?

Ben Just ill with something.

Ashely What? Tell me! I want to know!

Ben Something. Something! Just something!

Ashely What something Ben?

Ben (*shouting*) Sickle cell! Now just fucking go away!

Lighting change.

So she knows and now there is this whole sickle cell rigmarole in front of us. Will she quit or cope? I can feel she's swinging my way. I want that *so* much.

Ashely Oh Ben, I'm sorry.

Ben (*embarrassed*) That's all right.

Ashely I wish you'd told me before. Why didn't you?

Ben Well, I didn't want to put all this on you, you nar.

Ashely (*slightly smiling*) Did you think I'd run away?

Ben I, I dunno.

They look at each other.

Ashely But Ben, I don't get why some mis-shapen blood cells give you so much pain like this.

Ben It's something to do with the oxygen as well. I dunno.

Ashely How can you be so ignorant about yourself? Look how it's affecting you.

Ben I dunno all the little details Ashely.

Ashely You don't seem to know the big ones either. God, what sort of person are you?

Ben I just . . . Look, my mum knows all about it.

Ashely I'll ring her then.

Ben No, don't.

Ashely Why?

Ben I just can't handle her around.

Ashely Listen, Ben. You can't keep letting your life be interrupted like this. You've got to do something. It's terrible.

Ben It ain't terrible, serious. It ain't bad at all. I'm practically over it. Innit the first time you've seen me like this all the months you've known me, eh? It don't affect me much anymore. I used to be ten times worse than this. My uncle had it as well. He was worse than me.

Ashely Is that the chef?

Ben Yeah.

Ashely Where is he now? How is he?

Ben He's dead.

Ashely What?!

Ben Not of this. Something else. A stroke.

Ashely (*sighs*) Oh, right.

Ben I've been OK for a year. I used to be like this all the time.

Ashely Oh.

Ben I just get a small ache sometimes now. Not very often, then I take a pill.

Ashely Yeah?

Ben That's why I get tired at work, you nar, get headaches.

Ashely Oh, I see . . . (*Pause.*) Ben?

Ben Yeah?

Ashely How long you normally like this?

Ben Well, I ain't normally like this.

Ashely No, I know. But when you are?

Ben Three days, four days. Maybe a week.

Ashely Don't you think, well, we could try and find something out about this thing, this sickle cell?

Ben You can try.

Ashely (*putting on her coat*) No time like the present. And you know, Hayse'll be hounding you about your absence soon. You'd better tell him.

Ben I can't. Ash, be serious. He'd sack me on the spot. I need the money.

Ashely Well you better dream up a good excuse. (*She picks up the phone receiver, and gives it to* **Ben**.)

Ben What shall I tell him?

Ashely Tell him you've got the flu. (*She goes as* **Ben** *dials.*)

Ben Oh, hallo Captain. It's Ben Stranelle. Yeah, sorry I haven't been in, but I've got the flu (*Holds his nose.*) I'm sorry I didn't let you know earlier. Yeah, I know it's bad. I'll make up for it Captain, all the points I've lost. Promise. I'll be in sometime next week. I'll try. Sorry Captain. Bye. (*Puts receiver down.*)

Lights change.

When I keep taking six pills instead of the four it says on the bottle, and still the pain is only dulled like a cup put over the mouth of a blaring trumpet, two days going by seems a long time. Like doing time and waiting for your sentence to end. Ashely's vexed and impatient for my parole. She's even looking for hidden escape routes, but I know they don't exist.

Ashely *comes in with a carrier bag.*

Ashely I've got you some liver.

Ben God! I hate liver.

Ashely It's full of B vitamins, and I'd eat it raw if I knew . . .

Ben A'right. A'right.

Ashely My mum's lent me a book. How are you feeling?

Ben Same. Did you get my Tennants?

Ashely I forgot.

Ben Ah, Ashely. You forget everything!

Ashely No I don't. I got another prescription renewed.

Ben I told you to write it down.

Ashely The Doctor wanted to know why you haven't been for your appointments at the hospital?

Ben 'Cos I haven't been ill! Why did you forget Ashely?

Ashely You can't take pain killers, and drink alcohol at the same time, crazy! I don't like all these drugs you're swallowing. You know they might even be creating other problems we can't see yet.

Ben Oh why not cheer me up some more?

Ashely My mum agrees with me.

Ben I've got to have them for the pain! Don't you understand? That's all that matters. It's OK for you to talk.

Ashely I've been reading about blood and oxygen. We can try other ways.

Ben How can *we* do anything.

Ashely My mum says that Doctors just tend to look at the symptoms. It's true. Look at you. They're just covering it all up with all these. (*Shakes the bottle of pills.*) There's a cause for all this somewhere along the line.

Ben (*not convinced*) Yeah.

Ashely (*looking at the book*) And that's what I'm going to try and find out from books like this. See if we can find out about the bloody cause. Anyway we're going to make a start on your diet. It's no good saving up and spending all your money on one luxury meal and then living off beans for the rest of the week.

Ben *picks up his diary. He and* **Ashely** *are lost in their own thoughts.*

Ashely Vitamin B6 deficiency anaemia. I wonder if that's it? Vitamin E deficiency anaemia. Anaemia and stomach acid. No that's not it. Iron deficiency anaemia. Folic acid deficiency anaemia. Oh . . . sickle cell anaemia occurs in persons who seem to have an unusually high requirement for folic acid. Patients have been known to have made improvements when given 5 milligrams or more of this vitamin daily. Were you ever given folic acid Ben?

Ben (*making notes in his diary*) One luxury meal, yeah, I'll still make spinach soufflé and I'll also try an anchovy sauce with a hollandaise base. That can be a bit of a bastard. What is it? Two thirds of a cup of butter, three egg yolks, tablespoon of lemon juice, seasoning. Melt the butter, remove from the heat, beat the egg yolks into the butter and season. Return the mixture to the heat and keep stirring. That's when it can curdle. (*Now speaking alone.*) We'll probably get asked that at College. What d'you do if a hollandaise splits? I'll say what my uncle told me.

Ashely Ben!!

Ben (*surprised*) What?

Ashely (*slapping the book shut*) You haven't been listening to a word I've been saying, have you? I'm trying to help you here. The least you can do is to concentrate for longer than a minute.

Ben I have been listening, only I wanna catch up with my college work. My exams are in a few weeks.

Ashely It'll be your own fault if sickle cell catches up with you first, because you haven't done anything to prevent it happening again.

Ben Sorry, what does it say?

Ashely (*sighs*) It says folic acid and vitamin C help.

Ben (*dismissive*) God, folic acid! I had that, and then they took me off it when I was 16. It's rubbish. How old is that book?

Ashely 1968.

Ben *laughs.*

Ashely Well, here's something else, anyway. Sickle cell anaemia is a disease of serious proportions, with some sufferers having relatively minor symptoms, while others may become severely disabled in life. (**Ashely** *looks at* **Ben**.) Ben. Your uncle. The cook. What did you say?

Ben (*irritable*) A stroke. A stroke. I told you!

Ashely The majority are plagued by intermittent pain crises, bacterial infections, and fatigue easily. This will all result from chronic anaemia. That's why you must eat lots of liver. Everyone knows it's good for anaemia. (*She reads.*) It's been estimated that 50% of patients die before reaching the age of . . . (*She breaks off.*)

Ben (*turning to her*) What?

Ashely (*quickly, seeming tired*) Nothing. My eyes are getting tired.

Ben *grabs the book.*

Ashely Ben. It's out of date. 1968.

Ben (*reads*) It has been estimated that 50% of patients die before reaching the age of . . . 20, and most don't survive beyond 40.

Silence.

One and a half years. Is that all I've got? Is that what all this means? (*He looks helplessly at* **Ashely**.)

Ashely (*hugging him*) It says only 50% of people Ben.

Ben (*shaking slightly*) Jesus. It ain't fair.

Ashely (*rocking him*) No it's not fair babe, but listen, the book's out of date. We must get some more recent information.

Ben If it's all like this, I don't wanna know. Dead by 20! Christ! I can't believe it Ashely. I'm scared.

Ashely For all you know they might have found a cure by now! You haven't been near a hospital for ages, and if they can't help you, well that's what I've been saying, you should at least try and help yourself.

Ben (*after a pause*) Yeah, you're right, must.

Ashely Make a hospital appointment.

Ben Yeah. Not the one in Bushey, a new one round here. They might've found out loads of things since I last went for a check up, eh? (*Laughs nervously.*)

Ashely And can I come with you?

Ben Yeah, sure.

Ashely Good, we can pick their brains, and listen, if you've been suffering less and less as you've got older, imagine how much better you'll be when you start taking your health seriously.

Ben *has picked up a packet of cigarettes, and* **Ashely** *snatches them away from him.*

Ben For God's sake! (*Sighs.*) A'right. A'right. I'll try . . . and to prove it, why don't you go and make some of that delicious liver stew of yours. Yummy. I can't wait.

Ashely (*kissing him*) Your wish is my command.

Scene Three

The sound has faded away. The sofa is replaced by a desk, chair and anglepoise lamp. It is the hospital clinic.

From one side comes a female medical student with a **Doctor**. *She has a white coat, and is flicking through files.* **Ben**'s *name is called.*

Ben *and* **Ashely** *come on from the other side, towards the desk.*

Student Sickle cell anaemia?

Doctor (*thinking*) Mmmm sickle cell anaemia. Genetic disorder. Characterized by abnormal haemoglobin molecule; designated haemoglobin 'S'. Effects: distortion, hethrosites, RBC into sickle cell. Haemozygous state includes benign carrier form of 'AS'.

Student Gene expressive. And cause of the disorder?

Doctor Variable. Sickle cell gene and auto-somnal recessive passed on to both male and female children.

The **Doctor** *is now sitting.* **Student** *pulls up another chair and sits by him.*

Student And affects?

Doctor Negroes; Caribbean. African. Settled populations adjacent to Mediterranean and Indian Ocean. (*Looks through notes.*)

Student (*to* **Ben**) Take a seat please. (*Looks at* **Ashely**.)

Ben Is it OK if she . . . err . . .

Student I'll just get you a chair. (*She does.*)

Doctor (*glancing up*) Sit down. Oh isn't there another chair?

Ben } She's getting one . . .
Ashely }

Student *comes with another chair.* **Ashely** *sits.*

Doctor Right Ben, your first time with us. Is that right?

Ben (*quietly*) Yeah.

Doctor But not your first experience of hospitals, so I see from your notes passed on from Bushey. (*To* **Student**.) Have you seen their haematology department?

Student Yes. New Coulter counter.

Doctor Good chain synthesis studies too.

Student And gene analysis.

Doctor There's restriction enzyme analysis going on there as well. Mmm. (*Looks at notes.*) It's been quite a long time since you've been for an appointment there Ben, or anywhere else?

Ben Yeah, well, em . . . I haven't had any pains really, only a bit and then I take DF118 for that.

Doctor (*to* **Student**) A very effective analgesic in these cases. (*To* **Ben**.) How have you been getting that?

Ben My GP. He just renewed the prescription.

Doctor Hmmm . . .

Ashely Shouldn't he have done that Doctor.

Doctor Well . . .

Ashely (*brief pause*) Should he have gone for an appointment Doctor?

Doctor Try to keep them here. Relatively important.

Ben Umm . . . why Doctor?

Doctor To keep a check.

Ashely A check on what?

Doctor (*looking at* **Student**) Emm . . . transubstigations.

Student (*offering*) Occilations?

Doctor Occilations, or alterations.

Student (*offering*) Variations?

Doctor Yes. (*Looking at* **Ashely**.) Variations.

Ashely In what?

Doctor *and* **Student** *look at each other*.

Doctor Reticulosis count.

Student (*offering*) WBC differential?

Doctor (*glancing at* **Ashely**) Mm, yes various things like that, and of course to monitor full blood count.

Ashely Yes, what was his blood count this time Doctor? I mean it's important to have 13 to 15 gms of red blood cells isn't it?

Doctor Mmm.

Ashely But people with sickle cell anaemia only have 8 to 10 gms don't they?

Doctor Mmm.

Ashely And that amount of cells can fall as low as 2 to 3. That's when they have a pain crisis, isn't it?

Doctor (*head in notes*) Mmm.

Ashely Well, Ben was recently, emm, had some pains, didn't you?

Ben Yeah, yeah, but it wern't as bad as them times when I was in Bushey.

Ashely Yes, but you did say it was the first pretty bad attack you'd had for a while.

Ben Well, yeah, but it's all over now, isn't it.

Ashely Yes well, it still would be very interesting to see what your blood count is anyway. Could you please tell us what it is Doctor?

Doctor Mmm? Yes. It's OK. Pretty acceptable I should think. (*Mutters to the* **Student**.)

Ben (*to* **Ashely**) I told you I was OK.

Ashely Shhh! Listen.

Doctor (*now audible*) We've only dealt with minimal cases here.

Student But current information *is* passed on here?

Doctor Periodically of course. (*Flicks through notes*.) Quick resumé of this case shows a mis-diagnosis initially, and then a correct detection revealed through a sickledex test when patient was 9. Electrophoresis proved blood group was 'SS'. Then, as you can see he underwent a series of hospitalizations suffering from the usual 'A' plastic crisis and later a splenic sequestration which naturally lowers haemoglobin. (*Mumbles*.)

Ashely Did you get any of that?

Ben Nope. Now you can see why I don't know anything about it.

Ashely Don't give me that! We're going to find out something.

Doctor *sits up and sighs*. **Student** *smiles at* **Ben**.

Student Well Ben, you have got a lot of notes haven't you!

Ashely Doctor can you tell us if the iron that's in liver helps this kind of anaemia?

Doctor Mmm. Liver? (*Half laughing*.) No, no. Absolutely nothing to do with it. (*He writes*.) I'll make an appointment for three months time then.

Ashely Well, before we go, could you please tell us something about all the different blood groups. I mean, what exactly is 'SS'?

Doctor I'm sure Ben could let you in on that little secret, couldn't you?

Ashely Well, no he can't. Can you?

Ben (*embarrassed*) Well, I find it a bit confusing sometimes, you nar.

Doctor (*putting the cap on his fountain pen*) It's all very simple really. (*Rapidly.*) Because your mother and father were sickle cell trait carriers, they wrought all this on you, unwittingly of course, and it's all very simple to comprehend once you realize that there are over 280 million of these molecules.

Ashely What molecules?

Doctor *looks at* **Student.**

Student (*offering*) Colour matter molecules?

Doctor Colour matter molecules as in haemoglobin, that's right, and these are labelled 'A' for normal, 'S' for sickle, 'C, D and E' for other haemoglobin abnormalities. When 'C, D and E' are paired with the sickle gene this is referred to as a sickle disease, but the 'SS' combination only describes the anaemia, of course. The majority of your cells prone to sickling contain over 90% haemoglobin 'S' and it is within both Bater chains of the haemoglobin 'S' molecule that valine is replaced.

Student Valine?

Doctor (*to* **Student**) Valine, err . . .

Student Glutonic acid.

Doctor Or even the sixth amino acid, yes, the sixth amino acid is substituted and consequently produces the sickling phenomenum. Everything clear?

Ashely Well . . .

Student (*offering*) The five preventative measures?

Doctor Yes . . . they're all you need to know, and they are . . .

Ben I already know them.

Doctor I'm sure you do.

Ashely Well I don't. Could you write them down? I'd like to know what they are.

Doctor Very well. (*Scribbles.*) Drink six pints water per day. This helps the flow of the blood. PH balance, though this can be tricky. Avoid catching infections. Keep warm.

Ben (*half laughing*) I had a few pains last week 'cos I got cold cleaning out the freezer at work.

Doctor Mmm, avoid that. And last of all, bear in mind stress. We underestimate the role it can play in contributing to these attacks. Right. Here's a prescription for some more painkillers. Unfortunately, no miracle cures yet! Research a bit thin on the ground, I'm afraid, but you seem to have had a lot of luck in the last year or so. Let's hope it continues, eh?

Ashely I was wondering, doctor, if I should be tested for this?

Doctor (*partly to the* **Medical Student**) Well, if it hasn't reared its ugly head by now dear, I don't think it ever will.

Ashely No, I mean for the trait. That doesn't have any symptoms, but it could have some effect on children?

Doctor Could do. Could do, but there's always termination. (*Writing in file.*) Well, we'll see you in January Ben.

Ben (*taking card from desk*) Do I take this to the pharmacy?

Doctor (*writing*) Yes, yes. Ground floor, just round from the flower shop.

Ben (*hesitates*) Before we go, I'd like to ask you something Doctor. We read something in a book about a lot of sicklers dying before they get to 20.

Doctor (*moving papers*) 20? No, no. You've misunderstood I think. It's generally through infancy or early childhood that a disproportionate number of sickle cell patients die. Taking that into account you should have popped off a long time ago. Bye, bye!

Blackout.

Scene Four

A spotlight on **Ben**.

Ben When we came out of the hospital into the street I saw, saw so much! I see these weeds coming up through the pavement, and I see that halfway up the road the paving stopped and there's this tarmac surface, where no weeds can get through, see? I see how this Lockets wrapper in the gutter is the same colour as the yellow line it's laying on, and while I'm seeing that, I see this pound coin near the drain, and picked it up! I see the sun's out, bit weak, you nar, but definitely making a show. I see this tree with nearly no leaves left in someone's garden and I see the grass just cut in somebody's else's. But most of all, most of all . . . I see the street's practically empty. (*Hushed.*) Nobody about, and I want to run! Swing my arms round and round, and shout, then every few yards jump and run again and jump again, right up the road and into the next and the next! (*He stops. Smirks as he checks himself.*) But I never.

Asheley's angry and stomps along not seeing anything outside. Just angry. First, angry that she forgets to ask the Doctor about cigarettes. Second, angry that if she had, she probably wouldn't understand what he said anyway, and

third angry, what she did understand he said about having kids, she never liked that much. I try and be angry too. I say 'Go and get your blood checked Ash. See if it's OK.' So she went, and with her went my anger. And I went to college.

Scene Five

Ben *at college.*

Peggy Oh Ben, I didn't know you were waiting.

Ben S'alright. I was just looking at your photos. Isn't that one, err, Max Vernon? He's Suise chef to err . . .

Peggy That's right. He's under Anton Clark at the Carousel. I got a letter from Max the other day, telling me all's well. He wanted to know if I have any promising students this year.

Ben Oh?

Peggy I've an idea, but it's all in the future, and this is the present, with problems of its own. I want to talk to you about a proper job. I know you've got one of a kind in that fast food place, what's its name? The Star Trek Cafe, but come on Ben, that's not going to be sufficient training at all if you're thinking seriously about catering, and I know you are. You do realize that this course is meant to be in conjunction with a day release?

Ben (*adamantly*) I know, I know, I know. But I ain't gonna join no second rate outfit. Work in a London Transport canteen, cook-chilling and freeze-blasting my food.

Peggy They're both decidedly better options than the one you doing now Ben.

Ben When I join a brigade of chefs, even if I start as a kitchen porter, I'll be happy as long as I know it has a good standard and reputation. As long as I know I'm part of the best. That'll do me.

Peggy You might find you have to compromize a bit.

Ben No.

Peggy (*sighs*) Well, have you heard anything hopeful yet?

Ben I wrote off to some places last week, including one of my uncle's old restaurants.

Peggy Nepotism works in all professions. Is this the famous uncle we keep hearing about?

Ben Yes, he worked at the Mayfair.

Peggy Very good kitchens there. Good luck with that, and keep me informed about how it goes. I'm sure if you get into a really good kitchen like that it would help a great deal with your 706/2. You've coped exceedingly well during this year, even with very little real work experience. I can only put it down to aptitude for this trade, and what you might have picked up from your infamous uncle.

Ben *and* **Peggy** *laugh.*

Seriously, though, as long as you can see the importance of all this, especially when your exams are in, what it is it, only a few weeks from now. You failed them last year, or didn't sit them, or something. Why was that?

Ben I was ill.

Peggy Ah yes. That reminds me of the other matter I wanted to see you about. I noticed on your tutor's register that you weren't in last week. You missed a very important lecture on marinating, or was it sauces. No marinating, yes. Where were you?

Ben Err, I was ill.

Peggy You know what the college policy is on illness, don't you? It's irresponsible to miss a week at this important stage, on account of something like a cold.

Ben This *is* important to me. I wouldn't have had the time off for anything, but I had to. I was ill.

Peggy Oh come on Ben! Is a runny nose all that it takes for you to grind to a halt? If it is, then maybe I've got the wrong idea about you.

Ben I had pains as well.

Peggy What sort of pains?

Ben With my sickle cell.

Peggy Oh yes, of course, you do suffer from that don't you. It slipped my mind. I remember wondering what it was when I read about it in your report sent up from your school in Watford or wherever.

Ben I remember that report, yeah, and finding out what it said. It was the day I come up here for my interview. There was about ten of us in all sitting in the waiting room. No one knew anyone else, well, I never knew anyone anyway. Some guys were talking across from me, but I was so sick with nerves about what questions there'd be, I couldn't say nothing. I think we were all as nervous as each other, but some showed it in different ways, you know, by chatting. Anyway, as soon as that door opened everyone shut up and Mr Richards walked out. I thought he was going to call the name of the next person to be seen, like, but instead you know what he said? He goes to the whole room, 'Can the one with the sickle cell complaint come in next.' Can you imagine it? The way they all looked at me in that room. He might as well've come and put a big rubber stamp on my forehead sayin' it. (*He rubs his forehead.*) It ain't all come off yet. Some people're still reading it.

Peggy Well, I didn't read it Ben. I'd totally forgotten about it. I'm sorry about it though.

Ben Nar, don't be. I'm the one who's sorry for having a week off. I'm apologizing like Marcus did when he had time off for a cold, and Sophie did when she went to Benidorm, midterm.

Peggy But Ben, it's different with you.

Ben Nar, it ain't. Us three had a week off, and we all apologize equal.

Peggy But you're not . . .

Ben (*stressing*) Yes it is! OK? OK?

Peggy All right Ben, but if you don't remind us, you can't blame us for forgetting.

Ben (*smiling and bouncing out*) Peggy, I gotta go. I'm late for work. I'll see ya next week.

Act Two

Scene One

Bright lights on the rest bay at the Star Trek cafe. No one around, but noises from the bridge and kitchen.

Ben *comes in furtively. He's avoiding someone. Takes off his jacket and top, grabs his uniform and begins to put it on when* **Hayse** *enters with his watering can.*

Hayse Ben?

Ben (*surprised*) Oh, a'right Captain. Err, I was just . . .

Hayse You're late!

Ben Er, yeah, I was kept at college. We had this lecture, and it ran overtime.

Hayse College! What College?

Ben I'm doing catering. (*Pause. No reaction from* **Hayse**.) This great head chef, Anton Clark came in to give us a talk on . . .

Hayse Yes, yes, right, OK. What I want to know is, why you haven't been in for a week?

Ben I had flu.

Hayse Oh, flu, right. In that case it was a good thing you stayed away. I can't somehow stomach the idea of germs flying about. They not only contaminate the food, but also contaminate the other members of staff, and the next thing you know there's a hygiene crisis on your hands, and that's the last thing this branch needs. Now get up on the bridge right away. There's a crew shortage as it is and the orders are coming in fast and furious.

A phone rings. **Hayse** *goes to answer it. As he leaves* **Curtis** *comes in.*

Curtis 'And a car, ra ra! TWA TWA

TWA to the USA, hey!

Curtis *is waving the head of a mop about like a pompom. He chucks the mop down.*

Ben Curtis! Don't put it there! If Hayse sees it . . .

Curtis Hey, Bushman's back! Easy boy!

Ben A'right. Wha's 'appenin' man?

Curtis I jus' come from the bridge. I've been serving away with a smile and giving all that 'cosmic day' shit. Then I see Chantelle coming through the door. Nar man, that girl's distressed news, I can feel it. I could see her eyes were hunting around for me.

Curtis So I thought I'd just slip out of her visibility, down here, for a little bit. Ya know what I'm sayin'?

Ben Hayse is on the prowl.

Curtis Thought as much. So I brought these down with me. (*Waves papers in the air.*) The comment sheets you nar. C'mon, let's have a look at what some of these plonkers say. (*Scanning a paper.*) Food: good. They must be mad. Drinks: fair. That's more like it. Décor: good. (*Kisses his teeth.*) They must come from cardboard city! Service: good. I should think so! And listen, guess what crew member from this: 'He's OK, but pity about the haircut!'

Ben and **Curtis** (*looking at each other*) Michael!

Curtis (*shuffling the papers*) Oh, here's one for me! Food: fair. Drinks: fair. Décor: bad. Service: very good, and crew member Curtis, great! Ring me any time on 672 5564, signed Yasmin the belly-dancer! (*Folds paper and puts it in his pocket.*) Stingin'. Stingin'! Hayse ain't getting his hands on the little one.

Ben Jesus Curtis, don't mess around.

How can you seriously go out with a girl who does something like that!

Curtis I ain't gonna ring her and ask her to marry me am I!

Ben (*going*) Hayse is coming. Laters, laters.

Hayse (*coming in with his watering can*) Curtis?

Curtis Captain, I brought you some comment sheets down.

Hayse Thank you very much. (*He takes the sheets.*) I've just had a call from head office and they've told me that the success of the Captain Kirk Quarter Pounder campaign, coupled with the high percentage of favourable comments for this branch, have pushed us into second place in the ratings! I just had to tell someone the good news. D'you understand? We're actually in second place this week, and we've got a whole month in which to push ourselves into that top spot. I know we can do it with just that little bit more of a concerted effort from everyone.

Curtis Yeah.

Hayse And you know Curtis, I'm relying on you. If you see any of the Crew loosening their grip, and not giving 100% of their all, you mustn't let it pass without chastizing them for it. Understand?

Curtis (*becoming mesmerized*) Yeah.

Hayse It's like a tug of war between us and the Strand branch now. That's how I see it.

Curtis Yeah.

Hayse Being number one means the USA.

Curtis Yeah.

Hayse And next week you'll have been working here for nearly eight

months which qualifies you to take your third band exam.

Curtis Yeah.

Hayse And you know what that can do for you, don't you?

Curtis Yeah.

Hayse With this branch in that number one position and you a third-band crew member, that ticket to New York is practically yours.

Curtis And touch down!

Hayse What?

Curtis I, I mean, yeah.

Hayse And no one wants that more than me, because if it's this branch that sends its crew member to represent London at the fifth International Star Trek assembly, I automatically obtain promotion into the coveted realms of head office!

Pause, while they both indulge in their own visions of the future.

And Curtis, it means, when you come back from America there's every possibility that you can go on a day release management course and apply for a trainee manager's job here.

Curtis (*spell broken*) What?

Hayse Well, wouldn't you want that? (*Watering plant.*) I can see that you're suited for this kind of career. It takes a certain sort of person with drive and dedication, and I can see that you've got plenty of that.

Curtis Err, yeah, yeah.

Hayse You'd notice a vast increase in your income, and I'll tell you something; there's a very good superannuated pension scheme. (*Pats Curtis on the shoulder.*)

Curtis (*flatly*) Pension scheme.

Hayse Yes. It's always advisable to think ahead into the future for the day when you're married with a house, and children.

Curtis Well, yeah. But, err innit America first?

Hayse Just something to ponder on Curtis. But you're right. It's America first.

Curtis (*relieved*) Yeah.

Hayse Well, hadn't you better get back to the bridge?

Curtis Err, the bridge.

Hayse Yes, where you came from, isn't it?

Curtis Right! I'll, em, I'll go back to the, em, bridge.

Hayse Yes, the bridge.

Curtis (*going reluctantly*) The bridge. Right.

Hayse yes.

Lights fade.

Scene Two

Screen illuminated. The serving area. The Star Trek theme is audible. Droning and tinny. There are also kitchen noises. **Ben** *is running to and fro.* **Curtis** *joins him.*

Curtis Next order! Can you move up to the other counter please? Yeah, can I help you? Oh, it's you. I can't really talk now, I'm working. I haven't been trying to avoid you Chantelle. Shut up, everyone can hear you! OK. I'm listening. Go on, make it quick. I've got people to serve. What d'you mean! Jesus Christ girl, you sure? But Chantelle, are you sure it's me? Shut up girl! Everyone's looking at ya. 'Course I care, it's just that, look, my queue's getting longer. I do love you,

but, what you gonna do? OK, what we gonna do? Look, can't we talk about this some other time Star? I'll take you out tonight, up the Studio or something, right? Meet me there after work. Why not. Don't you trust me? But I weren't avoiding you Star. I was just busy. Nar what I mean. Nar, I don't mean with other girls. Well, I can't prove it. Nar, I ain't proving it like that! I can't Chantelle. I ain't ready for that. But can't your mum and dad look after it, if you want to go and get a career? A'right, a'right. Shut up! The whole place is checking you again. They'll both have to find out sometime girl, talk sense. Get rid of it? But they'll still know. Private! I ain't shouting! That's gonna cost me untold amounts Chantelle. Look, go on the National Health. Nar, I ain't gettin' rid of my responsibilities. I never even knew I had any. Jesus, look at the size of my queue. Listen. I see what I can do. I come back to you on it. But I ain't promising anything, right. Yeah, I'll see what I can do.

Curtis *sighs, and the high pitched signal sounds.*

Sorry, this counter's closed. Can you go to another one please.

Ben (*touching* **Curtis** *on the shoulder*) Coming?

Curtis I'll be down in a minute. I just gotta do something.

As **Ben** *goes,* **Curtis** *leans over the till.*

Blackout.

Scene Three

Lights immediately come up on the rest area, where **Ashely** *is pinning on her working cap.* **Ben** *comes in. He stubs out the cigarette he is smoking before* **Ashely** *can see.* **Ashely** *turns to him, and hugs* *and kisses him.*

Ben (*pulling away*) Slow down, slow down. Wha's happenin'?

Ashely Ben, I got the results from the Doctor!

Ben What results?

Ashely You know. That screen test for sickle trait.

Ben Oh, yeah, yeah. So?

Ashely I'm clear! My blood's normal! 'AA' Not a trace of sickle cell in sight. (*She laughs.*)

Ben Great. Aren't you the lucky one.

Ashely Yes, I am. (*Kisses him again.*) It makes all the difference now.

Ben Why?

Ashely Because, on one of those nights I stay over . . .

Ben And when does that become permanent Ashely?

Ashely Things can start heading that way now. Can't you see?

Ben But when?

Ashely Listen, as I was saying. On one of those times, if there's a small accident, then I've got a choice. I don't have to get rid of it, like that bloody man at the hospital said.

Ben Terrific, but when?

Ashely My Doctor was so nice. He actually looked at me when I was talking, and he really put my mind at rest about so much. How've you felt today babe?

Ben All right.

Ashely No pains at all?

Ben (*irritable*) No! Ashely, I was asking you when you're gonna move in?

Ashely I dunno.

Ben You said . . .

Ashely I know, but look Ben, I want to be sure about other things as well.

Ben What?

Ashely How well I know you for instance.

Ben Ashely!

Ashely . . . and your place is so horrible.

Ben Thanks.

Ashely We'll have to find somewhere else, somewhere bigger . . . speaking of which . . . (*Looking for forms and leaflets.*)

Ben Oh, if you're so fussy. I suppose we could look for somewhere else. Put our names down on the council list first, then try housing associations next and private places after that. Mortgage is out, though that'd be the best deal. Oh, this is gonna take untold years Ashely.

Ashely He gave me all these leaflets and things. The Doctor was *so* helpful, and he actually told me to go ahead and try all the other kinds of alternative medicines I mentioned . . . and he said 'Don't think of them as alternative to orthodox treatment, but complementary.'

Ben (*glancing through the forms*) You know, Curtis told me he was going to get in this place up his road and squat. Squat! Jesus, like some crusty rough neck. Nar, that's really out of order. What would people think of you if you said you lived in a squat?

Ashely (*staring closely at him*) It's amazing all the things you don't know about. If you get this green card, you could get help with your heating and your housing.

Pause. **Ashely** *waits for* **Ben** *to react.*

Ben 'old on. 'old on. 'old on! What's

all this kind 'a rubbish I'm seeing 'ere about disabled?

Ashely Well, you apply for this card and that proves you're disabled, and then . . .

Ben Watch it man! Who said anything about me being disabled?

Ashely Your sickle cell says you are. That's who!

Ben I ain't disabled!

Ashely What d'you call last week then?

Ben Sick!

Ashely Sick with a disability.

Ben Nar, nar, nar. This is really out of order!

Ashely You are! Look what that thing can do for you. You don't have to live in a gross room! You don't have to live in the freezing cold! And, all you can say is 'It's really out of order!'

Ben Oh Jesus, be serious Ashely! I can't apply for this!

Ashely You're entitled to it.

Ben But who'd believe it? Look at me. I'm all right now.

Ashely Now.

Ben Yes now, and for most of the time. Taking this'll be like stealing. How can I take money for all these things?

Ashely Well, as you said, finding a place is going to take untold years.

Ben I can't do it Ash. Sayin' I'm disabled. I've got a brain that works. I can see. I can hear. I can speak and I can walk around. Look Ashely. I'm walking around!

Ashely Oh hallelujah! The lame will walk, and the sickle celled shall not be disabled!

Ben Look, I ain't being accused of stealing. It'll . . . It'll be like them cars you see with the orange disability sticker in the window. I seen a car like that draw up, and this bird in six inch high stilettoes jumps out, about as disabled as I . . .

Ben *breaks off. They look at each other.*

Ashely Yes?

Ben Look Ashely, this wheelchair thing don't represent me. Right?

Curtis *comes in putting something in his pocket.*

Curtis A'right?

Ben *(folding the papers up)* A'right.

Ashely *(snatching forms)* Don't screw them up.

Ben *(snatching them back)* Give 'em here.

Curtis *(snatching forms)* What is it?

Ben *(trying to get them)* Don't mess around Curtis.

Curtis *(dodging. Looking at the forms. Then looking up)* Who's disabled?

Ashely *(sarcastically)* Who's disabled? Who's disabled? *(Shooting a glance at* **Ben**.*)* Where've I heard that one before? Guess which one of us is disabled Curtis?

Ben Ashely, shut up.

Ashely Is it me? Do I look disabled? *(Shakes her head.)* Nar. Could it be you Curtis?

Curtis It ain't me.

Ben Ashely. Keep your mouth shut.

Curtis *(pointing)* Is it you: *(Laughing loudly.)* Nar man!

Ben I warned you.

Ashely But Ben, is he laughing because he believes it or because he doesn't believe it?

Ben (*shouting*) I dunno! All I know is he's laughing.

Curtis (*laughter subsiding*) C'mon, what's wrong with you bushman?

Ben See, he believes it.

Ashely And what is wrong with that?

Ben Thanks Ashely.

Curtis What's your problem Benny boy?

Ashely (*sighing*) The problem is sickle cell anaemia.

Curtis Oh right. (*Pause.*) Ain't that like when you've got two personalities?

Ashely Jesus! No it ain't dear. It's like when you've got most of your blood cells a sickle shape, and they don't last very long and they don't flow along very easily, so they jam up in the veins and stop oxygen . . . no I'll say air . . . getting round the body, and that causes a lot of nasty pains. Got it?

Silence. **Curtis** *looks from* **Ben** *to* **Ashely** *and then back again.* **Curtis** *begins to giggle. Then* **Ben**. *Both laugh loudly.*

Ashely What are you laughing for? Don't laugh! This is serious. Oh Christ!

Curtis Well if you think you've got problems Benny boy, I've got some double rough ones at the moment.

Ben (*relieved to change the subject*) Yeah? What?

Curtis Well, it's Chantelle's trouble, but I suppose I had a bit to do with it, nar what I mean?

Ben Right. What's she gonna do?

Ashely Do you know if you and Chantelle are sickle cell carriers, Curtis?

Curtis I don't carry nothing but myself.

Ashely Because . . .

Ben Oh Ashely, what is this? Just leave it will ya?

Ashely Because, if you both are, then there's a one in four chance of you having a *disabled* child. I just thought I'd let you know . Right?

Ashely *goes.*

Curtis The girl's wasting her breath. I told Chantelle to get rid of it and she's doing what she's told. I got this stingin' lickle plan sussed out to help her, see. So she can go private, and that'll leave her uncomplaining. Safe. (*Pause.*) Anyway. Come on. Let's bust this three band exam crap. (*Gives* **Ben** *a sheet of paper.*) I gotta get this or I can forget the Super Bowl.

Ben (*taking the sheet*) You got some bottle you nar.

Curtis That's what life's all about sunshine. Seeing the chance and taking the chance.

Ben (*laughing and shaking his head*) How long does it take to fry one bucket of Trekian Chicken?

Curtis 5 minutes, 30 seconds.

Ben Correct. What side of the Kirk Quarter Pounder box has the Captain's face printed on it?

Curtis Left hand side.

Ben No. Right.

Curtis Shit!

Ben What is the correct call when you are about to grill the second side of a batch of Spock burgers?

Curtis (*exiting*) Zooming 12 regulars.

Lights change.

Scene Four

Ben (*in a spotlight, alone*) What Ashley said really freaked me out. I thought about it for days and days. Disabled? Nar man. I'm not having that! It ain't so much the thought of stealing, or getting that rubber stamp, but it's more giving up to it.

I had this dream the other night. I was in this huge kitchen with this massive wooden table in the middle. I was on one side and Curtis was on the other and I knew we had to prepare this colossal banquet for about five hundred people or something. There was all these butlers in black suits coming in, one after another to take the dishes away, and I was just getting mine ready in time 'cos I had my hands tied behind my back, see? I kept checking Curtis on the other side of the kitchen strolling around throwing together loads of this stingin' food, all ready to be collected. There was me trying to beat up some eggs with a fork in my mouth, and everything on my side boiling over, or breaking down. Yet, I was tight in there, just keeping my head above the chaos. Then suddenly Curtis starts chucking around all the food he's just made, laughing like some maniac and jumping all over his gateaux and pâté, mashing them all into the ground. He kept doing all these crazy things, like pouring water into his electric cooker, and then turning it on. I was too taken up with the havoc on my side to bother myself with the mess he was causing. Anyway, I could tell he was getting his quota turned out ahead of me. Then all of a sudden I realized my hands weren't tied no more. I could hear Curtis shouting 'It's ready. It's ready. Take it out of the oven!' I found myself going to this microwave and taking out all these steaming hot TV dinners. Then the butlers came and snatched them away. They were smiling all over their faces, and patting me on the head, saying 'Hasn't he done well'. Then I was there waiting for the next batch of processed beef to heat up and thinking to myself 'It's so simple, innit?' I woke up feeling double rough though . . . Anyway, that was the dream I had. (*Pause.*) I've told Ashely to sack this disabled shit and stop treating it as some big issue. The pains are so few now, I've nearly forgotten that time I was sick in my room. I say nearly 'cos I can't forget it totally, like I usually do. This time Ashely won't let me. She can't be like Curtis and never mention it again. She keeps dragging me round to see these weirdo medicine men. We've been to, what's it? Homeopathy? Anyway that ain't worked. I got an ache in my fingers and ankles. I took my DF118. We've been to acupuncture. I got an ache in my back and knees. I took my DF118. It's wicked, 'cos sometimes the pain stays away and Ash thinks all these untold treatments are working. Then I feel it. The teeth biting away round my elbow or somewhere, and Ashely dashes that idea and starts again. I don't mind. It keeps her sweet. But sometimes it all gets a bit out of order.

Scene Five

The Rest bay. **Ashely** *is sitting on the edge of the table, writing on a notepad from a text book.*

Ashely It's adopted from the yin and yang belief, and you know your hair analysis thing that was done when we went to the herbalist? Well, that showed that your PH level was more acid than alkali. D'you remember that Doctor at the hospital mentioned something about PH balance. This macro-biotic diet can deal with that. It shows you all the things you can eat to make your diet more acid or more alkali. I'm writing it out, so try to keep to it, just for a while to see if it helps.

Ben Two really strange things happened today Asheley. I got a letter from the Mayfair saying they had no record of my Uncle Andre ever working there as a chef. I don't understand. I'm sure he used to talk about that one a lot. And then, when I went to college today, I was really shamed up in front of everyone.

Ashely How?

Ben We got asked what to do if a Hollandaise sauce splits, and I went and told them what my uncle once said. 'Put it in a pan with melted butter.' The lecturer just laughed and goes, 'If I wanted an omelette, I'd be well on the way to making one!' I couldn't believe it. I was *so* sure. I just stood there stunned. I didn't even hear what the right answer was.

Ashely I'm sure you'll find out.

Ben But it ain't that. It's my uncle. Innit. It just don't make a drop of sense to me. I thought . . . oh, I dunno.

Curtis *comes in. He is unaware that* **Hayse** *is right behind him with a watering can.*

Hayse (*watering the plant*) Crew.

Curtis Jesus! (*Turning round.*)

Hayse Rest bay to bridge. Ten minutes.

Hayse *goes.*

Ben ⎫
  ⎬ Yes captain.
Ashely ⎭

Curtis (*speaking up so that* **Hayse** *can hear*) Did I catch you bunking freezer duty again Ben? You're really letting the crew down.

Ben ⎫ Sorry.
Ashely ⎬ Shut up Curtis.

Curtis *checks to see if* **Hayse** *is still in earshot.*

Curtis It's a cool yo'll, chill. No panic. He's gone. (*He offers* **Ben** *a cigarette, and* **Ben** *goes, automatically, to take it.*)

Ashely Curtis! He's given up.

Curtis I never knew.

Ben Er . . . (*Looking at* **Curtis**.) Yeah, I have. (*Looking at* **Ashely**.) Reflex, just reflex, you nar.

Ashely OK.

Curtis Why?

Ashely Because smoking contracts the blood vessels and it's hard enough for his blood to get through as it is. By the way, the same goes for alcohol.

Curtis You given that up as well?

Ben Sort of.

Ashely Yeah. He has.

Curtis Rough life.

Ben Double rough.

Curtis What's the point though?

Ashely What's the point in doing these things that are making you worse? If you stop, you're bound to benefit.

Ben Yeah, yeah.

Ashely Like this diet. I didn't finish telling you about it.

Ben Later Ashely, a'right?

Ashely What's wrong with now?

Ben *looks at* **Curtis**.

Curtis Don't mind me. I think it's all rather interesting. (*Exhales a long column of smoke.*)

Ben (*sighing*) Go on then.

Ashely As I said before, your blood is more acid than alkali, to balance yourself out you need to eat more alkali foods. This macro-biotic diet can help you with that. I've made a list of all of the alkali foods that I think you should stick to for a while.

Ben What sort of foods?

Ashely Well, there's beans . . .

Curtis First time I've heard beans means health.

Ashely Not those kinds of beans. Kidney beans. Aduki beans.

Curtis Er duki who?

Ashely Shut up!

Ben Go on. What else?

Ashely Carrots, cabbage, fish, (herrings, prawns), err, brown rice. Brown rice is one of the best things. It's got all the minerals you need. You could live off that, if you wanted to.

Curtis Yeah but who'd want to.

Ben Go on. What else?

Ashely Well, that's it really.

Ben What?!

Curtis *laughs.*

Ashely Surely you can create something out of those ingredients Ben.

Ben What about basic things, like eggs and butter?

Ashely Nope. Acid.

Ben What about meat or chicken?

Ashely Nope. Acid.

Curtis What's all this acid rubbish. I don't see no holes burnt all over 'im 'cos he's got big amounts of acid in 'im.

Ben You nar. (*Laughs.*)

Curtis And all this reading about it in books. You're just gonna come up with loads of things you think you shouldn't do, and then worry yourself mad checking on them.

Ben Yeah. It's like the self fulfilling prophecy we done once in a sociology lesson. You tell someone they're bad, or this is bad, and it is, 'cos you make it like that in your mind, and theirs.

Curtis Yeah, everyone's better off not worrying.

Ben Yeah. (**Curtis** *and* **Ben** *laugh.*)

Ashely So. You think being ignorant is being better off. If that was the case we'd still be covering ourselves with leeches and making human sacrifices to the gods.

Curtis Well look at you Ashely. I never see you smile no more. You're all vexed and worked up and you ain't even got it! As far as I can see knowledge don't give you nothing but more problems.

Ben It's true.

Ashely (*shrugging*) OK. (*Slams the book shut and puts the pencil and pad on top of it neatly on the table as if to say 'Case closed'.*)

Pause.

Curtis Err, I gotta move the bins.

Ben I'll give you a hand. (*To* **Ashely**.) I'll be back in a minute.

Ashely Do what you want.

Curtis You sure you can handle it?

Ben (*irritated*) Positive. Course I can. C'mon. (*To* **Ashely**.) Look Ash, I'll go through that PH thing with you later.

Curtis (*now offstage*) C'mon if you're coming.

Ben (*going*) OK.

Ashely begins to go through Ben's pockets. She takes out an address book and writes down a number.

Hayse (*coming in*) Ashely, where are Ben and Curtis?

Ashely Outside.

Hayse I want to see you three in here after clean-up duty.

Ashely But . . . we'll miss the last bus.

Hayse (*stopping*) Tough! If you're not here after swab duty, they'll be hell to pay. It's here or you'll be out. Understand? Tell the others.

Ashely (*goes to phone. Dials*) Hallo? Is that Mrs Stranelle? You don't know me, but my name's Ashely . . .

Lights fade.

Scene Six

Ben and Curtis are kicking a cardboard box around. Somewhere outside.

Curtis . . . and Hayse creeping about, you just can't relax. I dunno where he's gonna pop up next. I can't wait till I'm out of this fuckin' place.

Ben Nar what I mean.

Curtis Now I got this rubbish third band it's only time before this place reaches number one in the damn ratings. I know Big H's gonna nominate me for America, and then I'm out a' here and it won't be a day too soon. You nar what I'm saying?

Ben You nar. When I do my exam I wanna get this place out of my face for good. I'm just shitting, case I don't get a job somewhere decent before then.

Curtis Yeah. And I need Chantelle off my back. That girl is just extra,

with all her demands on me.

Ben Yeah. When I get my 706/2 and get settled in a good kitchen, then me and Ash can look for a flat.

Curtis She can just get off my case 'cos I'm gonna kick up some serious living for myself.

Ben Eh?

Curtis Some wicked living. Nar what I mean? That's what you need as well. Make some space for it in your diary Bushboy.

Ben Nar, nar. I don't wanna make no space for madness like that. Messin' everything up.

Curtis That's why you'll always be a sucker ragamuffin. (*Kicking the box off stage.*) Stuck in a food mixer job, with a mortgage and two point five kids.

Ben (*following*) I might, Curtis, I might just.

Scene Seven

The rest bay. Ashely has been clearing the table. Ben mopping the floor.

Ashely I saw you! With my own eyes, I saw you! Stop playing games. Tell me if I'm wasting my time. Admit you're not taking any of this seriously. (*Pause.*) You're not. Don't try telling me you are. I saw you.

Ben OK you saw me. One damn cigarette and you don't talk to me all night.

Ashely (*now clearing the table*) Thank God you didn't bother to lie.

Ben You don't see me dropping dead 'cos I had a smoke do you? Jesus you are making my life miserable.

Ashely Making *your* life miserable! What about my life? My time? My energy? Do you think I'm enjoying all this?

Ben You're just using me as some kind of practical experiment Ashely.

Ashely (*amazed*) Is that what you think? Can't you see why I've been reading books till I see dots dancing in front of my eyes? Making notes till I've got a permanent dent in this finger, and going with you to all those private Doctors has nearly cost me an overdraft.

Ben I never asked you to do it. I never wanted you to do it. You drag problems out of everything like you dragged this problem out of me. (*Pause.*) I didn't want to tell you.

Ashely I wish I'd never got myself involved.

Ben But you did.

Ashely That's because I care, and because I care, every time you say you're in pain, I feel it.

Ben But ain't that the pain of failing 'cos all the things you try don't work?

Ashely Ben, you bastard. Thanks for nothing.

Both look at each other. **Ashely** *stares him out.* **Ben** *begins to mop again.*

Ashely Remember Curtis said to me 'How come we don't see you smile no more Ashely?' Anyone who don't care can keep smiling. We can all be like Curtis and laugh and joke. 'Oh Bushman you've got a disease, but who fucking cares? Have another fag, have another lager. Kill yourself before you get to 20, but make sure your crazy girlfriend don't catch you. She's only going to make life a misery by trying to make you better.'

Ben But Asheley, this is all getting to be an obsession with you and its breaking us up.

Ashely Nar Ben, it's you! Your attitude.

Ben And yours.

Ashely I'm trying to help. I can't go on with you fighting against me.

Ben What d'you want?

Ashely Just some cooperation for once. It's important to believe we can fight this thing together, instead of ignoring it and putting on some big, hard man front. Just accept what you are.

Ben And what's that then, an invalid?

Ashely You know, I used to think you were a really together guy. Everything about you seemed to be sorted out. I thought that was a sign for everything else about you. I was half right. Your life's in order, but your body's not. That's where you go wrong. And because you can't see that, it's clear how immature you are, and irresponsible. You're going to end up the same way as your uncle.

Ben You're mad! What are you talking about?

Ashely How old was he? 39? I dare say you'll go the same way. Ignorance must run in the family.

Ben You're really cracked you know. He died of a stroke. What's that gotta do with me?

Ashely You know very well what it's got to do with you.

Ben It's got nothing to do with me.

Ashely Why don't you just admit it? You know he died of a stroke that was a result of his sickle cell. Didn't your uncle have a terrific crisis just before he died? The only time you saw him near a hospital was when he was carted there. He died because of blood sickling in his brain, causing a stroke.

Imperceptible ringing sound fades in and steadily rises in pitch until the end of the scene.

Ben So. Who told you all this?

Ashely What caused the last crisis he had?

Ben *knows* **Ashely** *has been speaking with his mother.*

Ashely You know what caused it don't you. Alcohol! He was an alcoholic. And yet despite that you drink and do all these bad things. Why aren't you scared like I am?

Ben That couldn't happen to me. My uncle was far worse than me. Just 'cos we had the same thing don't mean I'm as bad as he was.

Hayse *comes in.*

Hayse What's going on here? Haven't you finished this place yet? Where's Curtis?

Silence.

I said, 'Where's Curtis'!

Ben *sits down and rubs his leg.*

Ashely I dunno.

Hayse I told you I wanted to see you three in here after swab duty, so where is he?

Ashely He must still be cleaning the vat out in the kitchen.

Hayse Call him.

Ashely *goes off to fetch* **Curtis**. **Ben** *gets out some pain killers and takes two or three.*

Hayse What's that?

Ben I've got a headache.

Hayse You'd better have a few because what I've got to say isn't going to make it much better.

Ashely *returns with* **Curtis**.

Curtis Ay ay Captain. All present and correct.

Hayse Right you three, you're under suspicion of theft.

They look at each other.

Ben Nar man.

Curtis Ya lie.

Ashely It's got nothing to do with me.

Hayse One of you three, or maybe the whole lot of you have been putting fingers where they don't belong. In the till. The receipts show a 700% increase in cancelled orders. Now, by any standards that's abnormal, and it only goes to prove one thing. Those cancelled orders have gone into someone's pocket. I want to know whose pocket that is. If it isn't accounted for by head office it'll jeopardize our position in the ratings, and I'm not going to allow that to happen for the sake of some sticky fingered little night worker. I'm giving the culprit a chance he or she wouldn't normally get in a situation like this. We can either deal with the matter outside the law, or inside. I'm sure you realize which way is best? I'll give you a few minutes to think it over. (*He goes.*)

The three look at each other. **Ben** *sits down heavily.* **Curtis** *lights a cigarette.*

Ashely Why are we all under suspicion?

Ben (*quietly*) We share tills don't we?

Curtis I don't believe this. I don't believe this. Nar man.

Ben Don't you Curtis?

Curtis What's going on in this damn place. That man is extra. How can he accuse us of stealing? He ain't got the right. Damn rough neck. He can't prove nothing. This is just out of order I'm tellin' ya.

Ben Just shut up Curtis and give the man back his money.

Curtis What?

Silence.

Ben I said, give the man back his money.

Ashely What's going on?

Ben (*rubbing both legs*) You think I haven't guessed how you're handling Chantelle, Curtis?

Curtis OK Ben, maybe you ain't such a sucker after all? But listen right, there ain't no need for Hayse to know is there, eh? (*Pause.*) Is there, eh, Ben?

Ben (*in pain*) Yeah, yeah, OK.

Curtis *stands up and takes a long drag on his cigarette.*

Ashely Ben, you stupid! What are you sayin'? That he's the one, and you're not telling Hayse?

Curtis He's a mate. He ain't gonna, are you Ben?

Ben (*weakly*) I dunno.

Ashely Ben. Hayse's got to know or you and me are gonna get blamed!

Curtis Cool it babe. If no one admits it, no one will get the blame.

Ashely You fool.

Curtis Watch who you're calling a fool, girl.

Ashely If no one admits it he's gonna get the police in. Ben. You've got to tell Hayse.

Curtis You keep your mouth shut. Don't grass on me, right?

Ashely Don't order him about. He'll do what he's gotta do.

Curtis You mean he'll do what you say.

Ashely At least that won't get him the sack, or me. I want to walk out on my own terms. I don't wanna be kicked out.

Curtis No one's gonna get kicked anywhere, if we just play it cool. I wanna get to the Super Bowl. I ain't gonna ruin my chances 'cos of this.

Ashely Your chances should be ruined, seeing as you've caused all this. What d'you intend to do, eh? (*Pause.*) You'd better make it a smart one that leaves me and Ben clear. Right?

Pause.

Curtis A'right. Listen. Say we agree to give the money back to Hayse, but anonymous like, so that no one gets the finger pointed at them.

Ashely Then that's saying we're all guilty. Don't be mad!

Ben (*trying to stand, but in acute pain*) Is this enough excitement for you Curt? (*He stands for a moment.*) Ash, I've got to get home. (*He collapses.* **Hayse** *enters.*)

Hayse What's going on?

Ashely Ben, where's the pain?

Ben (*face distorted with pain*) Legs!

Hayse Which one of them is it Curtis?

Ashely Stand up. Try and stand up.

Curtis (*confused*) I dunno. I dunno.

Ben Hospital Ashely. Quick. This is a bad one.

Hayse You *must* know! If head office find this out, it's the end. The end!

Ashely (*to* **Hayse**) Shut up you mad man.

Hayse What's he doing?

Ashely Having a crisis.

Hayse That makes two of us!

Ben *cries out.*

Ashely (*to* **Curtis**) Get an ambulance, quick. Move yourself boy!

Curtis *goes to the phone and dials.*

Hayse (*perplexed*) What's going on? What's wrong with him? Was it the guilt. Is that it?

Ashely No it's not. He's suffering from a serious blood condition.

Hayse (*backing off*) What?! And he's been working here? In my branch? With my food? And he's got that? I didn't know he was that way inclined. I thought he was your boyfriend. God. I'm surrounded by crooks and perverted cripples.

Curtis The ambulance is on its way.

Blackout.

Scene Eight

The hospital. An accidents and emergencies unit. The sound is now high pitched above hospital noises. **Ben** *and* **Ashely** *are sitting on chairs.* **Ben** *is writhing around in pain.* **Ashely** *is looking about. The* **Nurse** *appears, and is walking across the area.*

Ashely Nurse!

Nurse (*not looking*) Can you just wait your turn please.

Ashely But you don't understand. This is an emergency. He's . . .

Nurse (*going*) They're all emergencies here dear.

Curtis comes from the opposite direction.

Curtis You still waiting?

Ben *moves over on to* **Ashely**'s *seat and cries out.*

Ben Ashely, get someone, please.

Ashely (*frantic*) Curtis, what are we going to do? We've been here over an hour.

Curtis Don't let him fall over. Keep him straight.

Ben *cries out.*

Ashely Let him go.

Curtis Well, I dunno . . .

Ashely Just try and find someone Curtis.

Curtis Yeah . . . err . . . OK. No panic Benny boy. It's cool.

Ashely Just go!

Curtis goes, and moments later returns with the **Nurse.**

Curtis . . . and he's in pain, and he's suffering, and he's gonna die. And you're gonna let him die. You're distressed, you know. What d'you call yourself.

Nurse Yes, yes, you can stop the Eddie Murphy now. I was coming over here anyway.

Ashely (*jumping up*) Look, he's having a sickle cell crisis. It's the worst I've ever seen him. You've gotta do something right now! Get a haematologist to see him straight away.

Nurse That's all very well, but we're really rushed off our feet tonight with all the accidents due to the bad weather.

Ashely I don't care. He needs something for the pain.

Nurse Well, if that's all he needs, I can give him some pain killers.

Ashely (*hysterical*) They don't work. The damn things don't bloody work any more.

Curtis (*taking her arm*) Calm down,

calm down.

Ashely (*shaking him off*) Leave me!

Nurse (*to* **Ben**) What's your name?

Ashely (*taking out the DF118*) Look, he's taken six of these in the last hour, and they haven't had any effect.

Nurse (*to* **Ben**) If you could just tell me your name lovey?

Ashely For God's sake! Get him a Doctor.

Nurse Name?

Ben (*through teeth*) Ben Stranelle.

Nurse (*writing it down*) Is that two ll's?

Ashely Yes.

Nurse Address?

Curtis *has bent down to comfort* **Ben**. *The* **Doctor** *comes in*.

Ashely Doctor we've been waiting for over an hour, and all she can do is ask stupid questions.

Doctor (*unconcerned*) I'm sure they're not stupid questions.

Ashely They are. You got all the answers when we came for his appointment. This is all a big waste of time. He's suffering. Can't anyone see it?

Doctor (*to* **Nurse**) What is it?

Nurse She says it's a sickle cell anaemia crisis.

Doctor (*interested*) Oh.

Ashely Ben, don't hold it back. Let them see what it's doing to you.

Something in **Ben** *snaps, and he collapses from the chair into* **Curtis**'s *arms*.

Curtis (*embarrassed and surprised*) Jesus!

Doctor Hmmm. Straight into a side ward I think nurse.

With great speed **Ben** *is put into bed. There is a drip. The high pitched noise continues.*

Nurse Here we are. A nice place by the window.

Ben Injection. Which one is it?

Nurse It's just coming now. What was I saying? Oh yes. And in the morning on a clear day, if you look over the roof of the garage and between the two tower blocks, you can just about see the river and the bridge, and people going to work and school. It's very nice. There you are.

Ben What was it? You didn't ask me about morphine when we went through the allergies.

Nurse It's just a little dose of something to make your pain go away. There's no need to worry. Get some rest, and we'll get your blood sample checked. (*She goes briskly*.)

Ben But I wanna know. I wanna know what it is. Is it the right one? Is it the one that's gonna rip through this ten tons of crushing concrete and smash it up? Blast it into little, little bits again. (*Note lowers slightly*.) All them smashed up tiny pieces, so small, with small little voices, screaming out their imperfection, and no one hears them but themselves. And as they scream, they come together. All them millions and millions of untold tiny bits. Crowding, hugging, and pushing together, till they're possessing all the space and there's no room for anything else, but their screaming. It's getting louder and louder, till it's one, manic, glass-cracking cry that's using my whole body for its mouth.

The sound increases for a moment, and then drops again.

So what is it? I wanna know? I wanna know?

Ben *becomes incoherent, and falls asleep. The sound begins to fade away, and the lights cross fade.* **Ashely** *comes in. She tidies the bed. Then* **Ben**'s *mum,* **Tessa** *comes in.*

Ashely (*smiling*) Hallo . . . Tessa?

Tessa Yes, and Ashely?

Ashely *nods.* **Tessa** *looks at* **Ben**, *and kisses him on the forehead.*

Ashely They're giving him something for the pain. It knocks him out.

Tessa I hope he remembered to tell them not to give him morphine. They give that to all the sicklers, but he can't take that.

Ashely I'll try and find out. (*Walks round the bed.*) I'm glad you came. (*Sits.*)

Tessa I would have got here sooner but all the trains've gone haywire.

Ashely The bad weather?

Tessa Yeah. We're never prepared for it, are we?

Ashely No.

Tessa Did they say what caused this crisis?

Ashely They haven't said yet. It could be anything. Maybe a blood infection, the stress of work and exams, or even because he won't stop smoking and drinking.

Tessa Oh dear me. I never liked him doing that you know.

Ashely He thinks it doesn't make any difference. He says he smoked and drank, and wasn't ill for a year. I said if he hadn't, he might've been OK for two years.

Tessa Yes, and his blood count? Do you know how that is now?

Ashely Creeping up day by day.

Tessa (*sighs*) Thank you for contacting me.

Ashely I had no choice. I didn't know what else to do.

Tessa I wouldn't have known otherwise.

Ashely He never seemed to want you to know. I don't know why.

Tessa He says I bug him. He thinks I'm a nuisance. I think I care.

Ashely I know, and I know he didn't want me to ring you. The first time I called, it was because I was angry. I know he didn't like that. This time it was because I was afraid. He can't mind that. He'll have to understand. I really needed someone to talk to.

Tessa Ashely, I know that need, and I know what it's like to have no one that cares to listen, except for God. (*Looks at* **Ashely**. *Pats her knee.*) It's good to know there's someone else.

Pause.

Ashely I had the test done you know. My blood's normal.

Tessa And you don't have the trait either?

Ashely No. My type's AA.

Tessa Oh, that's wonderful. You've done well finding out.

Ashely Yeah, and that's not the only thing I've tried to find out though. There's been all the ways of helping him to get off the drugs.

Tessa Drugs! What drugs?

Ashely (*half laughing*) No, no. I mean the powerful pain killers. You know . . .

Tessa Ah, I see. No, you mustn't do that. He needs them.

Ashely Yeah, I know, but I think that

you shouldn't just rely on orthodox, like, traditional doctors. There's so many other kinds of medicine that might have an effect. You just don't know unless you try.

Tessa Yes, that's true. I believe that too. I once took Ben to a faith healer. The reverend did the laying on of hands. It was such a lovely service.

Ashely And?

Tessa I still say a prayer for Ben every night like the reverend said.

Ashely Oh.

Pause.

Tessa Have any of the things Ben tried worked at all?

Ashely Ben tried! (*Laughs.*) *I* tried you mean. Ben's just been playing along. If he'd taken things seriously, he might not be here now.

Tessa So, Ben hasn't been keen then?

Ashely *shakes her head.*

Tessa Because he doesn't like to think of the sickness always being there?

Ashely He'd go along with that, yeah.

Tess (*after a pause*) Well, you did try.

Ashely But what I want is: 'At least *Ben* has tried.'

Tessa *flinches.*

Ashely If it wasn't for his stupid uncle . . . (*Looks at* **Tessa.**) Sorry, but Ben wouldn't feel so protected.

Tessa But that's good for him. Ben thinking like that.

Ashely What?

Tessa Look. Ben and André did suffer the same, but in different ways. André slowed right down, down till he stopped. Then he would sit in a chair, boozing and listening to his old Sam Cook records, while his legs swelled up as if someone had forced so much air into them with a pump. While Ben cried out with his pain. So much pain, like the pain I cried out with when I gave birth to him.

Ashely That must've been terrible for you. (*Pause.*) But why is it better that he thinks . . .

Tessa Listen. André could talk all these things about working in fancy restaurants to Ben, but I knew those times when he bothered to find a job, it had only been as a kitchen porter. Even when he was fit and well, it would be 'I'm sick Tessa. I can't work, I'm sick.' He was sick all the time! Or at least he said he was. André was just damn lazy, and used his sickness to cover it up.

Ashely Mmmm, I get why Ben thinks that now. He's not like his uncle is he.

Tessa Thank God. Thank God.

Ashely But he's just as sick.

Tessa If he doesn't think so, he *is* stronger. Can't you see?

Ashely But he's not facing the truth!

Tessa But you don't know what André was like, Ashely. You don't want Ben to be like that.

Ashely But look how weak he is now. Running round filling in all the cracks his disease makes. (*Looks at* **Ben.**) Then it bursts out one time making a hole so big, he can't ignore it no more. Well, I hope he doesn't ignore it.

Tessa And if he does?

Ashely Is that what you want?

Tess I only want what Ben wants.

Ashely This must make him check himself.

Tessa I've seen Ben like this plenty of

times since he was a boy.

Ashely Is he gonna end up like his uncle after all? I might as well've just gone and done my shiatsu!

Tessa What stew?

Ashely This massage course I've been wanting to do for a long time, but all this with Ben's interrupted things.

Tessa You shouldn't have let it get in the way.

Ashely I did it for him . . .

Tessa Did you? I'm sure Ben didn't want that. You know when Ben was going to leave home, soon after André died, my fears flourished like weeds, and sprang up everywhere. I didn't want him to go, and I said to him 'What's going to happen? You're going to be ill somewhere on your own, with no one knowing and no one to take care of you.' But I knew underneath it was because I wasn't ready for him to go. I wasn't thinking of what Ben wanted, but what I needed, and when I understood that, I let him go.

Ashely All right. Maybe I have been doing all this for me as well, because it's something I need, but in this case isn't it better than what Ben seems to want. Have I got to go along with that?

Tessa If you love him, and that's what he wants at this moment . . .

Ashely Nar. That's mad, that's mad.

Tessa But the boy's not ready for what you want Ashely.

Ashely When will he be ready then? What's it gonna take?

Tessa You'll have to wait and find out.

Ashely He might never be ready.

Tessa That's right.

Ashely (*shaking her head*) No . . .

Ben Mum . . .

They go to **Ben.**

Tessa Hallo son.

Ashely Listen Ben, I thought I'd, umm, call her.

Ben Hallo mum.

High pitched sound begins again as **Tessa** speaks.

Tessa Try and get back to sleep my love. We are here all day.

Intense sound and pain.

Ben How can I get back to sleep when the pain starts as soon as I open my eyes.

The **Nurse** *ushers* **Tessa** *and* **Ashley** *out.*

Ben Nurse! I need an injection!

Nurse Ben, this *is* an Oscar winning performance isn't it.

Ben I need something for the pain.

Nurse There's plenty of people here in just as much pain as you and you don't hear them screaming and shouting do you. Please have some consideration.

Ben But I can't help it.

Nurse I'm afraid you're just going to have to wait till its time for the next dose.

Ben I can't. I can't.

Nurse We don't want you turning into a morphine addict now, do we?

Ben But I ain't even meant to have morphine, anyway.

Nurse Look, I'll get the Doctor. (*She goes.*)

Ben *moves about in the bed to get comfortable. His head hanging over the* *edge. He is practically upside down. He lets one arm fall over the edge, and brings his right knee up. The sound reduces somewhat when he gets into this position.*

Ben (*slurred because of the morphine*) She says there's people in here in as much pain as this. She might be right. Every day I see them being wheeled back from the theatre knocked out and bandaged up. New hips. No cataracts. Bladders working again. Yeah, they're in pain, but at least they know their pain is payment for the repairs that've been carried out. Mine ain't. As their pains begin to ease off I hear them chatting in the day room about how wonderful, marvellous, amazing, medical science is, and because of it all the things they're gonna be able to do. Never looking back, always looking forward, and never having to see this place again. Even in hospital, man ain't equal.

Nurse *comes in. Sees* **Ben** *runs to him.*

Nurse Ben! (*Grabbing his wrist to test his pulse, and then dropping it.*) What are you doing? You gave me such a fright. Come on, get back into bed.

Nurse *sits him up and the note rises.*

Nurse The Doctor will be here in a minute and he says I can give you another dose if the pain is really that bad.

Ben Dose of what?

Nurse The same as you've been having.

Ben Is it morphine though?

Nurse Mmmm.

Ben But I can't take that. Makes me feel bad.

Nurse (*preparing an injection*) Does it? Oh well, at least it's going to give you some relief.

Ben There are other things that I can have that don't make me feel . . .

Nurse Come on Ben. Stop making a fuss. You did ask for it didn't you.

Ben I didn't know it was that.

Nurse This is the only thing we give to patients with sickle cell.

Ben But we ain't all the same.

Nurse (*preparing the needle for the injection*) Come on Ben, who knows best?

Ben (*retreating*) Nar, wait for the Doctor.

Doctor *swaggers in, and the* **Nurse** *goes to meet him.*

Doctor Ah yes. The sickle cell case. Bed 21. (*To* **Ben**, *cheerily.*) Hallo.

Ben Doctor I can't take morphine.

Doctor How is the young ummm. (*Gets* **Ben**'s *chart.*) Ah yes, Ben. How are you.

Ben I've been trying to tell the nurse I have to take something else. Not morphine.

Doctor *looks at chart.*

Doctor Your blood's looking good Ben.

Ben (*shouts*) I've got to have something for this pain!

Doctor Whereabouts is the pain then? Mmmm?

Ben In my legs. In my arms. In my head.

Doctor (*drawing back the covers*) In the ankles?

Ben No.

Doctor Knees?

Ben No.

Doctor Thigh?

Ben No.

Doctor Where then?

Ben In my leg. Not one part, the whole bloody thing.

Doctor (*to* **Nurse**) Have you given him anything?

Nurse I was just about to give him the extra dose of morphine.

Doctor Yes. Good. Just, er, three milligrams, let's say.

Ben Doctor.

Doctor Yes.

Ben You can hear me?

Doctor Yes.

Ben (*spelling it out*) I am allergic to morphine.

Doctor Oh. (*Pause. To* **Nurse**.) Is he?

Nurse I wasn't informed.

Doctor (*looking at notes*) Let's have a look. Ah, mmm, yes. Right. I think we'll transfer you to Pethadone. 75 milligrams I should think.

Nurse OK Doctor.

Doctor See you later Ben. (*Going with* **Nurse**.) It can be the case that morphine is a touch on the strong side, and can have an adverse effect.

Ben *gets into another unusual, but comfortable position.*

Ben And I just want to wriggle and struggle and kick, punch and tear my way out of this sack.

Ashely *comes in.*

Ashely Hallo Ben.

Ben *goes to sit up.*

Ashely No, don't move if you're comfortable like that.

She lays her hand on the bed, and then moves it away again.

Ben They were giving me morphine.

Ashely Why? (*Sits.*) Oh yes. 'Ours not to reason why. Ours just to do or die.' Isn't it?

Ben They're gonna put me on pethadone.

Ashely Good. How's the swelling? I brought you your Sam Cook tape.

Ben Thanks. (*Pause.*) They gave us our breakfast before our cup of tea this morning.

Ashely Mmm. (*Pause. Then.*) The electric man came to read your meter I started cleaning out your kitchen. I chucked that filthy old frying pan away.

Ben What?

Ashely It was in a disgusting state.

Ben That was my favourite frying pan. It took me ages to get it like that.

Ashely I'll get you a new one.

Ben (*sighing*) It'd built up a patina on it. I was gonna use it for my exam. Nothing stuck to it. Ashely, what did you do that for?

Ashely I never knew. I'll get you a Teflon one. They're non stick.

Ben Just forget it. I ain't gonna do the exam anyway.

Pause.

Ashely Curtis rang. He asked if you were out.

Ben Fat chance.

Ashely He's gonna come in. Either today or tomorrow.

Ben Tell ya the truth. I don't wanna see him. I don't wanna see anyone.

Nurse *comes in.*

Nurse Here's the menu card for tomorrows dinner and Wednesday's breakfast. Sit up properly Ben.

Ashely He feels better like that.

Nurse Do you Ben?

Ben Yes.

Nurse *smiles and goes.*

Ben D'you have to come in every day Ashely?

Ashely I want to.

Ben I wake up sometimes drenched in sweat. I can't have a bath. I feel rough. I feel disgusting. I know I look a state.

Ashely I promised myself I'd see you through this.

Ben Still on your mission?

Ashely I don't think so. (*Pause.*) I enrolled on my course today.

Ben Good, I never liked to think it was me taking your mind off of curing the rest of the world. (*Lighting up a cigarette.*)

Ashely Shut up Ben. Just shut up! Show off your self-destruction to yourself. Not when I'm here. (*Walking away from the bed.*)

Ben I don't care I never asked you to come. I don't care about anything.

Ashely Why not?

Ben Because the disease don't care. I don't care because the disease don't care. I don't take this sickle cell into consideration 'cos it don't take me into consideration. Right?

Ashely What about us? What about your consideration for us? This ain't a battle of wills. It ain't got conscious thoughts, like it wants to get possession of your body all the time. It's part of you. You've got to make room for it. It don't look like it's gonna be evicted, so you've got to learn to live in the same house with it.

Ben Very good. Very good.

Ashely If you can't see that that's it, then I can't take us seriously. I just can't.

Peggy *comes in.*

Peggy Hallo Ben.

Ben *sits up, and looks more alert.*

Ben Oh, a'right Peggy. This is my girlfriend, Ashely.

Peggy Hallo.

Ben Ashely. This is Peggy. She's from college. Head of department.

Ashely Oh. You must be the one who phoned up.

Peggy Yes. Ben I rang you at home because you hadn't been in. It was Asheley who told me you were ill. I'm sorry.

Ben (*forcing a smile*) Yeah.

Peggy How are you? When are you coming out?

Ben They don't know. When the pain eases up, and my blood's back to normal I suppose.

Peggy Let's hope that's soon.

Ben I think you'll have to cancel my exam.

Peggy Don't say that. There's still time. I'll tell you what. I'll inform the board, and we'll keep your place open right up to the last minute.

Ben All right, but I doubt it.

Peggy I came in to give you some news actually. I wrote and told Max Vernon about you, even though I thought you'd probably get into one of your uncle's old restaurants . . . how's that gone by the way?

Ben I think I got it all a bit wrong. A mix up with the names.

Peggy That's good in a way, because I recommended you to Max and he says he's willing to take you on as a comis chef.

Ben (*lighting up*) Really!?

Peggy Yes.

Ben (*souring*) I bet I have to get my 706/2 first.

Peggy That's the thing. I'm not sure how he'd feel about you working part-time, or doing day release to study it again.

Ben But I'd pass if I could take it.

Peggy I know you would, but bits of paper mean so much in this world.

Ben (*demoralized*) Oh God.

Ashely Can't you talk to this guy and tell him how good Ben is?

Ben Don't tell him I'm sick for God's sake.

Peggy (*flatly*) I already have.

Ben He knows?

Peggy Yes.

Ben And he still would've taken me?

Peggy Yes.

Ben Oh Jesus Christ.

Peggy Look. I'm going to do what Ashely says. I'll talk to Max myself. There may be a chance he'll make an allowance for the exam.

Ben Thanks Peggy.

Curtis *comes in dressed in American football kit. He leaps around with his football, and sings to the tune of Yankee Doodle Dandy.*

Curtis I have come to sing you this song

All the way from Uncle Sam
I have heard that you're not well
And came running quick to Balham

News from the Star Trek Cafe
Hayse got in a relief
He gave me the sack today
'cos he found I was the tea-leaf.

He finishes on bended knee in a typical High School hero pose. Others look in amazement. **Ben** *and* **Ashely** *laugh.*

Peggy Yes . . . well. I'll be getting along I think. (*Remembering.*) Oh. I brought you some chocolates. I hope you like them.

Ben Thanks.

Peggy (*putting the box on the bed*) I'll be in contact very soon. Bye. (*To* **Curtis**.) Er, well done. (*She goes.*)

Ben (*smiling*) Curtis. You're mad.

Curtis (*taking off the helmet*) Actually the lyrics is wrong. But I couldn't think of anything else to rhyme. It was a few days ago I tell Hayse, and he booted me out.

Ben You told him?

Curtis He was coming down on me with the pressure to grass you two up, nar what I mean? I thought he was gonna find out sometime soon anyway. So thought I might as well let him have it and skidaddle . . .

Ashely What about the money?

Curtis I give it back and told Chantelle to go National Health. I buy the girl some flowers and give her ten of them Starship models so she can get herself a free Kirk Quarter Pounder, without cheese that is. That shut her up.

Ben You got some front Curtis. What about the Super Bowl?

Curtis I'll see it on telly. Might go next year. I get untold amount of squids doin' 'is. Me and that Yasmin. Remember? We do it together now. She does a belly dancing singing telegram and I do this one. Then together we do King Kong and Faye Wray.

Ashely That's not too hard to imagine.

Ben What did Hayse say when you told him?

Curtis Threw a wobbly. (*Picks up menu card.*) What's Macedonian vegetables?

Ben Frozen veg.

Curtis Where's the nurses?

Ben Oh around. Finished paying off for your motor?

Curtis Yeah, but I wrote it off last week when I raced Errol into the side of this pub.

Ben (*laughs*) Wicked! Been training?

Curtis All the time now I sacked that rough neck job. (*Grabs headphones from the bed puts them on and sings.*) 'Tie a yellow ribbon round the old oak tree . . .' (*Takes them off.*) Where's CCR?

Ben Can't get it.

Curtis (*flings down the headphones*) Living deadstock! (*Opens chocolates.*) Ben, give us a chocolate.

Ben Take 'em.

Ashely Curtis, aren't you going to ask Ben how he is?

Curtis (*scoffing*) Oh yeah. When you coming out mate?

Ben Dunno yet.

Visitors leaving bell sounds.

Curtis Fire!!!

Ashely Shut up, idiot.

Curtis I can see you ain't changed.

Ashely (*to* **Ben**) I'll see you tomorrow.

Ben Right. (*Pause.*) Ashely.

Ashely What? (*She is ready to leave, but* **Ben** *takes her hand, then lets go.*)

Ben Nothing. I'll see ya.

Ashely (*kissing him*) Take care babe.

Curtis I'll try and come in again sometime, a'right?

Ben Yeah.

Curtis See ya mate. (*He goes with* **Ashely**, *throwing his football in the air.*) What you doin' later tonight then Star?

Ashely Don't call me Star!

Cross fade of lights. **Ben** *takes his diary from under the pillow and makes notes.*

Ben Blood count normal. Hardly any pain. I'll call Peggy and tell her I'm taking it. Day and night revision then plan menu. Get down to Smithfield early on the day of the practical. Yes! It might have been a dream for my uncle, but it won't be for me.

Lights change.

Ben *jumps out of bed.*

I discharge you Ben Stranelle. Comis chef one.

Curtis *comes in, in his football kit, crouches next to the bed ready to play.*

Curtis Curtis Sinclair. Miami Dolphins quarter back.

Boys in spotlight.

Right. We start. One down and ten! That's four attempts to make ten yards, so move!

They are running.

Pass incomplete. Three down and ten! Hand off into stomach and take it away into the end zone. Hit it!

Ben I dunno what he's talking about. I just do what he does, and try to suck up his energy. I see him reach up, duck, crouch and I'm trying to do the same.

Curtis 444.

Ben It's OK though. We're the same. Both running together. But nar, nar. Hang on. I think he's getting faster. He's beginning to edge ahead of me. Just a bit more push. Come on, and I'll be up there again with him. Running side by side, the same, but nar. No matter how much I'm trying, how much effort I'm putting in, I can't make up that gap.

Curtis C'mon. Faster. Faster.

Ben (*shouting*) I'm trying. I am! But the gap's getting bigger. More and more space. My feet are racing so fast they've vanished into grey smoke around my ankles, and my heart's banging a hole in my chest. But why ain't my body moving anywhere? It's fighting to move up an inch. It's been 19 years of this clawing to keep up.

Sound rises again.

19 years of struggling against this weight to fill in the gap.

Curtis Fill in that gap! Fill in that gap!

Ben I can't. I can't do it anymore.

Ben *collapses on the floor. Sound still high.* **Curtis** *jogs off easily throwing the football in the air. The sound drops again, and* **Ben** *speaks through his severe pain.*

Jesus Christ, why is it me chained to this fuckin' weight? I've pulled and pulled, but it only let's me go so far. What am I meant to do? I wanna let you in without you busting down my door. But I don't know how. I don't know how.

Nurse *and* **Doctor** *run on.*

Doctor Page Doctor Hughes and ask him to stand by. He'll probably need a transfusion this time.

Blackout.

Scene Nine

Ben's *room. He is sitting on the arm of the sofa looking much recovered. He is talking on the phone.*

Ben Thank you very much Mr. Vernon. I appreciate that so much sir. You don't know what it means to me. It's really kind of you to let me start. Yeah, much better. I'll see you on Monday then. Goodbye.

While **Ben** *has been on the phone* **Ashely** *has come in carrying a small case. She is putting her coat on. When* **Ben** *has finished on the phone, he goes to her.*

Ash, won't you change your mind?

Ashely Please . . .

Ben Why not?

Ashely I think we should just be apart for a while. You know the reason why. I'm not going into it all over again. I've looked after your place while you were away, and now you're back I'm going.

Ben You don't have to.

Ashely I do.

Ben Does that mean I ain't gonna see you any more?

Ashely Don't be silly. We can still see each other, but if you want more, you're gonna have to give more.

Ben But I said . . .

Ashely I need to see it.

Ben (*sighs*) What can I say? (*Pause.*) Look, you're forgetting something. (*Picks up some papers from the sofa.*)

Ashely They're not mine. They're the forms for the green card. (*She kisses him.*) They're yours if you ever change your mind.

Ashely *goes.*

Ben Ashely . . . (**Ben** *throws himself on to the sofa, lying on his back. He puts a cassette in the tape recorder.*) Prenty patience Ben. Prenty patience.

'Bring it on home to me' by Sam Cook begins to play. **Ben** *takes a cigarette from a packet, puts it in his mouth, lights the lighter. Waits. Puts out the lighter, and flings the cigarette aside. He picks up the forms and begins to read them as . . .*

Lights fade.

Job Rocking

Benjamin Zephaniah was born in Birmingham, England in 1958 but lived in Jamaica as a child. His early teens were spent in various approved schools and prison was a turning point in his life. In his late teens he earned his living by doing impersonations of famous stars and an encounter with the National Front started him thinking seriously about politics, his religious beliefs and his role as an African descendent in an alien society. He chanted about local events, characters and places in Birmingham and developed a strong following. His first book **Pen Rhythm** was published by Page One Books and his second published work, **The Dread Affair**, condemned the institution of law and order. His work in theatre includes **Playing the Right Tune**, performed at the Theatre Royal, Stratford, East London and **Hurricane Dub** made for BBC Radio. His records include **Big Boys Don't Make Girls Cry** and **Free South Africa** which he recorded with the Wailers on Upright Records. His latest album will be released in 1989 with Mango Records. He has taken part in a number of television programmes, made his acting début on Channel 4 in the Comic Strip film **Didn't You Kill My Brother** with Alexei Sayle and a documentary about Benjamin was shown on Channel 4 in 1987. Benjamin has toured in Europe and the Caribbean, was short-listed for the post of Creative Artist-in-Residence at Cambridge University and his poetry has been quoted in the House of Commons. In 1988 he was awarded Writers' Residence in Liverpool with the African Arts Collective.

Author's Preface

I would like to take this opportunity to speak about the performance of poetry. When I started performing (which was a long time before I started writing), I had not heard of the 'Oral Traditions'; I believed I was in a world of my own and I was full of ideas on how to use the voice, how to involve many people but of all these ideas I only had the chance to expose one – me performing on my own. Like any artist I want to take my art form to its limits and my first play **Playing The Right Tune** was a mixture of poetry and prose. For me it was a kind of half-way house because what I really wanted to write was a whole play of poetry, in effect, one long performance poem.

Charlie Hanson who was then Artistic Director at Riverside, gave me the chance to do this for the first time and **Job Rocking** was produced. As Mr Hanson said when we first discussed the project, 'We need a cast of Benjamin Zephaniahs'. He could well have said a cast of Mickey Smiths, Martin Glynns or Jean Breezes, what he meant was our performers had to learn the art of performing poetry; the rhythm, the timing, the breathing are of utmost importance, if you take the set away the poetry should stand on its own.

The first rehearsals were really workshops on how to perform the work, there was little talk about the set and 'blocking' was out until three days before the opening night, a bit confusing for the cast at first but they soon saw why this was necessary.

I wish I could now go on to give my tips on performing poetry, but I can't. Some people have it built into them, some have to work at it for a while but we all have a metronome called 'the heart'. What I can say is that I was very pleased with what came out of the Riverside collaboration and I thank them for allowing me to experiment with my new ideas, (but when you think about it these ideas are not so new; Shakespeare also believed poetry was theatre).

For any group that is considering performing **Job Rocking** I say go for the rhythm. If you feel comfortable and 'Drop Dat Riddim Right' your sound and good looks will make it work.

As I am writing these few lines a Liverpool based company called 'Catalist' are rehearsing **Job Rocking**. Fortunately we are in the age of rap so the idea is not so strange, but I still have to emphasise that we are not putting words on to music but making music with words, creating a theatre of rhythm; you should be able to dance to **Job Rocking** and this should be understood if you are performing it or just reading it. Rock On.

Benjamin Zephaniah

Job Rocking was premièred at the Riverside Studios, London on 23 September 1987, with the following cast:

Manager/Rich Man	Roger Griffiths
Sheila	Sakuntala Ramanee
Max/Leroy	Victor Romero Evans
Christine	Jo Martin
Rocky	Mark Aspinall
Keith	Jay Simpson
Kay/Traffic Warden	Yvette Harris

Directed by Charlie Hanson and Anna Furse
Designed by Jeremy Herbert
Lighting by Charlie Paton
Costumes by Jane Morley

Job Rocking is set in the Job Club, once the poet's fantasy, now society's reality.

*The Job Centre is hi-tec, with a large central computer, the staff (**Sheila** and **Manager**) are on a platform above the computer, the place for the job hunters is below.*

Lights up.

Sheila *is in the office.* **Manager** *enters.*

Job Club

Manager Oh what a jolly centre

Sheila we're open in a while

Manager I'm so proud of my Job Centre
it has a different style

I thought the place was getting empty
I asked where do people go?
Sheila thinks they go other agencies but no
the truth is I think people have lost faith
so they don't look
the other night I check for past attendance in our book
it was terrible and dreadful business was getting low
I said we must win back out custom we must make our presence show
then I had this idea as I lay in my bath tub
I thought that night, I'm really bright
let's start a Job Club

Job Club we really must start a Job Club
that is what I thought as I lay in my tub
unemployed youth will push and shove
I could see it everyone would want to join our Job Club

Manager } Job Club, Job Club, Job
Sheila   } Club, job, job, Job Club

Manager then I told myself that I must search down in my heart
air bubbles were surfacing as my legs went apart
I said we must give our customers a service that is great
a service that no service industry could imitate

Sheila free letters, stamp and envelope to make them feel at home

Manager so long as they don't phone abroad free use of telephone

Sheila free counselling so problem people then can problem share

Manager we'll be the best Job Centre that you can see anywhere
we'll be the best centre to be found in all the nation
then I'll stand a better chance of getting my promotion
we'll be the first Job Centre to reach out to all the masses

Sheila one day every week we can have writing classes

Manager Job Club we can act like we have some love

Sheila we can expand our business and use the room above

Manager but we have to wait till the walls get scrub
I told Sheila we can do it, our own Job Club

Manager } Job Club, Job Club, Job
Sheila   } Club, job, job, Job Club

Manager Leroy used to come here, he was here every day
Leroy, local lad made good he almost married Kay
but Leroy was a free spirit, as free as spirits are
now Leroy is a very, very famous superstar

Sheila Leroy left here with a job as a record company's cleaner

Manager but Leroy got promoted and now his is a singer

Sheila Leroy's coming here to open our Job Club today

Manager he told Kay he's coming, he said 'cool, right on, OK!'

Manager *descends to lower level into Job Club, dancing to chorus rhythm,* **Sheila** *prepares to open up and unveils poster advertising* **Leroy**'s *appearance.* **Sheila** *unveils posters on unemployment.*

so Sheila made a poster and put it on display
she wrote upon it 'Join our Job Club just walk this way'
free membership and she told them that there are no catches
she then got on the phone to order some job clubber badges
the ideas that I get when I'm bathing is amazing
I know that when you're unemployed it can be quite frustrating
I'll make this place a Job Centre where youths can voice their feelings
I will make this Job Centre a centre that's really appealing
and if it's appealing then I'm sure people will join
don't you think this idea's great another one of mine

Sheila every member must possess a Job Club member card

Manager we will help them look for work if looking work is hard

Sheila priority is given to those that join

Manager and privileges given if they're here a long time

Sheila and if there's a job clubber that makes a friend a member

Manager we'll give them a Job Club coin

Sheila that is not legal tender

Manager Job Club it is so original Job Club
we can get personal Job Club
it came in a vision as I lay in my tub

I've made a decision welcome to the Job Club

Manager } Job Club, Job Club, Job
Sheila   } Club, job, job, Job Club

(*Repeat three times.*)

As chorus is repeated other characters enter rhythmically. On final line of chorus **Max** *approaches office and joins in on word 'job'.*

Job Centre

Max I've been coming here now for going on three years
I use up all my dole money on this and a couple of beers
I don't want to get involved with a play on unemployment
I'm just like you; I've just come 'ere for a little entertainment

All at the Job Centre

Christine look at this luxury

All at the Job Centre

Keith we even have TV

Christine I left school six months ago to face the world out there
but every day since I left school I seem to be in here
I don't really like the people, the decoration's crap
I can decorate gissa job I can do better than that

All at the Job Centre

Kay you listen and they talk

All at the Job blah blah

Christine then they send you for a walk

Rocky I went for an interview the other day ask Keith
the interviewer asked me if I ever was a thief
I told him I was as straight as a plank

and I never did rob
I said that to him and then I told him
where to stick his job

Rocky *does one-finger sign, as in two-finger sign.*

All up his Job Centre

Max every day for some

All at the Job Centre

Sheila everybody's welcome

Keith my story's a sad story I never
had a trade
my family's a broken one my daddy
never stayed
my step-father was rough and drunk
and brought no money in
I am told that's why I'm out of hand
and I need discipline

All at the Job Centre

Keith we've come here to learn

All at the Job Centre

Rocky no we've come here to earn

Kay I've been a nurse and a cleaner
but I keep getting the sack
I come round here I get a job soon
enough I'm back
I think it must be something 'bout my
personality
I just won't let nobody take no liberties
with me

All at the Job Centre

Christine you have to stand your
ground

All at the Job Centre

Sheila there's one in every town
I am not unemployed I have a job my
work is here
I must take care and watch my step or
I'll be down there
I come here every day as well
sometimes we have a laugh
but unlike them lot I get paid cause I
am a member of staff

All at the Job Centre

Kay where opportunity's knocking

All at the Job Centre

Keith yes we are job rocking

(*Repeat three times. Chorus: all join in on
repeats.*)

Manager Job Centre's all right the Job
Centre is cool

Keith Job Centre's an extension of
school

Manager Job Centres are in – the Job
Centre's great

Rocky Job Centres are centres that
some people hate

Manager Job Centres are now
futuristic

Max Job Centre's a place where you
move slow not quick

Manager Job Centres are modern – a
cultural delight

Kay   } but Job Centres don't get
Christine } you work

All right.

*Lights change as computer job console starts
functioning.* **Manager** *operates it.*
Christine *receives first print out.*

Footballer

Christine What is this? that's not for me
that is not my category
I want a job that really shows my
masculinity

Rocky electronics

Christine boring game

Keith building trade

Christine just the same
I'm looking for something to make my
name a household name

Kay painting

Christine waving all day long
I am young and fit and strong
you see these jobs now I can tell you
where they all belong
I don't need a diary 'cause all my time
is free
I don't need to look 'cause I know
what I really want to be,
a footballer a footballer

All she wants to be a footballer.

Christine I want to earn my living by
scoring goals
not painting or printing or mining coal
a footballer a footballer

All she wants to be a footballer.

Christine I want everyone to see me
on the TV screen
kissing men covered in mud and
acting mean
a footballer, a footballer

*Chorus join clapping in rhythm to football
fans' chant (ie 'Christine, Christine', clap,
clap, clap.)*

Max she wants to be a footballer

Christine don't gimme no bull about a
job that's proper

Kay 'cause you can earn good money
as a footballer

Rocky you can sell your story to a
newspaper

Max or you can climb the ladder and
become a manager

Keith you can have an affair with an
actress or a swimmer
to boost your career when you are a
beginner

Christine I want a job with a future
and progression
but I can't see no football section.

All a footballer a footballer
she wants to be a footballer

Christine I've never played for money
but I have the skill
I have the stamina and the power of
will

All a footballer a footballer
she wants to be a footballer

Christine *dribbles imaginary ball in and
out of other characters.*

Christine you will see me on the field
a flashing head
and what a dribble
when they ask me for my autograph
I'll do a funny scribble.

*Chorus chant 'Christine' and clap as they
carry her across stage triumphantly.*

All a footballer a footballer

Christine I want to be a footballer.

Chorus continue to chant with **Christine**
as cheerleader.

Christine I've been doing what I've
been told

Manager } she's been doing what
Chorus } she's been told

Christine why am I still on the dole?

Manager } why is she still on the
Chorus } dole?

Christine I should be out scoring
goals

Manager } she should be out scoring
Chorus } goals

Christine yeah, why am I still on the
dole?

Manager (*to* **Sheila**) why is she still on
the dole?

(*Repeat three times.*)

Rocky *interrupts with sound of car hooter,
to same rhythm as chant.*

Am Hard

Rocky I wanna Cortina you know

what I mean I wanna drive something
flash
ask me why I'm here I'm not looking
no career
I'm just looking some easy cash
'cause round our end you go round
the bend
if you can't raise a little bread
when I'm dating a bird I don't wanna
look a turd
I wanna look hard instead
Am hard and rough and I don't bluff
am tuff I ain't no weed
but I do need money and my eyes get
bloody
if I don't get what I need
ten pints a night is my intake of
alcohol fuel
when I'm out of my mind I then go
and find
a table and play pool.

Sheila he's *hard*

Rocky am hard

Christine he's tuff

Rocky so tuff

Kay and he don't care about no
career

Keith the DHSS said he won't get no
cash if he don't sign
so he's here

Christine he fights

Rocky I fight

Kay he drinks

Rocky I drink

Manager }
Sheila } really unemployable

Kay It's true that every interviewer
says

Manager he's unsuitable

Rocky some people call me Edgar but
my real name is Rocky
I go the gym every Tuesday night so

don't you mess with me
I change my clothes two times a week
and fortnightly I bath
I have BO and no one knows I'm
serious don't laugh
oh what a mess at the DHSS when
they cut my money down
this guy said 'your fault go get a job'
so I kick him on the ground
he pressed an alarm but I stayed calm
the police came in no time
now I need money 'cause the judge
gave to me
a two hundred and fifty pound fine.

Sheila *he's hard*

Rocky am hard,

Christine *he's tuff*

Rocky so tuff

Kay and he don't care about no career

Keith the DHSS said he won't get no
cash if he don't sign up
so he's here

Christine *he fights*

Rocky I fight

Kay *he drinks*

Rocky I drink

Sheila really unemployable

Kay it's true that every interviewer
says

Manager he's unsuitable.

Rocky we went for a drink one night
last week
to a night club in Mile End

*Chorus come to life in disco dance in
corner.*

there was me and Shirley and some
other girly
with some other girl's boyfriend
well I don't dance I was cool in a
corner
talking to my beer.

Keith *steps out of disco light and mimes to* **Rocky**'s *story*

when this guy came up to me and said
'Surely I've seen your face somewhere'
he looked at me intensively as I sipped
my pint of bitter
he said 'That's right, couldn't see in
this light
you're the guy from the Job Centre.'
he said 'You're Rocky and you're quite
hard
you stabbed someone didn't you?'
I said 'Listen shoo or you know what
I'll do
I'll do the same to you.'
well he went away and the very next
day
I saw the bloke in here
he walking around walking up and
down
trying to find a career
I said 'hey mate I was out with a date
last night
remember me?'
he said 'yeah sure you were by the fire
door
oh yeah you're name's Rocky
I had a few drinks I was drunk I
think'
but I won't forget that stink
then I gave him an upper cut and
then a headbutt
before that guy could blink

Keith mimes receiving blows and ends
up on his back.

Keith *he's hard*

Getting up

Rocky am hard

Christine he's tuff

Rocky so tuff

Kay and he don't care about no career

Keith and the DHSS said he won't get
no cash if he don't sign
so he's here . . .

Christine he thinks

Rocky I think

Max he stinks

Rocky I . . .

All *stink*

Max really unemployable

Kay it's true that every interviewer
says,

Manager he's unsuitable.

Sheila *sprays air freshener in* **Rocky**'s
*vicinity. Chorus make noise of blowing
away smell which develops into sound of sea
breeze.*

Lights change.

Keith *is discovered in a spotlight in a high
place.*

I Want To Be A Fisherman

Keith   After leaving school I found a
job
working as a painter's mate,
I had no 'O' levels but school was over
and I thought that was great,
painting factories and painting houses
each and every day,
climbing ladders, having long tea
breaks
I thought this was OK
then I left that job for a life in the
market
selling fruit and vegetables
but it wasn't my thing and I was aware
this job was not stable
but now I know what I want to do
to earn my daily bread
I want to go to sea where the sun
shines free
and the breeze can reach my head

I want to be a fisherman
and spend my time at sea
I want to be a fisherman
only fishing can satisfy me

I don't mind work and I like to be
occupied

but factories are not for me
and I won't drive a bus too much
violence and fuss
I would rather get drowned at sea
I used to want to be a plumber and fly
a helicopter
but pipes and heights don't go
and I could work in a park or be a
watchman in the dark
or throw road grit on snow
but I know what I want to be
a fisherman's life is for me
now I know what I want to do
I want to earn my bread at sea

I want to be a fisherman
and fish my weekly keep,
I want to be a fisherman
and cast my net to the deep

*Fade lights to Job Club and computer starts
up again.* **Kay** *takes printout.*

Rocky   now Kay's had opportunities

Kay   yes I've been quite lucky

Rocky   she got all these flash
qualifications

Max   you know why? It's education yes
education is the key

Sheila   most employers would agree

Christine   but don't you feel quite lost
and sad when you think of all the jobs
you've had.

So Many Jobs

Kay   So many jobs I've had so many
jobs I've had
some were good and some were bad
there's been so many jobs I've had
I used to work down Park Lane in a
hotel
some think it's fiction but it's fact a lie
I would not tell
I spent much time in the kitchen
'cause that was where it was at
but I ate so much that I got fat and
then I got the sack

then my agent phoned me with a job
from the Sun
he said all they want is a picture with a
little tit and bum
a little tit and bum I said you must be
out your mind
and that was that I was on my way
another job to find
my next job was in theatre with a
group based in King's Cross
they said it was a co-op but this co-op
had a boss
one day I spoke my mind about the
way things were running
I was democratically kicked out and
I've done no more acting

so many jobs I've had so many jobs
I've had
I pass through them like fashion fads
So many jobs I've had

Christine   she's been a hostess in a
classy club

Keith   she's been a barmaid in a rough
pub

Sheila   she's been a cleaner all day
rubbing and scrub

Rocky   she's been a DJ with some
heavy reggae dub

Christine   she's worked in a church
with a radical priest

Keith   she's worked in the garments
industry in Aldgate East

Sheila   she's worked as a secretary to a
mega star

Rocky   she's worked with an astrologer
who studied Jupiter.

Kay   so many jobs I've had and none
of them have lasted long
sometimes I think I'm doing great and
then something goes wrong
so many jobs I've had but I can never
hold one down
I've worked in every super store that
you can see round town,

I've worked days and I've worked
nights I've worked part-time and full
I've worked in some dodgy jobs and
some respectable
I've had my share of money so I really
can't complain
but now I'm broke and out of work
so here I am again

Max so here you are again looking for
work and you have knowledge
these youngsters make me sick I had
no chance to go to college

Sheila well Mr Simms there's always
time for adult education

Keith that's why we're here

Max why are we here?

Keith they call it job creation

Max well job creation's good if you
are 19 and you're single, my eyes
are old with age but in your eyes I see
a twinkle.

Rocky he's done his bit

Max I've done my bit son I have done
plenty

Keith those were the good old days

Rocky when we ruled the waves

Max now my pockets are empty.

Redundant

Max I did tink I have job until
retirement come
I work 20 years for Matthew and Son
before de nuclear age when dem used
to mek gun
I used to earn some money yes I used
to earn some
I did tink I was cool at Matthew and
Son
till de management put de union pon
de run
at dinner time we play dominoes, dat
was fun

now me have a bad back 'cause every
day me lift a ton

Chorus Lord dem mek me redundant

Manager *creates rhythmic sound with coins
in pocket as he fiddles with computer to the
beat of chorus.*

Matthew and Son med me redundant

Rhythmic noises disturb **Max.**

Max attention attention attention I say

Kay listen to an older one. He's come
a long way

Silence.

Max for a person a pension a pension
I did pray
I neva want fe beg because I know I
pay
de youth of today must pull up dem
sock
'cause dem nar get a job through
politician ballot box
de only ting you get is job creation
scheme
but nu job nu get created, full
employment is a dream

Chorus dem mek me redundant
Matthew and Son mek me redundant

Max me have a mortgage me car get
sell

Kay he used to have a caravan he sold
dat as well

Max dish washer, spin dryer all on
HP
and at my age no employer want me
but me feel young and strong
me could work much more years
when me tink of de future me end up
in tears
'cause me children growing up I did
want
give dem de best
I did want mek me children betta than
de rest
but Lord dem mek me redundant

Matthew and Son mek me redundant

I di tink I have a job until retirement
come
I work 20 years for Matthew and Son
dem used to tell there was security
but de only ting dem give is
redundancy
the only job I've had was with Matthew
and Son
when dem mek me redundant dem
give me a sum
but it neva last long when de tax man
heard
now I'm looking for a job, I tink dat
weird

Lord dem mek me redundant
Matthew and Son dem mek me
redundant.
you know why

All why

Manager *is operating computer in rhythm
to poem.*

Max to do my dob dem have a
computer
to turn on de lights dem have a
computer
to sweep de floor dem have a
computer
to open de door dem have a computer
de foreman is not Fred it is a
computer
the fight for rights is dead 'cause of a
computer
dem don't pay so much wages cos of
de computer
de computer last for ages so dem
taking over

Lord . . .
dem mek me redundant

*A single file is formed as they walk round
the set like robots.*

Computers

All Chorus Computers computers

computers (*echoes.*)
taking over the workplace

(*Repeat three times.*)

computers computers computers
taking over the factory floor

(*Repeat three times.*)

Rocky the robots of the future are
living here today
workers are not needed when
computers play
don't complain to the union computers
have the right
because when they are working
computers do not fight

All Chorus computer computer
computers
taking over the workplace
computers computers computers
taking over the factory floor

Max first they ask you nicely to go
voluntary
or they order you to go and give you
some money
technology is moving they say it cannot
stop
human factors go below computers are
on top

All Chorus computer computers
computers
taking over the workplace
computers computers computers
taking over the factory floor

Sheila in the Social Security there is
nothing spared
dem sey Scotland Yard has the best
one
with that nothing else compares
if you pay by mail order cheque or
American Express
be sure without a doubt the computer
has your address

Kay Computers will do anything
management say
they don't get pregnant and they
never demand higher pay

Max computers they are present all
over the earth
with computers management say they
get their money's worth,

Keith computers are now everywhere
who knows where they come from

Christine they computerize the
kitchen they computerize the bomb

Kay they computerize the wrist watch
now we have computer time

Rocky in schools uptown we have
computers doing nursery rhyme

Manager has Leroy arrived? What car
does he drive?

Rocky I bet it's something flash
(*Said with a hint of jealousy.*)

Manager does he have in-car phone?
Is he accident prone?

Rocky bet he's got fancy lights on his
dash.
(*Said with a hint of jealousy.*)

OK

Manager You said that he would be
here
you said he'd be here for sure
and now we waits and he's so late
and now we wait some more
you told me that he had no more
engagements
for today
If so why has he not arrived
If so where is he Kay
this PR exercise is really crucial can't
you see
Leroy started here now Leroy's a
celebrity
you said he'd launch our Job Club
with a bang
and right on time

Kay well superstars are always late
and it's no fault of mine

Manager OK you've let me down

Kay It's no fault of mine

Manager OK you've let me down
look at the time
was he this late when you had dates
when he was your boyfriend

Sheila you're getting personal
beware you don't offend

Manager I'm just trying to check up
on his punctuality

Kay well if you're checking up on him
don't bother checking me
you asked me to invite him to come
here and I said yes
I could not know he's let us down tell
me how could I guess

Manager you were the one who said
you know him I quote 'outside in'
or was it just another case of your
exaggerating.
well be Leroy or no Leroy
this club will be a success
you'll see our hearts get full of joy
as we expand and progress
he might come and he might not
still this club goes in motion
the big hand now has passed the dot
so this Job Club is open
but OK you've let me down

Kay It's no fault of mine

Manager OK you've let me down
we're out of time
and you . . .

Manager *runs upstairs to office where*
Sheila *has frozen into a pose.*

Everything For Me

Manager (*to* **Sheila**) You've been
sitting on your backside
you've been doing no good
you're not doing nothing that you
know you should
you've been wasting your time like
there is no tomorrow
but I know something that you should
know

Sheila *types to rhythm of poem.*

I want you to do everything for me
I want you to do everything for me

gimme that document gimme that report
and think a little while 'cause you never have thought
order my dinner and my cup of tea
I want you to act like a real secretary
keep the show running show some commitment
remember we work for the government
be perfect there is nothing you should lack
and I have the power to give you the sack

I want you to do everything for me
I want you to do everthing for me

sit up on your chair girl try look smart
you look so sad you could break my heart
it's a real good thing my heart is tuff
I look smart you look so rough
I have high hopes I am manager
a real exclusive pen pusher
I have a house I have a car
and I control dis job centa

I want you to do everything for me
I want you to do everything for me

Rocky he wants you to

Manager change the display cards in the window
we have no work but don't let it show

Max he wants you to

Manager work for your money 'cause you are lucky
to have the privilege to be working for me

Christine he wants you to

Manager answer the phone speak loud and clear
if it's my wife tell her I'm not here

Keith he wants you to

Manager be my servant be my slave
'cause you'll get the sack if you don't behave
I want you to do everything for me

Christine did you hear what the man said

Manager I want you to do everything for me.

Kay boy you going to end up dead.

Chorus he wants you to

Manager I want you to (*descending stairs.*)

Chorus he wants you to (*building momentum and imitating* **Manager**.)

Manager you will do

Chorus he wants you to

Manager you must do

Chorus he wants you to

Manager you must.

Ad-libbing until **Manager** *exits.*

Manager *changes into* **Rich Man** *backstage.*

He Wants You

Kay He wants you to do everything for him

Keith that's what he said

Max boy dat man dread

Kay he wants you to everything for him

Christine he must be really off his head

Kay who give him the money

Christine and who give him the power

Kay who gives him the right to control you

Max well he is the manager

Kay more like a *dictator*

Christine you have your job and *he* has his job too

Rocky he's a big head brute that's what I say

Kay and you must face him every day

Sheila that's right so let's forget it it's my job

Christine well I've seen his kind around before
I am used to them I know the score

Rocky give them a suit and tie and they think they're god

Christine does he always talk to you like that

Kay I've never seen him smile the rat

Christine if there's a judgement day he'll be destroyed

Kay if that's the way he'd talk to me
if I was an employee
I'd kick his balls and just stay unemployed.

Keith he wants you to do everything for him

All he wants you to do everything for him.

Christine surely you won't stand for it

Rocky I know what I'd do to the twit

Christine I'm not talking to you so just stay cool

Kay he can only threaten with the sack
surely you're not afraid of that?

Sheila (*shouting*) now just listen to me you bloody fool.

Kay *exits to change into traffic warden.*

Sheila (*more intense and slow rhythm*) a job is a job and the job is to keep it it
might not be full of prospects hope and joy
a job is a job and you see this job I need it
or I would never take that verbal from that boy
I was born to work from washing dishes
now I fulfill his master's wishes
I have to work yes every day
for most of it I get no pay
a lazy man leaves me no choice
when I get home I play housewife
but you lot never see me then
when this places closes it don't end
and I've spent much time looking work
I looked until I went berswerk
but these things I keep concealed
see I know just how you lot feel
see when I do an interview
I see a piece of me in you
I don't get no job satisfaction
this job does not have that attraction
a job is a job and the job is to keep it
so don't be fooled I'm only here for the money
a job is a job and you see this job I need it
and I don't think I'm really that lucky.
from nine to five to stay alive
that's the way I must survive
and thousands out there envy me
thinking I have security
they say 'You're indoors nice and cosy
a weekly wage and things are rosy'
at first I thought that was true
until I worked a month or two
now he sees me as quite inferior
but don't you see me as superior?
because deep down we're all alike
tomorrow I could be on my bike
an office job that was my dream
I wanted to return home clean
but once again I made a blunder
I'm on the carpet you're swept under
a job is a job and the job is to keep it
just like you a wage is what I seek
a job is a job and you see this job I need it

that's why I'm here for six days a week.
no I don't have to take that but I must take my money home
'cause I'm sure I won't be fed by friends or some persons unknown
no I don't have to take that but I bare it and I grin
if I'm not here I'll be round there
so there's no way I can win.

Rich Man *enters, breaking the tense atmosphere.*

Wimpey Homes

Rich Man Excuse me sir do you think you could help
I am trying to find a place
I was told it was near this Job Centre
but I just can't see no trace
my Rolls Royce is parked up outside
in a 'No Parking' zone
the place I want is an estate agent
called Uptown Wimpey Homes

All *Uptown Wimpey Homes*

Rich Man yes Uptown Wimpey Homes

Kay perhaps you should ask at the newsagent
they deliver all round here

Christine Or ask a cop or a road sweeper
I am sure there's one out there

Sheila Are you sure you're in the right place sir
why don't you check your map

Rocky you know something I have never seen
a real live bowler hat

All *Here this one he's never seen a real live bowler hat*

Rich Man oh I am dressed like this
'cause I am celebrating
my wedding date is near

I am buying a house it's a real surprise
my fiancee don't know I am here
she thinks we might live near Hampstead Heath
in a flat we can expand on
but I'll spend a few pounds and we'll have our own grounds
and we'll live in a Wimpey mansion

All *They'll live in a Wimpey mansion*

Rich Man yes we'll live in a Wimpey mansion
we'll live a life of love and laughter
we'll live a happy ever after

Rocky he looks a right one don't he Keith

Rich Man you looks to me just like a thief

Rocky I am not the kind to just take that

Keith forget it leave it where it's at

Rich Man I am not like you can't laze all day
get on your bike that's what I say
and thanks I'll find my own direction
I can make the right connection
'cause all of you, yes all not some
yes every one of you is scum

Rocky I am not the kind to just take that

Keith forget it leave it where it's at

Rocky you could get killed for saying that

Keith forget it Rocky he's really fat

Rich Man you don't want to work you live off the state
and your kind's the kind I really do hate
you could find a job but you don't have a clue
your brain cells are dead 'cause you been sniffing glue
I don't have to speak to your kind
'cause I see the light and you people are blind

you're moaning minnies so learn to
stay quite
I know you're the kind that will go on
a riot

Rocky riot?

Sheila could you please leave sir

Rocky hold on just a minute
forget it leave it where it's at
could you please leave sir
let me speak to the idiot
forget it leave it where it's at.

You Don't Riot

Rocky *taunts him with a pointed finger
and sly looks.*

Rocky You don't riot if you have a
nice job
and a home to come home to at night
you don't riot if you have a nice job
and a home to come home to at night
you don't riot if you are well fed
and unemployment does not pressure
your head
you don't riot if you live in the city
but you have country cottage
where the view is pretty
you don't riot if you can have a
holiday
you can afford to have plenty to say
you don't riot 'cause life is swell
with the media on your side as well
you don't riot if you can safely walk
the street in peace
you don't riot if you have video games
to let your anger release
you don't riot if what car you drive is
the only problem you got
you don't riot if you have your share
and by change you have a lot
you say there's no such thing as a riot
you say it's purely crime
you say 'You're a moaning minnie
don't riot stay quiet
'cause our country's doing fine!'
the country's doing fine

Keith
Christine } yes, our country's doing
fine

Rocky we have a great army
to protect you and me
yes, the country's doing fine
no U-turn time

Keith
Christine   no U-turn time

Rocky inflation rules
no milk for schools
but the country's doing fine
why should you riot
do you get dole money
and I bet you fiddle tax
why do you riot
we do not riot
we're British, are you proud of that?
you don't get riots on Hampstead
Heath
or even in Handsworth Wood
so we don't riot

Keith
Christine } no we don't riot

Rocky we're very very good
you don't riot if you have a nice job
and a home to come home to at night

Keith *and* **Christine** *join in where
underlined*

you just don't riot if you have a nice
job
and a home to come home to at night
you don't riot with a big bank account
with American Express you can always
pay out
you don't riot
you choose a better choice
like rolling around in a big Rolls Royce
you don't riot
riots happen too late
and that's South Africa Britain is great
you don't riot
that sounds like hatred
and my people never get frustrated.
you don't riot if you have a nice job
and a home to come home to at night
all right.

Traffic Warden

Traffic Warden *enters to the centre and is very happy.*

Warden Oh Lord kiss me behind
I never think the pleasure would be mine
I've booked cars that were ugly and cars that were nice
but I never had the pleasure to book a Rolls Royce
oh Lord kiss me neck
dis is a day I will not forget
I have the ticket copy in my book
someone in here is a very rich crook

Rich Man what you mean you've put a ticket on my roller

Warden yes sir, and sir what a very nice bowler

All well sir you must pay the price
if you drive a mini or you drive a Rolls Royce

Warden well ever since I work in this area
de biggest thing I get is a Granada
I never ever got a Jaguar
so to book a Rolls Royce is a real pleasure
well sir you look like a real city gent
so you must pay the fine it is money well spent
'cause the money you pay goes to the police
wages must be paid to the protectors of the peace
and sir what a nice bowler hat
I wish us traffic wardens had ones like that
it really is quite something it has character
it's shaped just like a dumpling it goes with the car
yes sir you're looking real fine
but you should not park your car on a double yellow line
you should park it in a side street

Rich Man but the side street is too small

Warden well I'm telling you the High Street is no place to park at all
but you want to see him car de car really shine
that man must own a diamond mine
that car cost money the amount over me
and him looking for a job, that man greedy
you want see the seats dem is real leather
wid telephone, stereo and computer
that car have everything is real luxury
de only ting it no have is a lavatory

Rocky he's lost and he looking for a Wimpey home seller

Warden he doesn't look like a lost fella

Keith he's getting married soon so he's planning out his future

Warden oh now I know the reason why he has a car computer

Rocky he don't need to buy a house
he could live in his car

Rich Man looks like you've made your home here

Keith we're waiting for a star

Rich Man he's not turned up then should I take his place

Sheila no way

Rocky no way

Keith no way

Christine no hey he's got a singer's face

Rocky he hasn't got a human face
his face is just money

Keith and he's never without a job

Rich Man no I work for my daddy

Christine do you ever play football

Rich Man oh no but I play tennis
and once upon a time I played golf
with a star from Dallas

Warden well now I must be on my way to do another booking
I want to use up all this pad so I must keep on looking

Rich Man is there no way that I could pay in cash and right this minute

Warden I hope that's not a bribe dear sir
if so I'm just not in it

All well sir you must pay the price
if you drive a mini or you drive a Rolls Royce

Rich Man I'm off, I'll send you a cheque, I think 12 pounds is the price.

Rich Man *exits and changes to* **Larry**.

Warden well sir, that's the price of one
but sir, I've booked you twice

All nice.

Warden *exits and changes to* **Kay**.

Max why you handle him so rough? Why not show him some respect?

Rocky he looks down on the unemployed, so what do you expect?

Max It takes all kinds to make the world, not everyone's the same

Rocky he don't care about our kind
he only has himself to blame

Max de youth of today dem no have no manners
dem go to dem bed and no sey no prayers
my generation we have manners
every night we say our prayers
de youth of today dem no have no discipline
dem choose a world of darkness and a world of sin
dem need punishing, to produce discipline

I came here from the West Indies in 1958
everybody tell me Britain was great
but I still looking for dis greatness
but all I see is one great big mess
I don't want to preach no politics or tings like dat
but in dis world you have big fish and you have sprat
we are small fish in dis rat race
now I must state my case

nothing never come easy nothing ever come cheap
dem following dem leader like dem is blind sheep
nothing ever come easy you reap what you sow
most of these kids have never done a day's work don't you know

de youth of today have no understanding
dem never want to give but dem keep demanding
de result is quite astounding as unemployment keep on mounting
de youth of today have it easy I would say
dem never want to work and yet dem still get pay
when I was young dis was unheard of
you would have never heard a word of
please don't mix me up 'cause I'm not like dem
'cause I have worked for all my adult life my friend
I would still work but dem lot lazy
dem tink life easy but dem crazy
now de big boss come up with dis Job Club theory
he thinks he can solve the problem but look clearly
dis problem is here to stay
dat is what I have to say

dis job clubbing is madness just like a bad joke
we are being strangled and em giving us more rope
dis job clubbing is like a game of kids monopoly
even if you get somewhere you get redundancy

dis Job Club business is a stupid ting
what you youth need is some discipline
give them two years in de army
send dem to sea in de navy
de youth of today really need a
beating
none of dem can wash dem clothes

Kay *re-enters.*

or do house cleaning
dem only follow fashion
but I, I deal wid action

so I'm out said I won't play dis game
yes I'm out 'cause in de end it's all the
same
you work like mad, or you don't work
at all
It makes you sad, de system make you
feel so small
de youth of today are making such a
bad impression
I'm sure dem getting dem ideas from
television

Max *exits and changes to* **Leroy.**

Keith he's gone

Kay he's upset

Rocky (*posing*) he's off to place a bet

Sheila he don't gamble

Keith like he said he thinks our Job
Club is dead

Christine he's getting old

Kay he's wise

Rocky he said we're just girls and
boys

Kay he's wasted and he's so bright

Sheila he's upset and he's all right.

Larry's Gym

Chorus makes panting noises in rhythm.
Rocky *adjusts his hair, squeezes the odd
pimple and advances on* **Christine** *in a
macho style.*

Rocky (*to* **Christine**) Have you ever
done any stamina training
been really pushed when you really
straining?
push ups, sit ups, jogging and leg curls
It'll make you a better footballer man
or football girl
down at Larry's gym they have the
best in equipment
to exercise your body in every
department
if you really want to be a football star
why don't you come and work out it's
a mile or so not far

come to Larry's gym come to Larry's
gym
keep your energy up keep your figure
in trim
come to Larry's gym come to Larry's
gym
and when we've finished training we
can go for a swim

Larry *runs through in boxing gown and
cigarette in mouth.*

Larry was a world champion in karate
now he has retired his gym is his hobby
every now and then you see his face
on the telly
he might be really famous but he
always talks to me
if you gotta dole card I can get you in
cheap
the dressing rooms are separate so no-
one will peep
oh yes and he has got a place for five-
a-side football
with cushioned artificial turf just in
case you fall

Keith } come to Larry's gym come to
Rocky } Larry's gym

Rocky and if Larry's around I'll
introduce you to him

Keith } come to Larry's gym come to
Rocky } Larry's gym

Rocky there you can get you share of
exercising

have you ever thought of boxing?

Christine yeah

Rocky well this is the place
we could start a woman's team if that
be the case

Christine are you serious?

Rocky of course I am it's a serious
thing

Keith people would really pay to see
women boxing

Rocky if you really like to see yourself
there's mirrors all round
if you like aerobics they will play a
disco sound
there's a sauna and a massage if that's
what you like
and if you like to cycle there's a
standing still bike
you want to be a footballer
well this is where to start
you must speed up your reflexes
and slow down your heart
you want to be professional
it takes dedication
if you have plans one day to represent
the nation

Kay you'll be a pioneer because its
male dominated

Rocky you know your gonna have
hard times
but don't get frustrated
you'll be all right if you stick with me
you really will appreciate a muscular
body

Larry *runs up to* **Christine** *and looks at
her lustfully.*
come to Larry's gym come to Larry's
gym
Larry's a real nice bloke

Keith and he's married to Kim

On being reminded of being married **Larry**
raises his eyebrows and runs off.

Rocky come to Larry's Gym come to
Larry's gym

Keith Kim won an Olympic gold in
trampolining

Rocky many people look at me and
say I am not fit

Sheila smoking fags and gettin drunk
is not a good habit

Rocky but I need a training partner
to spur me on
we can tell each other when we're
doing something wrong
you look to me like somebody who's
got some motivation
you look to me like somebody who's
got determination
you look to me like somebody who's
got just what it takes
we could really have some fun when
pushing heavy weights
we could really have some fun but
that's not the motive
what we really want to do is keep our
bodies active
it's much better than wasting time it
really is creative

Keith you could even get a grant and
call it a collective

Rocky come to Larry's gym come to
Larry's gym
if you're serious 'bout football or are
you just joking?

Keith ⎫ come to Larry's gym come to
Rocky ⎭ Larry's gym

Rocky every Tuesday night I go
you should come along you know
I'd like to see you next week so
start participating
and come to Larry's gym.

*They run on the spot counting to eight. One
by one starting with* **Rocky** *they all
collapse leaving only* **Christine** *running.*

Lights come up on **Sheila**, *looking down
over a collapsed* **Rocky**.

Soft as a Pillow

Sheila *about* **Rocky**.

Sheila He came from up north to seek
a new life
all he needs is a job and a serious wife

Kay you're starting to sound like you
fancy him

Christine well it's me that he offered
to take to the gym

Sheila he came from up north to seek
something new
and all I want to do is help him
through
he needs personal attention that's all I
say
he had a rough upbringing that is why
he gone astray
because so many people stab him in
the back
he gets all defensive ready for an
attack
he's a product of society he's not to
blame
he needs a new identity so he changed
his name
he needs someone to talk to and some
understanding
what he really needs is some careful
handling
I'm getting to know him I tell you no
lie
deep inside he has his pride and he's a
nice guy.

he's as hard as a rock but as soft as a
pillow inside
he has a hard exterior but there's a
softer area inside

there's been no institution that gave
him a chance
and everyone gets nervous when in his
presence

Keith that's because when he talks he
talks with his fist

Kay and anyway most of the time the
guy's bloody pissed

Sheila now you're taking the mickey

Keith no she takes the edgar

Kay I bet you wouldn't call him dat if
he was round ya
everyone's so scared of him and you
are scared too

Sheila no way no I'm not scared of
him no way is that true
all I know is all he need is a little care

Christine you're a married woman
married woman beware

Sheila you've got one track minds you
think its all sexual
just because I may have used the word
personal
I was never thinking of nothing of that
sort
it's just he needs a gentle touch that all
that I thought
he needs the softly softly

Christine you can say that again

Others get up slowly starting with **Keith.**

Keith give him the softly softly and
you'll excite his brain

Sheila he's hard as rock but as soft as
a pillow inside
he has a hard exterior but there's a
softer area inside

Kay he's corruptible

Sheila yet lovable
with the right job he's well able

Kay if he could get his life stable

Sheila he's really be an example

Keith in principle it's workable

Kay but he so unpresentable

Christine the mission is impossible

Sheila that guy's just unemployable

Keith you don't have to be
unemployed there's work out there
you know
there's many ways of getting cash

Christine oh yes, then tell me how

Kay oh yes Keith, I bet you want us all to go and rob a bank

Rocky he's always got these ideas

Kay If you ask me he's a crank.

Off the Cards

Keith (*clicking fingers*) Off the cards get a job off the cards
off the cards get a job off the cards

you don't need no insurance card
you can still sign on and be a part-time bard
you can still claim your money with a job on the side
if you see an inspector then you have to hide
people do it all the time on building sites

Christine it all sounds good but is it morally right?

Keith forget about morality and just think of your spare money
when you check it that way I'm sure you will agree with me

off the cards get a job off the cards
off the cards get a job off the cards.

the tax man will not get you if you do not leave a clue
if you're late when you sign at the dole tell them you had the 'flu
employers like it also when they're fiddling accounts
if you work and claim your dole money you'll have a good amount
the place to look is launderettes and back-street timber yards
most of the time you're sure to find that you will need no cards

Rocky my mother used to do it at the Ranking cinema

Kay you should never say them things not in the Job Centre

Keith off the cards get a job off the cards
off the cards get a job off the cards

I was working in a second-hand shop
business was bad then business went flop
but I still had the security
of knowing I would get my dole money
Rocky won't talk about it but he did it too
once he was a part-time cleaner in a zoo

Rocky well it was money to spend and I won't pretend
but you should never tell an enemy only tell a friend

Keith off the cards get a job off the cards
off the cards get a job off the cards
the money that you get will never show
you will have bus fare ever you go
if you save hard you can travel abroad
you can start buying things you could never afford
to be sure of this financial gain
for the job on the side use a false name
you will find when you check it weekly
you're much better off financially
the money you get can't be checked out
you just stop working for a while if in doubt
some poeple say its robbing the tax-payer
I would rather do that than be a beggar
I don't believe in staying poor
If I have a little then I want some more
I believe when you're working in this rat race
every penny goes back to the very same place

off the cards get a job off the cards
off the cards get a job off the cards.

Sheila (*interrupting*) Here are brand
new jobs here today
take one Christine and go away
you need a proper job and a job like me
admit it would you not like to be a
secretary?
not yet advertised take an interview be
wise
forget about that football crap you
gotta realise
you really are quite feminine
but you want to be masculine
you're more suited to housekeeping
forget about that football ting

Christine balls I want to play at my
footballs

Sheila the same to you
just you take a look at these vacancies
you'll see something that you fancy
an agency wants someone for
modelling
you could see the world it could be
exciting
take this one for example a job in the
city
oh you're not quite young enough oh
what a pity
come just take a look 'cause you are
bound to see a job for sure
and when you have a job you will not
come in this place anymore.

Christine jealous now I see it you are
jealous
now I see
jealous would you believe she's jealous
of Rocky and me,
jealousy will get you nowhere
it can only hurt your pride
I think jealousy is something
that people should try to hide
you're jealous of me and Rocky
well your jealousy will grow
there is nothing going to stop me
to the gym with him I'll go

All to the gym with him she'll go

Christine and I'll be thinking of the
future

you are stuck around that desk
and it seems a kind of torture
and you're bound to be quite vexed
'cause we'll be working at our leisure
you say he's such a nice lad so
I think it will be a pleasure

Sheila jealous me you must be going
mad or something jealous me

Christine *Yes you're full of jealousy*

Sheila I am not jealous over nothing
jealous me?
pure fantasy
I am here to do a job that's gettin' a
job for you
and to help make this task easy you
know what to do
when you register your trade be
realistic
and don't say your ambition is to score
a hat trick
the world out there is hard and
competitive
you must be realistic if you really want
to live
forget about that football crap
come on we've heard enough of that
that idea should be left as scrap
a proper job is where it's at

Christine footballer footballer

All she wants to be a footballer

Flash explosion as **Leroy** *enters through
his poster.*

Keith Take a look folks Leroy's here

Manager who said Leroy? is Leroy
there?

Christine dressed to kill

Keith he's looking good,

Rocky If I had his money I would

Manager well Leroy good to see you
lad
a little late but we are glad
to have you so I say welcome
make yourself at home my son.

Superstar on Guitar

Rocky Hey, Prince Leroy, how are you?

Keith we ain't see you for a year or two

Leroy *descends stairs. Each step lights up as his foot touches it.*

Leroy cool

Kay said Leroy

Leroy cool I say

Christine then Prince Leroy went away

Rocky hey Prince Leroy came back here

Keith we use to run wild out there

Kay in the blues dance in the ghetto don't tell me that you forget now

Kay once it was Leroy and I

Manager now Leroy's a modern guy

Christine Leroy looking very slick

Rocky wait till Kay gives him some stick

Kay Leroy said

Leroy say who are you
I can say I am superstar
I found fame with my guitar
go and ask my manager

Kay Keith said

Keith Leroy this don't matter
we can still be cool together
we can still sing songs of praise

Christine Leroy looked slightly amazed

Keith Kay said

Kay Leroy think again
don't let money buy your brain
don't let stardom buy you out
Leroy man don't mek me shout

Manager listen Leroy you stand tall

Kay Not too tall 'cos you might fall

Christine Leroy said

Leroy I now live good
I have a house of brick and a cottage of wood
I have a real fast car and a real slick chick
I can earn my money quick,
I take 'coke' and go to Mars
I have gold like chocolate bars

Kay check this all you Leroy's now
he who rise must fall somehow
nice of you to play guitar
but why should you turn superstar
hope your guilt now burns inside
have you lost your ghetto pride?
one time Leroy was my spa
Leroy now is

All superstar.

Don't You Wish

Kay OK you've made the money
you have fancy girl and car
and no one can deny it
you're known as a superstar
your manager said it can be quite hard
to track you down
'cause every time you're wanted you're
always out of town
touring here and touring there now
touring is your life
I'm glad our plans did not work out I
could have been your wife
but you live and learn and you get
wise as you are growing old
and I was really glad to hear when
your last record went gold
but silver and gold will vanish away
but the respect you earn won't decay
you're looking quite uncomfortable
do you really want to stay
silver and gold is not what it takes to
be street credible
I think the damage that you've done to

yourself is irreversible
and don't you wish you had not sell
out
deep down, don't you wish?

OK you've made the money
and that's reality
you're always in the charts now
and always on TV
but are you a commodity always up for
sale?
and are your friends really real
friends?
and who answers your mail?
'cause people who were close to you
don't see you so it seems
and now we start to wonder
what does this stardom mean
if you cannot walk the streets where
you were born and bred
something's wrong, so change your
song
with pride hold up your head
'cause silver and gold might shine
bright
but what do you do when alone
'cause when you're seeking happiness
you must start looking at home
silver and gold might shine bright
but in reality
silver and gold is bought and sold
and life is not that easy

and don't you wish you had not sold
out
deep down don't you wish
no Leroy no I'm not impressed

Leroy I don't want to impress I'm cool

Kay remember now I know you best
I've known you since at school
no Leroy you tink you're cool
but where there's a rise there's a fall
you're rated big but sometimes it is
better staying small

Leroy Is it trouble you seek

Kay you know that I'm meek

Leroy then why give me all this chat

Kay I wanted you to be someone
but you can do better than that

Leroy It is trouble you seek

Kay well things look quite bleak
If you can't understand what I say
well I'm no critic but you look pathetic

Leroy and I suppose you are doing
OK?

Kay I'm not doing bad

Leroy oh really I'm glad
but you don't have a penny to show

Kay well money can't buy everything
you need in life you know
and you're doing good

Leroy why not so I should
'cause I have ambition and drive

Kay you have the connections

Leroy you're full of objections
'cause I have learnt how to survive
yes I have learnt how to survive

Kay have you now?

Leroy yes I have learnt how to survive

Kay maybe I'm not superstar
but I still walk the streets I'm alive
money is short but I cope

Leroy oh yeah

Kay money is short but I cope

Leroy but you still hang round here

Kay where do you hang my dear?

Leroy I'm going 'cause there is no
hope

Rocky like the shades

Leroy what did you say?

Rocky like the shades man

Leroy cool ain't they?

Keith how much did you pay?

Leroy I got them from a girl fan I
always wear a pair nowadays

Kay do you need to hide mate?

Leroy no that's not true but I tell you they make me feel great.

Glasses

Leroy I don't care about the weather be it rain or shine
I always wear these glasses of mine
when I can see you but you can't see me
I tell myself that I look sexy
I don't care if its bright or dark
I like to take my glasses for a walk in the park
I walk around the roses doing all these funny poses
I know I'm really cool and I know everybody knows
cool in me glasses me look so cool in me dark glasses
I wear them when I'm eating I don't want to see my grub
and then I go and pose around this poser pub
cool in me glasses me look so cool in me dark glasses
when I'm chatting up a partner my eyes don't hesitate
I'm not shy I get straight in 'cause I know I look great
cool in me glasses me look so cool in me dark glasses
I'm not showing off I'm just being me my eyes are really beautiful so I won't let you see
and if you see me naked I'll have my glasses on
I've tried so hard to see myself but I can't see no one
when I wear shorts and tee-shirts I even look cooler
I'm in a gang and we are hard and I'm the ruler
so when I pass through your town you'll know me by my hair
'cause when I can look you up and down and you can't see me stare
cool in me glasses me look so cool in me dark glasses
I went to see my doctor I could not see his house
I walked into his garage door and talked to mickey mouse
cool in me glasses me look so cool in me dark glasses
I watch the world cup on TV I could not see a ting
I could not hear 'cause I was drunk, but didn't England win?
cool in me glasses me look so cool in me dark glasses
you see me in the disco and in the trendy place
I'm a phallic symbol I have that kinda face
when I'm playing easy watch me how I lean
you never hear me saying yes it's cooler saying seen
you never hear me saying good it's cooler saying bad
am always talking 'bout the cars I think one time I had
I never wear a seatbelt it's much cooler without
but I won't let my mum see 'cause my mummy will shout
my friends don't talk behind my back I know because I'm told
sometimes I wear a tee-shirt when I'm really bloody cold
sometimes I'm standing in the bar I have a funny grin
it looks impressive tell the truth I can't stand the taste of gin
so now you know me better all except my eyes
I bet you cannot tell if I'm telling truth or lies
bet you cannot tell if I'm real or I'm fake
that's up to you that's a decision you must make
when my eyes are covered it helps out my body
until I had these glasses no one would dance with me
sometimes I have a cigarette it makes

me look all right
I never seem to light it 'cause I cannot
see the light
cool in me glasses me look so cool in
me dark glasses
when I wear them I get notice and I
feel confident
although it can be costly every day an
accident
cool in me glasses me look so cool in
me dark glasses
I know I'm cool it's natural I was born
like dis somehow
one time I was like everyone but I'm
different now
I have no problems problems are
yours and hers and his
I'm perfect but I'm no one without
these dark glasses
cool in me glasses, me look so cool in
me dark glasses

He dances off with **Christine. Keith** *starts imitating his dance moves.* **Christine** *turns back and embarrasses* **Keith.**

Leroy *changes back to* **Max.**

Kay that man's finish that man dead

Rocky well he's making loads of bread

Kay we don't live be bread alone
when he's broke he'll soon run home
that man really makes me sick

Rocky he made a load of money quick

Keith it all down to who you are
I think one day I'll be a star.

Michael Jackson

Keith I want to be like Michael
Jackson
I want a hair cut I want it fast
I want religion but one with class
I want a hero like spiderman
I need a fan

Rocky like Ronald Reagan

Keith I need good health care I need
to pose

Christine you need an operation upon
nose

Keith I need your money I need a hit
and just like you I need to get
someone who loves me into my life

Rocky you're bloody right you need a
wife

Keith when I see her she will not pass
you're bloody right I'll feel her class

I want to be like Michael Jackson
not just any millionaire
I want tight trousers that never split
yes
I have a problem I need a pair

Rocky will you scream?

People scream.

Keith I love those screaming people
to make me feel like I am wanted
I am really strong I might look feeble
I need a house that is haunted

some people think there's ants in my
pants
not at all it's the new American dance
and I mean it Billy Jean was not my
lover
I never touched her tell the truth it
was my brother

I want to be like Michael Jackson
this would give me plenty joy
If I can't be like Michael Jackson
then I want to be like Leroy

Kay who wants to be like Leroy?

Christine In his dreams I think he
tried

Rocky Keith wants to be like . . .

All Leroy

Kay I'd rather be unemployed.

Part-Time Unemployed

Kay The part-time unemployed the
part-time unemployed

no one knows the pressure of the part-time unemployed

Rocky she saved hard and bought a stereo

Keith that is filled with an equalizer and radio

Kay I saved hard yes I can prove that all you got to do is come and look round my flat

Sheila holidays holidays

Kay I do love a holiday
I work and save my money up and then I go away
to places that are sunny when in England it is cold
'cause I want to enjoy myself before I get old

All the part-time unemployed the part-time unemployed

Christine no one knows the pressure of the part-time unemployed

Kay I never claim my dole money

Sheila some people say it's pride

Kay but I always make my way 'cause I take things in my stride
I never want to be a slave each day of the year
so I slave a while there's time to smile when I disappear

Christine she spent last year in Spain

Sheila before that Trinidad

Kay next year it will be India I'm told it's not bad

Sheila she thinks it's really trendy

Kay but I like to move around
'cause staying in one place for long can make me feel down

All the part-time unemployed the part-time unemployed

Keith no one knows the pressure of the part-time unemployed

Kay it's my style I like to be versatile
it's my thing because I like travelling
I am told that I should sign on the dole
not me I like independency
I thought of marriage and then I thought again
I don't need marriage I just need good friends
very soon now I might emigrate
but not right now 'cause I'm in quite a state
money is what I want money is what I need
it's a matter of survival not a matter of greed
money is what I want money I must get
money really is a very funny subject

Christine 'cause you can't live without it and you always need some more

Rocky and rich people are greedier than people that are poor

Sheila when you have it you just spend it never thinking of tomorrow

Keith and then you have to ask around to see if you can borrow

Kay and when money comes your way
the money that you get
is accounted for already 'cause you must pay back the debt
old time people said 'it's easy come and easy go'
mine never come easy and its hard to let it go

All the part-time unemployed the part-time unemployed
no one knows the pressure of the part-time unemployed

Max *re-enters with bottle in hand, drunk.*

Max I did think I have a job until retirement come
I work 20 years for Matthew and Son before de nuclear age when dem used to mek gun
I used to earn some money yes I used to earn some

Kay welcome back to the Club

Max no I was just passing through

Manager welcome back to the Club

Max hey I am not one of you
but I just go to de Social and dem tell
me
If I don't come to dis place I get no
money
I could lose me temper I could lose
me cool
but me know dem people out to try
and turn me fool
I lived through war, I'm old, but I
won't get pushed aside
regardless of de system I will get
employed

Rocky come on we're not that bad

Max go wey you bloody mad

Manager come on brother Max

Keith it's time to face the facts
I'll keep coming here until the day I
make it big
then you'll have to pay a price to get
into my gig
or I might be a fisherman riding the
waves so free
at my interview Sheila said, 'listen
Keith we'll see'.

All at the Job Centre

Keith my future's in their hands

All at the Job Centre

Sheila 'cos we have futures planned

All she wants to be a footballer

Christine but I must train some more
but one day I will make it, I can't wait
'til I first score
until then I'll be here or sweating
down at Larry's gym
but I will make the team one day 'cos I
am out to win

All at the Job Centre

Manager it seems we are at home

All at the Job Centre

Max you're surrounded but alone

Rocky the bright light did not fool me
when I come to join this Club
really this Job Centre's just an alcohol-
free pub
they're all drunk on fantasies about a
living wage
I have learnt nothing's a cert I'll take it
stage by stage

All at the Job Centre

Keith you can sign and do your cards

All at the Job Centre

Rocky you don't have to look too hard

Kay I'll be here tomorrow now it's
nearly time to close
I feel sure I'll get a job but really no
one knows
Leroy is a memory he chose a
different way
but I won't do what he's done no I'll
earn some decent pay

Manager a government that's three
terms old supports my new idea
to see the centre of the future take a
look round here,
we're modern and computerised and
we are in control
we'll soon find a scheme to get you off
the dole

All at the Job Centre

Manager we're all job rocking

All who's job rocking? are you job
rocking? (*Repeat three times.*)

Manager job clubs are the future
there is no retreat

Rocky It's just an idea to keep us off
the streets

Manager let's face it job clubbing is
needed today

Max you haven't joined but still you
get pay

Manager unemployment figures get
lower each season

Rocky unemployment figures are
fiddled

Kay yeah that's the reason

Manager you youth are so lucky to
have us who care

Keith If we were that lucky we
wouldn't be here

All first it was a dream first it was a
fantasy
or a man that is known for his poetry
it was planned as fiction now it is
reality
go to your Job Centre pick up a leaflet
and see
we did not know that one day it would
really be for real
someone from society said

Manager jobless here's a deal

All now there's Job Club on your telly

Sheila　﹜ now Job Clubs are
Manager　 advertised

All now you've seen the poets play
go out and see if we tell lies.

Titles in the
Methuen Modern Plays series
are listed overleaf.

Peter Handke	*Offending the Audience* and *Self-Accusation*
	Kaspar
	The Ride Across Lake Constance
	They Are Dying Out
Vaclav Havel	*The Memorandum*
Kaufman & Hart	*Once in a Lifetime, You Can't Take It With you* and *The Man Who Came To Dinner*
Barrie Keeffe	*Gimme Shelter (Gem, Gotcha, Getaway)*
	Barbarians (Killing Time, Abide With Me, In the City)
	A Mad World, My Masters
Arthur Kopit	*Indians*
	Wings
Larry Kramer	*The Normal Heart*
Stephen Lowe	*Touched*
John McGrath	*The Cheviot, the Stag and the Black, Black Oil*
David Mamet	*Glengarry Glen Ross*
	American Buffalo
David Mercer	*After Haggerty*
	Cousin Vladimir and *Shooting the Chandelier*
	Duck Song
	The Monster of Karlovy Vary and *Then and Now*
	No Limits To Love
Arthur Miller	*The American Clock*
	The Archbishop's Ceiling
	The Golden Years and *The Man Who Had All the Luck*
	Two-Way Mirror
	Danger: Memory!
Tom Murphy	*A Whistle in the Dark & Other Plays*
Percy Mtwa	
Mbongeni Ngema	*Woza Albert!*
Barney Simon	
Peter Nichols	*Passion Play*
	Poppy
	A Piece of My Mind

Joe Orton	*Loot*
	What the Butler Saw
	Funeral Games and *The Good and Faithful Servant*
	Entertaining Mr Sloane
	Up Against It
Louise Page	*Diplomatic Wives*
	Golden Girls
Harold Pinter	*The Birthday Party*
	The Room and *The Dumb Waiter*
	The Caretaker
	A Slight Ache and other plays
	The Collection and *The Lover*
	The Homecoming
	Tea Party and other plays
	Landscape and *Silence*
	Old Times
	No Man's Land
	Betrayal
	The Hothouse
	Other Places (A Kind of Alaska, Victoria Station, Family Voices)
Luigi Pirandello	*Henry IV*
	Six Characters in Search of an Author
Stephen Poliakoff	*Coming in to Land*
	Hitting Town and *City Sugar*
	Breaking the Silence
David Rudkin	*The Saxon Shore*
	The Sons of Light
	The Triumph of Death
Willy Russell	*Educating Rita, Stags & Hens* and *Blood Brothers*
	Shirley Valentine and One for the Road
Jean-Paul Sartre	*Crime Passionnel*
Sam Shepard	*A Lie of the Mind*
Wole Soyinka	*Madmen and Specialists*
	The Jero Plays
	Death and the King's Horseman
	A Play of Giants
C. P. Taylor	*And a Nightingale Sang . . .*
	Good